Investing for the Utterly Confused

Investing
for the
Utterly Confused

Paul Petillo

McGraw-Hill
New York   Chicago   San Francisco   Lisbon   London
Madrid   Mexico City   Milan   New Delhi   San Juan
Seoul   Singapore   Sydney   Toronto

1 2 3 4 5 6 7 8 9 0   FGR/FGR   0 9 8 7 6

ISBN-13: 978-0-07-148046-8
ISBN 0-07-148046-3

This publication is designed to provide accurate and authoritative information in regard to the subject matter covered. It is sold with the understanding that the publisher is not engaged in rendering legal, accounting, or other professional service. If legal advice or other expert assistance is required, the services of a competent professional person should be sought.

> —From a declaration of principles jointly adopted by a committee of the
> American Bar Association and a committee of publishers.

McGraw-Hill books are available at special quantity discounts to use as premiums and sales promotions, or for use in corporate training programs. For more information, please write to the Director of Special Sales, Professional Publishing, McGraw-Hill, Two Penn Plaza, New York, NY 10121-2298. Or contact your local bookstore.

Library of Congress Cataloging-in-Publication Data

Petillo, Paul.
   Investing for the utterly confused / by Paul Petillo.
      p. cm.
   Includes bibliographical references and index.
   ISBN 0-07-148046-3 (alk. paper)
   1. Investments. 2. Securities. I. Title.
HG4521.P44 2007
332.6—dc22   2006028008

Alla mia moglie: ti amo

Contents

Acknowledgments

I want to take this opportunity to thank the amazing number of people who not only were kind to me as I navigated the period after the publication of my first book, but probably saw their effort as something that was second nature. While many of these people profess to have been only doing their job, their help and kind words meant a great deal to me.

Special thanks to Mary Glenn and Melissa Goldner, who worked with me on the first book. Thanks to Janice Bangs, Leslie Martin, Helen Raptis, Carl Click, Ken Akerman, and the whole staff at KATU (Portland, Oregon), who guided me through my first experience with live local television. Special thanks also to Nicole Hart for her insight.

Thanks also to Eva Rosenberg, Gerri Detweiler, Mary Goulet, and Heather Reider. Roberta Yochim also deserves a nod of thanks, along with Chris Malta, Joe Trembley, Larry Swedroe, and *Oregonian* columnist Julie Tripp.

Introduction

◆◆◆

When You Invest, You Win

I want to assume that you are the reader who will become the next Warren Buffett.

Outside of the world of investing, Mr. Buffett is just another grey-haired midwestern man approaching his eighth decade, living in a modest home in Nebraska. But to those who know of his accomplishments, he is something of an investor's idol. He has a sort of matter-of-fact, gee-whiz approach to investing that many have written about and more than a few have worshiped. In the world of investing, this man is an icon.

But why would I want you to become like him—to achieve success and become an investor's idol? Buffett is an opportunist who searches for values where others find none.

Do I suppose that with a basic education in investing, you could one day be worth billions? Hey, it could happen. And if it did, wouldn't that be cool!

Can I make the seemingly outlandish claim that if you harness the simple ideas that Buffett and numerous others who are also educated in the school of value investing use, they could work for you as well? I can.

Unfortunately, no icon, no successful investor, no one, including Warren Buffett, has done it overnight. Nor has anyone done it without repeating some basic concepts to himself, whispering in his own ears, recalling everything that he has learned and the mistakes he has made, and then using that information without fail over and over again.

And that is a talent that is learned only with time. Time—that abstract measure of success or defeat, the difference between winning and losing, or, in the case of investing, the single greatest asset you will ever own—needs to become your ally. In the Utterly Confused series, you will find that time is your guideline, your template to achieving success, your friend, and your benefactor.

Investors fall into three categories. Investors of the first kind understand that investing is something that they should be doing, but they haven't quite got around to it. Those in the second group, which is equally as large as the group of those who know little or nothing, invest in a haphazard way, often using what is available to them, usually an employer-sponsored retirement plan like a 401(k). And those in the third group, by far the smallest, know quite a lot about investing—or so they think—and can engage you with their philosophical approaches, talk at length about their strategy, offer sage advice on the direction of the marketplace, and ultimately tell you only about their winning picks.

For those of you in each of these investor groups—the "want-tos," "the know-somes," and the "smart-ones"—the only thing that separates you from a feeling of accomplishment is a grasp of the basics.

Drivers can be grouped very similarly. Think back to the days when you first entertained the idea of driving. No one simply tossed you the keys and let you get behind the wheel without making sure that you had some basic knowledge. Instead, people would take you with them and give you an education about the rules of the road. They would take the time to point out the bad drivers and the traffic hazards (often one and the same). They would instruct you on traffic signs and road etiquette, how to use the mirrors to see what was behind you, and how to scan the horizon for possible problems ahead. They would, hopefully, teach you how to be defensive and counsel you to be aware of your surroundings. They would instruct you on the finer points of braking and signaling your intentions.

These people would ease you slowly into the world of driving because they understood that they would be sharing the road with you some day. You are a beginner, a novice, an empty canvas.

After all of the instruction, after the months of practice driving accompanied by a mentor, you get your license to drive. And you enter into the world of the second group. You now know how to drive—the state you live in says so. But are you a good driver simply because you have in your wallet a piece of laminated plastic with the worst picture of you ever taken on it?

Once you are behind the wheel, you are in charge of over a ton of metal that is capable of transporting you from point A to point B with the mere turn of a key. How you get there, which road you take, and how you evolve as a driver depends on how much you remember from those early years of instruction.

And from those humble beginnings, a few of us find the act of driving to be so thrilling that we end up racing around an oval at speeds that would not be legal on any highway, challenging our skills as we compete with other racers to get to the winner's circle first. In this third group, the truly experienced drivers ply their skills. We hear about the Earnhardts and the Pettys, we hear about the Foyts and the Unsers. But while these drivers are praised for their accomplishments on the track, their wins pale in comparison to their losses. A. J. Foyt, for example, has won the Indianapolis 500 four times in 35 attempts. The late Dale Earnhardt, despite having won over $27 million in his career as a NASCAR driver, started 676 races while winning only 76 times.

In other words, no matter how little we know, how much we think we understand, or how experienced we like to think we are, the challenges of the road ahead of us are the same for investing as they are for driving. Investing is what you bring to it.

Using time to explain these concepts does not necessarily allow you to skip over the material that you think you have already learned. As I lay out the way to become an investor, a better investor, or, in some cases, a more knowledgeable investor, I will occasionally pay homage to those who have learned from their mistakes, turning missteps into success.

Although we are always inclined to celebrate our winners, it is our losses that will teach us the most. We will explore the basics with more than just statistical jargon. Instead, we will act as your driving instructor, the experienced driver in the seat alongside you, the extra set of eyes on the road ahead. Although this vehicle comes with only one brake and one accelerator, we will give you the tools to make informed decisions.

And one of those investors, who learned how to metaphorically drive his investing career at his father's knee, was Warren Buffett. Mr. Buffett, for all of his renown as a billionaire 36 times over, still uses some basic principles when deciding how to invest. He is most famous for taking a struggling textile mill in Bedford, Massachusetts, and turning it into a stock worth $107,000 a share. He did this by using the available capital inside this undervalued company to buy numerous other companies. He has the ear of Wall Street and the absolute loyalty of the people who own his Berkshire-Hathaway stock.

Mr. Buffett bought his first shares of a company's stock at age 11. Working at his father's brokerage firm allowed him to see how stocks work. Employed as a board marker, he invested in Cities Service Preferred, whose shares at the time were trading for $38. The story goes something like this: young Warren purchased three shares and was stunned when the price went down to $27. He held on to the shares until they recovered enough to sell. (Cities Service no longer exists. On December 3, 1982, Occidental Petroleum Corporation— ticker symbol OXY—acquired it.)

The story of that purchase doesn't end there. Eventually, the stock hit $200. Buffett had sold at $40. The experience of that hasty move taught him a great deal about patience.

Before we move on, though, Mr. Buffett, who is often referred to as the "Oracle of Omaha," offers investors a classic example of the cult of personality that often surrounds the stock market and the most successful investors.

There will always be super-investors, people who have taken their talents to the next level, providing us mere mortals with a lofty goal, a far-off destination, if you will, where fortunes become legendary. Investors, to their credit and more at their expense, often look for any crumb of knowledge that they might glean from these elite players. Even when, in many cases, we have many of those skills already, we still look to the few for the answers.

Seeking to expose the truth behind these super-investors, Mr. Buffett suggested, in an appendix to Benjamin Graham's book *The Intelligent Investor,* that we try to imagine a national coin flip. Each American, he asked us to suppose, would ante up a dollar, then step outside one morning and flip a coin. A seasoned mathematician, Buffett suggested that each time a coin flipper called the wager correctly, he or she would be allowed to stay in the game; losers lost their dollar, and their losses were distributed among the winners. In the short space of 10 days, the entire population of the United States would be whittled down to a group of winners numbering several hundred thousand.

Each of these investors' share of the losers' pooled money would be slightly over a thousand dollars. But the story goes on: 10 days later, those several hundred thousand winners would be further culled to just over two hundred winners. By having been able to call the coin flip correctly 20 consecutive times, the winners would each have a kitty worth more than a million dollars.

These winners would receive undue praise, he explained, based solely on those individuals' ability to simply flip a coin and became wealthy. While investing requires much more than flipping a coin, those who rise to the top do so with more than just skill. Sometimes a little luck, the right flip of the coin, helps.

We won't pander to the coin flippers, however. We will rely on building a skill level in each of you that will help you understand how the markets work, your role in them, and how you can benefit from them.

It is pretty easy to assume that you don't consider the act of driving to the grocery store something that requires luck. Instead, you use all of the things you learned as a beginning driver and all of the experiences you have had since you got your license, and turn them into a trip that you don't give too much thought to—you just do it.

This book will put you in the driver's seat, so to speak. But first, we need to give you some rules of the road. Instead of starting with the nitty-gritty of how the markets work, what stocks are, and how you can jump in with both feet, we'll begin with what you know—not what you know about investing, but what you know about yourself.

For many of us, our first exposure to any sort of investment comes when we land that first job out of high school or college. After the interview, after the orientation, after the training, you will most likely be faced with your first exposure to investing: the company-sponsored retirement plan.

After discussing retirement plans, we will move methodically to a discussion of mutual funds, followed by an insightful look at how the equity and bond markets work and, more importantly, how you can profit from them. You will move from learning how to drive to becoming confident in your skills. While good investing has little to do with coin flipping and more with understanding risk, value, and, most importantly, yourself, becoming a proficient investor, one who can do so with great conviction, is the ultimate goal of this book.

Who knows, you might become the next Buffett.

Investing
for the
Utterly Confused

PART I

Building Lifetime Wealth

CHAPTER 1
Learner's Permits

◆▬◆◆◆◆◆◆◆◆◆◆◆◆◆◆◆◆◆◆◆◆◆◆◆◆◆◆◆◆◆◆◆◆◆◆◆◆◆

So what is investing? While there are thousands of books and Web sites that attempt to describe exactly what investing is, including my own, it is not as complicated as you might think. In this book, we will explore investing in comparison with something that we all have in common: driving.

It is my hope that we can explore investing in the same logical progression that you used during your early experiences with a car. While driving is a universal experience, investing, for all of its positive attributes, has not become so ingrained that we do it automatically. However, this is not your fault.

Imagine driving down a road with ever-changing road signs and shifting terrain in all sorts of weather. Imagine driving as not being just a trip from point A to point B. Instead, imagine it as an experience that requires nerves of steel, the courage of your convictions, and the need for superhuman concentration.

Investing can be all of that and more. It is fraught with perils and potholes, littered with strategies and theories, and prone to sudden shifts in the landscape. At the same time, it can be puzzling and rewarding, risky and necessary, and, above all, both dangerous and safer than you might think. Investing will require you to have all of your senses acutely tuned to the journey. Like driving, it can become second nature, and with luck and the perseverance to take it one step at a time, we can reach this point. We can go from being utterly confused to being completely competent investors who are capable of successfully driving our investments forward, one step at a time.

We will start with your 401(k) or similar retirement plan for two reasons: these plans are easy to access, and almost everyone needs to have them. This will be your introduction not only to the world of investing, but to the idea of yourself as an investor.

The epiphany, someone once said, is solely the domain of men. Women's ideas, that same someone quickly added, take time to evolve. What separates women from men is their method of enlightenment. The way women make rational decisions turns out to be a far better approach than the sudden realizations that men often have. While women plan and strategize, educate and elevate their understanding, men have epiphanies. Men are left with the nagging realization that something could have or should have been done, while women simply know better.

The basic difference between men and women has been explored by a wide variety of researchers. While the Mars and Venus debates on a variety of topics rage, people in the financial world are most interested in how they can dissect the investor's brain.

All investors, male or female, epiphany or not, fall into the same three categories. It isn't how or when they discover the fact that they need to invest, but how they advance their goals that makes the difference.

 What the Experts Say

The market does not beat them. They beat themselves, because though they have brains they cannot sit tight.

Jesse Livermore

In the introduction, I cutely referred to these three distinct categories of investors: the "want-tos," "the know-somes," and the "smart-ones." The first phase of an investor's life is as a want-to. These are the novices, the beginners, the ones who want to learn how to drive their investments because they see the need to do so. They know they should be investing. They understand the importance of it. Or worse, they have shelved the notion of investing for some future time when they can pursue it. The problem is, that time is now.

The idea of investing seems to hit this group suddenly. They realize that they have a future that will need to be financed. If you are in this group, you understand the importance of doing this, but you have yet to take that first step. This book will be your driver education.

The know-somes have read books. They have listened intently to talking heads and market strategists—the media are full of them—and they have pondered the markets and perhaps even made some investment moves on their own. However, in many cases, they are not that far removed from the want-tos. They are experienced investors, but they are not experienced enough to be confident that what they are doing is the best thing. This book will show them something about themselves that they may not have known. While "the market" is often referred to as if it were some sort of living and breathing entity, it is simply a vehicle, an inanimate object that needs you to propel it, steer it, and ultimately take control of it. You are the driver.

The know-somes review their investments on a regular basis, often tweaking and adjusting, buying and selling, moving and realigning their portfolios. While this is a good thing, in a way it is unnecessary. The only group that benefits from all of this activity is the financial community that encourages you to do so. They are the ones that receive the commissions for all of that activity.

The know-somes are often plagued by doubt. They want to do a better job when it comes to investing. They want to understand themselves, their risk tolerance, and how much of a role that tolerance plays in their investments. They want some straightforward guidance, but they realize that, with so many different possibilities, a move that seems right may actually shave valuable time and profits from their investment goals. They want to get it right the first time, but they often find doubt rearing its ugly head, and they try again. The know-somes know better, but they do it anyway.

The smart-ones, ironically, are often not as smart as they think they are. They are confident about their investment decisions. They may have made a lot of money. They may have lost a lot as well. They live for growth and gain. They are always on the hunt for a bull market. While their hearts may be in the right place, their minds are often clouded with the same doubts that the know-somes have. They may be more experienced than the want-tos, but they suffer from the same inexperience when it comes to investing. Knowing how to drive is not the same as knowing how to drive well and safely.

What's the difference between bulls and bears?

The terms *bull* and *bear* are often used to describe two different attitudes toward the stock market. If you are a bull or bullish, you are looking at a market and expecting its value to increase. Being a bear or bearish simply refers to looking at a market and expecting its value to decrease.

The smart-ones love a bull market. A bull market is a period during which there is an upward trend in prices. The reason Wall Street likes this analogy, aside from the powerful appeal of such a strong animal, is the simple fact that bulls thrust upward. Bear markets, conversely, refer to markets in which there is a decline in prices, and that analogy suggests a hibernating market. In market parlance, bull is good; bear is bad. In the world of the utterly confused investor, the opposite is truer.

Chances are, you know a smart-one. Smart-ones, for all of their expertise, all of their failures (which they often fail to mention), and all of their successes (which they often do), can offer all of us some important information about the road ahead. They have become experts, involved, informed, focused, and committed to their investments and strategies.

Unfortunately for the smart-ones and the know-somes, the only true investor is the novice. Investing is a learning game. You grasp a little more about it every day.

For all of its complications, investing is a learning experience that continues teaching us throughout our entire lives. Even when we are recognized as licensed drivers, the road teaches us something every day—something about ourselves, something about our driving and our approach, and, more importantly, something about our skill.

The first signs that you have reached the point where investing seems like the next logical step usually hit you as an opportunity. Over the course of this book, we will look at the opportunities that all of us have to either enter the world of investing or become better participants. We will explore the pros and cons, the attitudes and the risk factors, the costs and the fees, and how to profit from something so essential. We will do this in a gradual progression from retirement investing to mutual funds to long-term investing, and, reluctantly, we will look at the short-term variety of investors. Once we have grasped these concepts, we will have the foundation to be able to explore, to take an in-depth look at stocks, bonds, mutual funds, and any of the numerous other ways in which you can turn a dollar into a profit.

CHAPTER 2
From Point A

◆◆◆◆◆◆◆◆◆◆◆◆◆◆◆◆◆◆◆◆◆◆◆◆◆◆◆◆◆◆◆◆◆◆◆◆◆◆◆

R emember the first time you got a real job? Not the hamburger-flipping job that gave you your first spending money, but the first job you got when you left college, the first employment that meant you were on the road to a career, the first job that seemed to matter. You had interviewed and were screened by an army of human resource personnel. You filled out paperwork, signed documents, took drug tests, and sat through orientation. The job was described to you, you met your coworkers, and you were suddenly hit with the realization that your childhood was over. You were an adult.

Many companies take a proactive approach to their employees' future. Your employer may offer you more than just a paycheck for a job well done. It may hold the key to your future decades down the road. Yet far too few of us understand this when we begin working. A company's offer of a defined-contribution plan such as a 401(k) or some other form of self-directed retirement plan is an opportunity that should not be passed over.

There is no single better introduction to the world of investing than these plans. They have all of the confusing jargon, mystical possibilities, tossed-about percentages, pie charts and graphs, and indecipherable choices that the world of investing can offer—and all this comes courtesy of your employer in a way that is often easy to take advantage of.

So why, then, if these plans are so easy to use, do so many of us do such a poor job of utilizing them to their fullest? The sad truth is that many employer plans are underused by the very people who need them the most. About 30 percent of those who work at large companies have turned down the opportunity to participate in their company's 401(k). The number is far greater at small companies that offer these plans to their employees.

Worse, the percentages get even more troubling when you look inside these plans. People often fail to do anything really constructive with them. Most of that stems from the complicated nature of these types of plans. But some of it stems from just bad decisions. It's time to change that by starting over—from the beginning.

Think back to the first time you wanted to drive. It doesn't matter what part of the country you were raised in; the feeling is the same everywhere. Wanting to drive may seem to come from some desire for independence, but in truth, it comes only from envy.

Sure, you might think that the freedom to go anywhere and do anything would be increased by the simple ability to drive, and you would be right. Yet the desire to drive is driven by envy. You might be envious of those who can take a car where they are going instead of relying on public transportation. Those people can travel far greater distances than someone who can't drive.

Investing does the same thing. It allows those who have grasped even the smallest fragment of knowledge, the tiniest of investment subtleties that come with enrollment in these types of plans, to do things and go places far beyond where those who have not done so can go. No amount of chiding or coaxing, warning or foreseeing, can make you take advantage of your company-sponsored retirement plan. No one can force you. But if a moment of envy ever serves you for your own good, such a moment that gets you involved in your retirement plan is one of the best.

 Fear melts when you take action towards a goal you really want.

Robert G. Allen

So what keeps people from participating in these plans? What keeps people who are already involved in them from understanding how they work? (Not only are the statistics on those not yet enrolled high, but the numbers of those who do not use their plans wisely are just as alarming.)

Those who have failed to enroll use a collection of old standbys such as "I haven't gotten around to it" (which is the embarrassed brush-off) or "I have bills to pay" (which doesn't put you in any sort of exclusive group by any stretch of the imagination), and then there is one group that says, "The company doesn't match" (which in some circles is considered a reason not to participate). Add to that, "The plan isn't that good," "I was never told about it," and "It's too much trouble," and you have a basket full of excuses, none of which has any real merit.

But envy might do the trick. Despite its inclusion as one of the seven deadly sins, envy might just be the push that we need. We openly envy someone else's success. We envy owners of enormous houses, folks on tropical vacations, red carpet opulence, and the parade of wealth that signifies success. We envy those with talent and those who can do what we could never do. That's okay. Why, then, don't we envy those who have taken the initiative to invest in their future?

When it comes to investing, of course, envy may prove to be among the worst traits you can have. But if we can utilize envy to prompt you to take action on this unique opportunity, then so be it.

 Every now and then, the stock market reaches stratospheric heights. It becomes the talk of the town. Everyone wants in. When the crowd moves in one direction, envy can make an investor follow. A good investor will use those signs of enthusiasm as a signal to stop and think. Buying anything while the price is appreciating does not give you bragging rights. Living long enough to profit from it does, however.

No driver ever began the learning experience without first envisioning him- or herself behind the wheel, driving a car. They pretended. They sat on a parent's lap as he or she pulled the car into the driveway, they made car noises, and they may have even seen themselves cocooned in a fire-engine red sports car. They may have learned to appreciate a car by helping to wash it or maintain it mechanically. Envy *made* you want to drive.

But we need a beginning. Before we throw you behind the wheel, we need to take a walk around this mode of travel. Let's take a walk around the 401(k) plan. These plans are often referred to as defined-contribution plans. To appreciate this type of plan for what it is and explain why it isn't the be-all and end-all of retirement plans, we first have to understand it, exploit its strengths, and work on its weaknesses.

We'll look under the hood, although you will be under no obligation to get your hands dirty. It is just that the mechanics of your 401(k) can provide some surprising opportunities.

Good luck is what happens when preparation meets opportunity. Bad luck is what happens when lack of preparation meets a challenge.

Paul Krugman

I want to take a moment to inform you about several things before we go too far. The first and most important is the fact that when I use terminology like "looking under the hood" or anything else that might refer to the actual mechanics of an automobile, I am not intending that you do anything more than appreciate how things work. If I made any additional analogies, I would reveal a fundamental shortfall in myself: I know nothing but the absolute basics about cars. And while I know a great deal more about investing, I prefer to let the trained mechanics do the dirty work and scrutinize their efforts.

I am much like John Sutherland, the traveling companion of Robert Pirsig, the author of *Zen and the Art of Motorcycle Maintenance*. I prefer to trust the mechanics of an automobile—no motorbikes for me, thank you very much— rather than be the kind of person who might pop up the hood for a look.

Pirsig does say that cars present challenges that motorcycles do not. Yet the concept of willingly ignoring the technicality of maintenance, as his friend John Sutherland did, presented philosophical problems for him. I fully understand. Having purchased quality engineering, John was counting on his bike much more than Pirsig believed was wise.

That is the philosophy I want you to consider when it comes to investing. Instead of constantly tweaking a portfolio—from the Italian word *portafoglio*, meaning "to carry"—full of funds and stocks, you should concentrate on picking quality investments. While there are many methods of picking the best investments, and we will discuss the pros and cons of many of these further on, such as avoiding the top of the category, the best of the best, and instead looking at the performance of a stock or mutual fund with peripheral vision, we will be trying to achieve two things: better than average returns and a good night's sleep.

A Good Idea...

Inside your 401(k), you will generally find the stock of the company you work for and a basket of mutual funds. Each of these will be explained in depth further on, but for the investor faced with 20 or more choices, the baffling concept of suddenly taking some of those hard-earned dollars and putting them away for use 40 or more years in the future is hard enough to grasp on its own without having to pick something you know little about to get you there.

Many companies have made improvements in how they educate their employees about their self-directed retirement plans, but in many cases, they still fall woefully short.

The numbers of enrolled employees in companies where the plans are available still point to a lack of understanding about how these tools work.

 As Americans age, they come to understand two very important things: they will be responsible for their financial future, and they will live longer.

Over the last 25 years, the 401(k) plan has changed the landscape. You can read a timeline of this tax-deferred section of the tax code by visiting the Employee Benefit Research Institute and downloading the following document: www.ebri.org/pdf/publications/facts/0205fact.a.pdf. (Throughout the book, I will be giving you resources to further educate you. You can use them if you like or rely on my explanation of their content.)

When Ted Benna uncovered that particular section of tax code while he was working on improving a banking client's savings plan, he had only the faintest idea that what he had uncovered would grow to its current size and importance. Thrift savings plans, which have been referred to as the 401(k)'s older cousin, were already available. But with the discovery of the 401(k), the cumbersome thrift plans were quickly replaced.

The 401(k) was never intended to be the primary form of retirement benefit. A 401(k) plan is a type of defined-contribution plan that allows you to take a predetermined amount or percentage from your paycheck, deduct it before it is counted as taxable income, and invest it in the way you believe is best.

...with Consequences

Choosing the best way to invest is not as easy as it sounds. Even Benna failed to foresee employees' reaction to these plans. As corporations rushed to embrace the notion of allowing employees to direct their own plans, employees froze. It was hardest on new employees who had little understanding of how the plans worked.

Older employees were faced with age considerations, risk assessments, and investment choices that had previously been the responsibility of pension managers. New employees were faced with a new paycheck and someone suggesting that they take a piece of that new-found windfall and invest it in a plan with an often-dizzying array of choices. Both groups found the experience chilling.

Major decisions like these are akin to driving at night in a rainstorm. For the youngest employees, the idea of deferring money for some time in the distant future when their tax bracket would be lower, blah, blah, has proved to be not such an easy sell. For still other employees, playing catch-up at the halfway point of a worker's career was equally unappetizing.

How We Got to This Point

These are the plans that are available to you. You need to make them work. But to make these plans a success, you first need to understand what is happening.

What is a pension?

Once upon a time, as the story goes, companies lured employees to their ranks with the promise of a pension. Without any real obligation to make or even keep those promises, these companies told their employees that they would receive a defined-benefit pension, a form of deferred income that increases each year that they work, is managed by the company in many cases, and uses actuarial tables—estimates of life spans—to determine how much the company needs to contribute to keep the plan solvent. Pensions bred loyalty. That loyalty was fostered by the company's "guarantee" of a fixed benefit payment for the rest of the retired employee's life.

Each year an employee covered by a defined-benefit pension plan worked, that employee's retirement income would increase. Pensions worked best for older employees. The defined benefit that was promised rose with each salary increase, as it was generally a percentage of your income multiplied by the number of years you had worked. The idea was that the longer you worked for a company, the larger your "defined benefit" would be, according to the Federal Citizen Information Center (http://www.pueblo.gsa.gov). These plans, however, had numerous problems.

One glaring one was transportability. If you left the company, you might forfeit many or all of the retirement benefits that the company had accrued for you. Those plans could become quite sizable, giving the retiring employee a sizable monthly check.

The real problem, however, lay with the company itself. Although employees fail to realize this, no company expects to last forever. Lasting through the generations has become more the exception than the rule, and even those companies that have lasted have grown through mergers and acquisitions. After that kind of activity, companies usually are just a fraction of their original selves.

Chances are that your 401(k) is safe, largely because of your ability to transport it from one job to another. Pensions are quite another thing. If you have a defined-benefit plan, find out who your plan administrator is. From there, you can find some basic facts about the health of your plan. If you're an older worker, your questions should be about the plan's health. For instance, ask the administrator if the company "smooths" the plan. This is a big word for averaging the value. Some years, when things are good and the investments in the plan do well, the company shifts some of those gains to years when it didn't do so great. Between you and me, smoothing gives the plan a surface like ice: thin, fragile, and ultimately dangerous. If you are new, ask the administrator when you will be vested.

When a company is bought, sold, or dissolved, something that seems to happen every day, its pension plan and the promises made by the original company to its employees are often cancelled. Sometimes, but not often, the obligations are carried forward. Most mergers look at existing pension plans as cumbersome or worse, a necessary evil.

Once these plans are eliminated, those employees who expected them to cover their golden years now look to the protection of the Pension Benefit Guaranty Corporation.

The PBGC acts as a sort of insurance for these plans. What it does is guarantee that the pension participants will get something for their service. The maximum benefit it will pay was around $3,900 a month last time I checked. If you were promised more than this, as some airline pilots were, a PBGC takeover can make quite a difference in your retirement plans.

Along came the 401(k), and companies could turn the cumbersome problems associated with pensions back to the employees. Employers needed only to provide their employee with access to a defined-contribution plan and they could move on to doing whatever it is they call their business.

To sweeten the deal, employers enticed employees with matching contributions. This means that when an employee saves a dollar, the employer puts another dollar in for free. Companies usually do this up to a certain amount or percentage. In their thinking, this was far better than dealing with pensions. There was no more guessing how long an employee might live. No more actuarial tables or funny accounting maneuvers. No more obligations to keep the plan fully funded.

Few employees realized exactly what this meant. Now, the employee was faced with questions of not only how much to invest, but where and how.

 How do pensions differ from one another?

Retirement plans usually are structured in one of two ways: defined-benefit plans or defined-contribution plans. Defined-benefit plans pay a certain fixed retirement income to the employee after he or she retires. The amount is based on the number of years worked, with the last years of the plan providing the employee with the largest contribution to the plan. Defined-contribution plans rely on *you* to save money for your own retirement; once you become eligible to withdraw your benefit, you will determine the amount of the payout.

What the employee now had was a defined-contribution plan, a self-directed plan that depended on the employee's grasp of what was available.

Easy Money

This is how these plans work. Suppose you earn $500 a week and you have put nothing away for your retirement other than the mandatory social security withdrawal done by Payroll. Now suppose your employer makes this offer: it will contribute up to 10 percent of your pay if you do the same, and all you have to do is put it away in an account that can be used only when you reach $59\frac{1}{2}$. (You can access it earlier for various reasons such as first-time home purchases, medical bills, and so on.)

So with a matching employer contribution, when you put $50 in the plan, your employer does likewise. Each pay period, your $50 is taken from your paycheck before taxes are calculated, your employer matches that contribution, and your retirement account gets $100.

 When you leave one job for another, take your 401(k) plan with you. You will not be able to put the assets in your new employer's plan, but you will be able to put it in a traditional Individual Retirement Account (IRA). The penalties for taking your money out of the account are prohibitive. There is a 10 percent penalty for early withdrawal, plus your contributions to the plan (and your employer's as well) will be taxed at your current rate.

While pensions lacked transportability, if you leave a job with a 401(k), you can take all of the money with you. However, you will be penalized if you fail to roll it over into another tax-deferred account. Many times, the plan administrator, usually a representative of a mutual fund family, can help you roll it over with very little effort. Roll it over into another retirement account as soon as you leave.

 With a 401(k), unlike a pension, you can determine how the money is invested. For the beginning investor, the one with the learner's permit, that might not be the best possible situation. But that's why you're here.

Unfortunately, unlike learning how to drive, learning how to invest for your future involves precious little time spent riding in the passenger's seat.

Remember the running commentary that the person teaching you how to drive offered as you navigated through traffic. There are twice as many things to consider when you're behind the wheel of your retirement plan. Outliving your money is one.

In the next chapter, we will look at how defined-contribution plans work and introduce you to some of their positive effects.

CHAPTER 3

To Point B

People in this nation are poised to live longer, and as a result, we face the possibility that we will outlive our money if we fail to save enough. The 401(k) plan is just one piece of this complicated puzzle, albeit a very important one.

The question isn't at what age I want to retire; it's at what income.

George Foreman

If you are fresh out of school and just starting a job, you could be looking at a career that spans more than 50 years. Retirement ages are being pushed back. Those actuarial folks in the federal government, the ones hired by the people who sign the social security checks to determine just how long we might live, are all over this particular issue.

If you are 50, you might be in the workforce until well into your seventies. The kind of retirement our parents know will be reserved for the select few who can actually say, with all honesty, that they have enough money to live on until they die.

Age is one thing. We understand that we will get older. Utilizing your 401(k) plan to give you enough money to live well is quite another. That will involve some risk.

Even if it has been 20 years since you filled out your application, the person you need to speak with about your 401(k) or similar plan is your human resources or personnel representative. Ask that person for the particulars on your company's retirement plan and who to contact to get started. If you are joining the company for the first time, ask when you can begin saving and, most importantly, whether your company matches what you contribute. With matching, the company helps you save more for your own retirement while providing a benefit as well. However, even if the company doesn't match—and many have stopped doing so in recent years—enroll as soon as you can. These plans are at the heart of *your* retirement.

There are two ways to save money. The first has no risk involved and is by far the safest way. Stuffing your cash under a mattress or squirreling it away in a cookie jar keeps it close at hand. Unfortunately, this safety is actually whittling away at the value of the money. In Part III we will talk about the effects of inflation on your investments, but for now, we will just say that savings that earn no interest are being slowly made worth less by inflation.

To counteract this inflationary pressure, your money needs to earn at least as much interest as the inflation rate. If inflation is running around the 3 percent range, your savings will need to earn at least 3 percent in interest just to keep even. To do better than even, you will need to earn more money than the inflation rate. That means more risk.

Although we want to separate the two questions, age (how long will I live?) and risk (how much reward can I expect for the risks I take?), they are not unrelated. They move in opposite directions.

For now, let's just say that you will live to be 100 years old.

To have enough saved to get to 100 years old, your investments will need to be vast and diverse. That said, how do you place your bets? How do you make sure that you have enough saved to make it that far?

Good health is as important as a healthy portfolio. The inability to enjoy what you have achieved as an investor and retiree is among the top concerns for the superwealthy. It should be your concern as well.

We are notorious when it comes to wishing for something without thinking the whole request through. In ancient Greek mythology, Tithous asked for long life without considering the need for youthful vigor to help him enjoy those years. So how do we achieve what would amount to economic youthfulness to accompany our golden years?

Carefully and with due diligence. Americans tend to be neither when it comes to retirement. Stories of woe-ridden investors who had been dreaming of early retirements filled the pages of newspapers and magazines for several years following the market meltdown in 2000. These investors gambled their economic youthfulness and paid dearly.

So the questions are: how and when? How do you finance a life that may be incredibly long? How do you anticipate the dangers on the road ahead?

Suppose I am beginning late. What should I do?

If you are beginning late, don't worry. Take into consideration all of your assets, all of your bills, and how long you plan on working. If your assets far outweigh your debts, then you should be fine. Begin saving now, and do it aggressively, budgeting for the remaining years of your career and focusing on your retirement needs.

For every thousand dollars that you expect to receive annually—not monthly—from your retirement savings, you need to have $50,000 saved. Add in the cost of taxes, deferred until you supposedly are in a lower bracket, and inflation, and you are facing quite a hurdle. One way to resolve this dilemma is to work until a very advanced age. The other option requires you to take on some risk for those savings dollars.

That said, at the time of your retirement, you will need to have a cool $2.5 million socked away if you want a $40,000 annual income after taxes. That's a lot of money. Assuming a conservative 6 percent return, consider Table 3–1. This table and any other examples throughout the book are exactly that: examples.

Let me finish the math for you. You have to invest $1,346 a month, or $337 a week, for 40 years just to receive an average income at age 65. Scary, huh? You

Table 3–1

Year	Total Annual Contribution	Total Fund Value
1	16,153.77	16,154.83
2	32,307.55	33,277.90
3	48,461.32	51,428.34
4	64,615.09	70,667.82
5	80,768.87	91,061.66
6	96,922.64	112,679.13
7	113,076.41	135,593.65
8	129,230.19	159,883.05
9	145,383.96	185,629.80
10	161,537.73	212,921.36
20	323,075.47	594,229.31
30	484,613.20	1,277,093.76
40	646,150.93	2,500,000.00

will have compounding on your side. You will have time on your side. But you will need to take at least enough risk to achieve a 6 percent gain.

Consider $2.5 million for a moment. It is a daunting number all by itself. The 6 percent we used in the calculation of that 40-year figure is, in most cases, considered conservative. Overall, the markets do slightly better than that over that length of time.

 For the last 40 years, the Standard & Poor's 500 (S&P 500) index of large-capitalization stocks has been the benchmark used by many investors to determine how well or poorly they have done. Over that period, the S&P 500 it has returned 10.3 percent, dividends included.

The Essential Tool

Let's quickly recap where we are. We understand how these types of defined-contribution plans work. You put in pretax dollars, and those dollars are invested for the future. We also understand that investing in your retirement plan will require you to take both your age and risk into consideration. You will do this by using the tools at hand inside your plan. You will use mutual funds (a full explanation awaits you in Part II) to get the best return on your investment dollars. But which ones do you use in a 401(k)? More importantly, how do you determine which ones will serve you best?

Inside virtually every retirement plan, there is an index fund of the 500 largest companies, the S&P 500. This group of companies offers you a broad exposure to the markets while giving you a wonderful place to start your investment life. The S&P 500 is also a good benchmark for judging how well you have done.

The index contains 500 of the largest companies. It is supposed to reflect the state of business in this country. These companies, two-thirds of which pay dividends, provide investors with a broad market perspective. (A dividend, which we will talk about later, is basically a share of the corporation's profit that is returned to the shareholder.)

What is the S&P 500?

You will hear references to the Standard & Poor's 500 index often—perhaps too often. It is an index of big companies only. In recent years, there has been a push for more specific benchmarks so that investors can properly compare the performance of their investments with an inexpensively run index.

The S&P 500 index is widely used by mutual funds. While many mutual funds compare themselves to this group of stocks, many of them are wrong to do so.

Almost every 401(k) offers an index fund for this large group of companies.

Almost every 401(k) offers a money market fund of some sort as well. Unfortunately, this is often the default investment. Signing up for a 401(k) plan does not mean your money is automatically directed to the best place possible. You are in charge of your future. You are the pension fund manager.

The S&P 500 would serve an investor who plans to work 40 years and is willing to put away $1,346 per month quite well.

To achieve that $2.5 million nest egg used in Table 3–1, you would need to invest more than the maximum currently allowed in a 401(k) plan. The legal deduction allowed by law is $15,000 a year or 25 percent of your salary, whichever is greater—unless, of course, you are over 50 years old, which means that you can take advantage of the gradually increasing contribution rate.

Using the 10.3 percent return for the S&P 500 for the past 40 years (although this is no guarantee of future returns), the amount needed to achieve that $2.5 million nest egg is greatly reduced. As Table 3–2 shows, instead of needing contributions of $16,000 a year or more, an annual contribution of only $5,205.23 could net the same result.

Table 3–2

Year	Total Annual Contribution	Total Fund Value
1	5,205.23	5,206.33
2	10,410.45	10,947.81
3	15,615.68	17,280.66
4	20,820.91	24,265.79
5	26,026.13	31,970.40
6	31,231.36	40,468.57
7	36,436.58	49,842.06
8	41,641.81	60,181.02
9	46,847.04	71,584.89
10	52,052.26	84,163.36
20	104,104.53	308,485.97
30	156,156.79	906,385.43
40	208,209.05	2,500,000.00

Adding some additional risk can keep your goals in sight while lowering the amount of money needed to achieve similar results.

Why plan for such a long life span? Because you never know how long you may live, what social entitlement programs (social security, Medicare, Medicaid) will be available when you are elderly, and what your health might be during all those years.

Even without the aid of medical science, we are capable of great age. Consider Jeanne Calment. In 1997, she passed away at the ripe old age of 122. Hailed as France's oldest citizen, she was a fan of port wine, cigarettes, chocolate, and olive oil. She fenced, she rode a bike, and at age 121 she released a rap CD. In an Associated Press release following her death, she was quoted as saying that the key to staying interested in such a long life was the ability to dream, to think, and to review her life.

Consider Adwaitya. He lived to be 250 years old. On March 15, 2006, he died in the Calcutta Zoo, his home since he arrived there in 1875. This Aldabran tortoise, taken from an atoll north of Madagascar, gives us reason to wonder about longevity. Gilbert White, an eighteenth-century naturalist, called the time given to these animals a "seeming waste," suggesting that tortoises "relish it so little." Saving for a long retirement allows you to do more than waste time in old age; it gives you the freedom to relish it.

Now that you have come to grips with the very real possibility that you could live to be really old, the goal is to do so without outliving your money. There is only one way to do that.

Investing will provide the means, but you must determine the risk. In the next chapter, we will ask ourselves a few questions about what is commonly called *risk tolerance*, a catchy phrase that always seems to suggest that there is some knowable level of risk that you are willing to assume and that from there you can begin investing.

I prefer to think of risk as an evolving and ever-shifting event that no one can accurately pinpoint—although some may try. In the following pages, we'll make an effort at a little self-examination and discuss what to do if you are who you think you are.

CHAPTER 4

Risk and the Retirement Account

I f your 401(k) is the only investment you have, you should not be very aggressive at all. Even if you have other investments, as an utterly confused investor, you should approach this account as if it is the only one you have. For that reason, you should take on less risk than that you would in a portfolio that was not part of your outside retirement savings.

You should take just enough risk to allow for growth without exposing you to outsized losses.

 If things seem under control, you are just not going fast enough.

Mario Andretti

Risk is wonderfully moderated by an index fund such as an S&P 500 fund. The returns have outpaced inflation. The index is diversified, exposing you to investments in a large number of companies in a wide array of sectors.

Investing requires you to do several things at once. As with driving, you have to balance a number of different skills to get from point A to point B safely. You must determine your speed. Speed is risk. The faster you go, the greater your chances of arriving at point B faster than the rest of us. But increasing your speed also increases your chance for mishap.

You have to consider the wide variety of conditions that will confront you on the road. The weather, the road surface, and the traffic conditions all play a role in how you conduct your journey. This requires balance. You make a plan to take the safest route, the one that avoids slowdowns and traffic jams that will impede your progress.

And you incorporate diversity by plotting different routes and anticipating the worst. Using risk and balancing that risk with diversity is the ultimate goal of your 401(k) or IRA investments.

What Is Risk?

Among financial writers worth their words, risk has been the subject of one of the greatest running debates. How do you determine how much or which amount of risk is right, for whom and when? How do you calculate risk? How do you measure it?

The Dow Corporation has a risk calculator that it uses for business. The company uses this tool to try to estimate profit projections for a business given the potential human casualties and environmental problems, and the severity of those problems. The answer is based on where and when these problems may arise, how litigious the people involved may be, and whether the problems are likely to lead to civil unrest or political fallout. The Acceptable Risk Calculator determines the exact price point at which profit is jeopardized by danger to the public.

Similarly, the American Heart Association offers an interactive calculator to calculate your risk of heart attack and stroke. Harvard University offers a cancer calculator, and while Soft32.com offers an interesting risk calculator, it requires more math than I think either of us wants to bother with right now.

The subject of risk is at the heart of every business decision. Your investments are a business decision. Determining how much risk you can handle will be discussed throughout this book, but your retirement account is not the place to take on a lot of risk. The cost of a misstep is far too high.

Yet risk and time are intertwined. At one point in your life, you can be allowed to take on more risk and be forgiven for any missteps, while at another time in your life, risk can punish you by forcing you to work years or decades beyond your plan.

It is impossible to separate time and risk, much as common sense and intuition should always be joined. They act to balance each other. The more time you have, the more you risk you can assume. And, of course, vice versa.

Consider the following questions. Although I have taken the liberty of answering them for you, they are an assessment of risk. Most investors have a difficult time wrapping themselves around a concrete definition of risk. Metaphors abound, but words are somehow inadequate for defining what is essentially an emotion.

But first, a word about what "the markets" are. They are places where investors go to buy a stake in a company; when they do so, they become financial partners who are entitled to a piece of the profits. Investors buy what other investors sell. Because people are involved, moods and sentiment play a role in how business is conducted. Bad moods translate into sluggish markets. Good moods, on the other hand, provide the markets with the enthusiasm needed to make them rise.

 Understanding your own personal risk tolerance is an evolving and gradually unfolding event that should take place over many years. But be warned: you will come across people who will try to pinpoint your risk tolerance, and they will be very persuasive. Brokers can be advisors and advisors can be planners, and they all have a separate agenda. When you speak with your 401(k) plan administrator, you probably will be talking to a representative of a mutual fund company that employs all of the above-mentioned professionals. Such representatives, however, have no interest in selling you a product, so their advice will be much more succinct, and if you are unsure about how much risk you can handle, they will lead you to a product that will give you time to develop a strategy.

Over a long period of time, the markets will be in better moods more often than they'll be in bad moods. Over a long period of time, an investor can survive the down-in-the-dumps stretches because the sunny ones will outnumber them by a considerable amount. That said, an investor with a long time horizon can take more chances or risk with investments than an investor with a shorter time horizon.

The investor with a short time horizon may actually witness more bad market moods than good ones. You can never predict when the market, which looks at and reacts to all sorts of economic data, will turn sour. An investor with a short time horizon might not have enough time to recover from those down periods or enough good times to make up the difference.

Take this little risk test and see if your answers align with mine.

1. What is your age?

A. Are you 35 years or under? (Insert your answer here _____)

My answer: If you are, you can assume more risk. Time is on your side. It is commonly believed that a young investor will be able to weather many changes in the markets.

Most financial folks believe that during this period, you should take the top down and let your hair blow in the wind. An investor in this age bracket can use an age-adjusted fund that targets an employee's retirement age. These types of funds are rebalanced over time to give the investor the right exposure to stocks and more conservative investments such as bonds. These investors can also use indexes that expose their investments to sectors of the market other than large companies, such as small and mid-size companies.

B. Are you between 36 and 54 years of age? (Insert your answer here _____)

My answer: This period, often considered the middle years of a career, is a time when the temptation to play catch-up is most likely to appear. Time is running short. If you started investing when you were young, now is the time to adjust the balance in your 401(k) to protect whatever gains you have made. This means that you need to add some more conservative investments to your choices, such as a total market index fund or an S&P 500 index. If you are just starting out, these are also good places to invest. [More on how the inside of your 401(k) plan should look a little further on.]

C. Are you 55 or older? (Insert your answer here _____)

My answer: Even if you are just getting started this late, you should still be very careful, indexing much of your savings or choosing a balanced approach. If you have reached a time in your life where your kids are gone, all the bills are paid, and perhaps you own your home, you can invest a good portion of your income in your retirement. Unless you plan on working well into your seventies, take modest gains for what they are— gains—and invest conservatively.

2. The markets are down and have been falling steadily for the past several days. Investors, the reporters tell you, are heading for the door, selling everything in sight. Everyone has lost confidence. You log on to your investments via the online access your 401(k) plan administrator provides. Your investments, even the conservative ones, are down, some of them significantly. What do you do?

    A. Should you sell your investments and, in doing so, cut your losses? (Insert your answer here _____)

    My answer: This is a knee-jerk reaction that does not help your long-term goals. One of the key ingredients in a plan such as a 401(k) is the ability to dollar cost average. This unique investment tool, which we will discuss later in the book, allows you to buy shares in the investments you choose at varying levels. When your investments are down, you are able to buy more shares. When your investments are high, this approach forces you to buy less. It is human nature to want to jump in when the markets go up and sell with the crowd when they decline. Dollar cost averaging does not allow this human emotion; you simply continue to buy even when you might otherwise consider selling.

    B. Should you hold on to your investments and wait for them to return to their former price? (Insert your answer here _____)

    My answer: Owning individual stocks, even (or especially) your own company's stock, in a 401(k) is a risky business. (We will discuss the hows and whys of individual equity ownership in Parts III and IV.) Suffice it to say that inside your 401(k), you should never rest on your laurels. Things do change. No matter. But by all means, stay invested. In the long term, some downturns, often called bear markets, can seem quite long, while their counterparts, the bull markets, when they return (and yes, Virginia, they always return), usually last much longer. Revisiting your strategy at least once a year is generally considered wise. Tweaking your retirement portfolio frequently has been proven to be not as profitable.

C. Should you buy more of the same investments because the lower price makes them more attractive? (Insert your answer here _____)

My answer: Understanding what you have invested in, which is the goal of this book, will give you the confidence to make this decision. It will help you identify when things have changed for the better or for the worse. It will make the decision to buy more much easier. Using dollar cost averaging will get you a good investment at a lower price—automatically.

3. You are on *Deal or No Deal*, a popular game show exported worldwide by a Dutch company after significant success in the Netherlands, that pits the contestant against unknown quantities in closed briefcases. Hidden within the briefcases are dollar values ranging from $0.01 to $1 million. You are asked to choose one briefcase. You then open and thus eliminate case after case. After you have opened the allowed number of cases, the banker, a shadowy figure who phones in, makes you an offer to quit. This "game" has inspired economic papers internationally largely because of its wide-open experimental nature. (Economists are always looking for ways to conduct experiments. One of the most difficult things to test is risk aversion. There is never enough money to conduct and measure the true reactions of the people involved—that is, there wasn't until *Deal or No Deal*. While you are being entertained, there are economists out there studying the contestants' reactions, their strategies, their ages and occupations, and so on.)

How would you assess your risk when confronted with the unknown?

A. After choosing your case and opening six others, which contain the million-dollar prize, the $750,000, the $500,000, the $400,000, the $300,000, and the $200,000, would you take the offer that the banker phones in? (Insert your answer here _____)

My answer: The contestant is asked to determine, through numerous commercial breaks, the utility value of his or her choice. Utility value is an attempt to measure numerous probabilities and determine how much risk is worth taking. For a particular contestant, the banker's offer might represent a full year's salary, as was the case with a teacher who was recently on the show. The offered sum might seem insulting, literally challenging the player to continue on with a "what have I go to lose" defense for his or her actions. According to a paper written by Richard Thaler, Guido Baltussen,

Martin Van den Assem, and Theirry Post, the ultimate goal for the contestant should be to "break even."

B. If, after you opened those six cases, the banker offered you a large amount of money that would substantially increase your standard of living, pay your creditors, help with needed remodeling, and so on, would you take it? (Insert your answer here _____)

My answer: You need to consider this: the banker is supposed to offer the mean difference between the total amount of money in the game and the amount of money that remains in play in the unopened briefcases. Because there is no strategy, no test of your knowledge, just you and your assessment of how much risk you are willing to take, you probably would turn down the banker's offer. The banker usually offers low amounts when larger-valued briefcases are open, and higher amounts when the low-valued cases are initially revealed. But the name of the game is excitement, and most contestants know that unless they are down to only a few cases and none of them is worth much, the risk is gone, but the utility (what you would do with the winnings) is gone as well, so you might as well just keep on playing.

C. There seems to be little chance that you will win any huge amount of money. Most of the cases with larger amounts have been opened already, and the offers that the banker has made have continued to drop. Do you take the offer even if it is significantly lower and leave? (Insert your answer here _____)

The paper by Thaler et al. used a cross section of contestants from several countries. What the authors determined was that the contestant needed to be able to make some simple computational guesses, an ability that, it turned out, was higher among more educated contestants. These contestants assumed that these are basically utility valuation calls. They understood what was at stake, whether the offer would make a difference in their lives, whether it would affect their goals, and whether it would be worth walking away with nothing as opposed to something.

4. Here's a last question about risk: a truck is traveling down a two-lane highway just shy of the speed limit. As you approach the truck, you must make a decision about whether to pass the truck or stay at the lower speed and continue your journey behind it. You notice that there is a second truck in front of the one in front of you that is driving slowly. Would you pass both trucks or wait for the lagging truck to pass first?

A. Would you take into consideration your car's mechanical ability, the road surface, the time of day, and the condition of your own reflexes, and then make a split-second determination to pass the truck anyway? (Insert your answer here _____)

While all of those factors play a major role in how well you will be able to perform the act of driving, making the decision after simply assessing all of those little pieces of data and determining your skill level implies a certain willingness to embrace risk in a measured way.

B. Would you decide that your abilities as a driver, regardless of the car's condition, the road, the weather, and any number of other factors, some known and others not, would allow you to take the risk and simply gun the accelerator and try to pass? (Insert your answer here _____)

My answer: You, my fellow traveler, may need to educate yourself in the fine art of computation. It can become increasingly important to use utility—an understanding of the advantages of making or not making a certain move—and risk—the ability to weigh the reward for the action. Besides that, you are frightening the pants off your passengers.

C. Would you pull back and allow the truck to make its own move around the truck in front of it, knowing that you will still get your opportunity to pass further down the road? (Insert your answer here _____)

This is the clearest understanding of how taking a risk when none is needed can affect you in the long run. Any number of unknowns could have entered into the previous two questions.

There is no scorecard for this little "test," and I would not go so far as to call it scientific, but it can be helpful in getting you to think about how you would react to some of the situations on your investment journey—and on the open road. With any luck, it has given you a little deeper insight into your risk tolerance.

Risk Has a Role and a Price

Understanding risk is extremely important when it comes to your investments. Shortly, we will peek into your 401(k) and discuss diversity, balance, and asset allocation, if only briefly, and the kinds of investments that are available to you. There is just one final word about risk that I'd like to offer.

The idea behind risk is to take responsibility for your investments. No matter what they are, you should never be faced with the possibility of losing all or the majority of what you own. Risk comes with a price. The greater the risk is, the higher the cost of taking it.

The Dow Jones Industrial Average lists 30 companies across a wide swath of industries that best represent the United States economy. It is debatable whether this benchmark is still valid—the S&P 500 is a much better index, and given the DJIA's ability to be volatile, it should probably be retired. The DJIA is price-weighted, meaning that when a stock increases by a dollar, that change has the same effect no matter how much the percentage advance is. For instance, a dollar increase in share value for a stock worth a hundred dollars a share (1 percent) would have the same effect as a dollar increase in a stock trading at ten dollars (10 percent). When the Dow was first introduced by Charles Dow in 1896, it contained the following companies with an average of 40.94:

American Cotton Oil Company (now Unilever)
American Sugar Company (now Amstar Holdings)
American Tobacco Company (divided in 1911)
Chicago Gas Company (now People's Energy Corporation)
Distilling & Cattle Feeding Company (now Millennium Chemicals)
Laclede Gas Light Company (now The Laclede Group)
National Lead Company (now NL Industries)
North American Company (changed to Edison and divided in the 1950s)
Tennessee Coal, Iron and Railroad Company (absorbed into U.S. Steel in 1907)
U.S. Leather Company (dissolved in 1952)
United States Rubber Company (formerly Uniroyal, bought by Michelin in 1990)

Markets can get expensive. When the Dow Jones Industrial Average climbs above the 12,000 mark and is heading higher each day, those who understand risk will realize that this market is on the way up. The cost of owning a piece of it has increased, and so has the risk that you will not be as handsomely rewarded for your investment. Creating a balance between risk and reward should always be the underlying goal of any investor.

There is probably no better analogy for how you should look at rising stock markets than a trip to the grocery store. Suppose you buy hamburger for $1.99 a pound one day. The next day, when you go back to purchase another pound of the same ground meat, you find that the price has gone up to $2.99 a pound. You will probably think that you should have bought more at the lower price the previous day. But if you have a recipe that calls for hamburger, you probably will swallow your objection to the increased price and buy it anyway. However, if, on a third trip to the store, you find that the price has jumped yet another dollar a pound, you will probably would seek a cheaper type of ground meat ingredient or not eat ground meat at all until the price drops.

As for contestants in the *Deal or No Deal* game show, weighing probabilities and consequences is key to deciding how much risk to take. The same is true of passing the truck on the highway. When it comes to investments, inside or outside your 401(k) plan, you need to keep three things in mind:

1. *There's always someone who knows more than you do.* In the world of investing, if you are buying something, the seller probably has a reason for unloading what she owns. You may or may not know the reason. If you are the seller, the buyer probably assumes that he knows something that you do not, since otherwise you wouldn't be selling.

2. *Your level of experience plays an important role in your decisions about risk.* If you ever feel that you are unsure about your risk tolerance, opt for the least risky investment. That usually means choosing an index fund that covers a wide range of companies. Do not, however, choose the default investment, which in many 401(k) plans is some sort of money market account. Keep your rainy day account in those; don't keep your retirement money there.

3. *Even the best strategies, advice from the most highly regarded financial gurus, and the surest investments can fail.* If you have analyzed the investment, done your homework, and invested with a margin of safety in mind at all times, you will be better able to accept some temporary defeats at the hands of the unknown.

Putting this newly found knowledge about risk to work will be quite another thing altogether. Today, 401(k) plans are evolving, just as you are evolving as an investor. Some plans may offer you brokerage services and opportunities that the vast majority of us do not have. But the key ingredient in your defined-contribution plan will most likely be the mutual fund.

In the next chapter, we will explore how mutual funds help both those with a great deal of investment savvy and those with little achieve great things for their future.

CHAPTER 5

Navigating Your Company-Sponsored Retirement Plan

◆◆◆◆◆◆◆◆◆◆◆◆◆◆◆◆◆◆◆◆◆◆◆◆◆◆◆◆◆◆◆◆◆◆◆

Inside every corporate-sponsored 401(k) plan is the company's stock, a selection of mutual funds, and usually some sort of money market account. This is where it all comes together. You understand the dashboard and the controls. You have been on the road and seen what you need to understand about yourself, how you will make decisions, and hopefully, how you will act in the face of an unknown future.

The hardest concept to grasp and the most important is the "you" inside. You can make many investment mistakes if you don't have a firm handle on not only who you are, but also where you are headed.

There are three kinds of people: those who make things happen, those who watch things happen, and those who ask, "What happened?"

Casey Stengel

Most 401(k) plans offer only a small fraction of the alternatives available outside of your plan. You won't have 8,000 mutual funds to choose among. You won't have the unlimited number of brokerage choices, such as individual stocks and bonds, options, and other investments that are available to investors outside the 401(k) umbrella.

In many cases, the offerings inside your 401(k) plan will amount to a basket of mutual funds and, of course, your company's stock. You should avoid your company's stock, if possible. You should do this for two reasons. The first is that putting individual stocks in your account increases your risk. Your company's stock is prone to volatility. Stick to the index funds offered.

The second reason you should avoid the stock is diversity. It is possible that the company's stock is already included in another part of your portfolio, such as an index fund. Using an index fund spreads your risk and increases diversity. There is a good chance that the place where your company's stock will do the best for you is inside your index fund.

What is balance?

Your retirement plan should always be balanced. Balance is the combination of time, risk, and diversity. Diversity involves putting your money in a wide variety of investments to reduce your vulnerability to volatile market changes. Even the most youthful investor should protect a portion of a retirement portfolio from harm.

Diversity is the act of spreading your money among a variety of investments. This is extremely important in a 401(k) plan. You are in this for the long term, even if you do not intend to stay in your job for the long term. Always approach your 401(k) as if you will be managing these investments for decades.

Index funds provide both a certain protection against risk and a good level of diversity. In addition, they provide those qualities at the cheapest price possible. Index funds work on autopilot. They change their holdings only occasionally.

When a company like Standard & Poor's changes its index, an index fund will sell the stock that was removed from the index and buy the new addition. Sometimes, if the company being added is too large, some of the shares of other companies may need to be sold to readjust the weights in the index. Weighting refers to an internal balance mechanism designed to keep the index somewhat reflective of the group it intends to mimic.

What is weighting?

Whatever the index you are looking at, some form of weighting is used to arrive at the average price. The Dow Jones Industrial Average, which is price-weighted (the share prices are averaged), uses what is called the Dow Divisor. This number, available at the Chicago Board of Trade, is used to determine the published average. It changes daily as a result of stock splits and other events that do not necessarily affect the value of the stock. A two-for-one stock split of a $100 stock would result in two shares worth $50 each. The company and its total value remain the same, but there are twice as many shares. The S&P 500 is weighted based on market capitalization (the worth of a company, determined by multiplying the number of outstanding shares by the closing share price).

Because age and risk play a determining role in your plan, the younger you are, the more you should attempt to balance your funds for the maximum benefit. Age plays a defining role in that balance. In the next step, we will look at not only the when but the where and how to get your 401(k) set up for the best results years down the road.

CHAPTER 6
The Role of Age

◆━◇◇◇◇◇◇◇◇◇◇◇◇◇◇◇◇◇◇◇◇◇◇◇◇◇◇◇◇◇━◆

Investors between Age 25 and Age 35

If you are *between the ages of 25 and 35*, you should look for a balanced fund that offers some exposure to bonds, or fixed-income investments, as well as stocks. Invest 25 percent of your allocation (payroll deduction) in this fund. Expect an expense ratio of about 1 percent or less. Fees tend to run slightly higher in a 401(k), a cost of convenience. Less is better.

Take, for instance, the Fidelity Balanced Fund. Fidelity is a big player in the 401(k) world, and chances are good that a fund like this, often referred as a hybrid, will be included among your plan's offerings. This fund has a five-star Morningstar rating (more on the significance of that in the next part of our investment journey), an investment strategy that includes a ratio of 60 percent of assets in stocks, with at least 25 percent of the remaining investments concentrated in fixed-income investments or preferred stocks.

 Many mutual fund families now have targeted balanced funds. For instance, if you were a 30-year-old employee and wanted balance, you would choose a fund that targets the length of your working career. For example, T. Rowe Price has a fund called the 2040, which assumes that you will retire in that year and gradually rebalances the portfolio from moderate risk to conservative over the lifetime of the fund.

Because a fund like this generally focuses on large-cap stocks—*cap* refers to capitalization, or the total market value of the company's stock—you should be careful about carrying other funds in your portfolio that might expose you to the same holdings that are in your asset allocation or balanced fund.

Inside the Fidelity Balanced Fund (ticker symbol: FBALX, 82 Devonshire Street, Mailzone Z1c, Boston, MA 02109, 800–343–3548), there are companies such as General Electric (GE). In fact, GE is one of the fund's largest holdings at the time of this writing. Owning both the Fidelity Balanced Fund and an index fund of large-cap stocks like those in the S&P 500 would expose your portfolio to GE twice, and in large enough quantities would interfere with your efforts at diversifying your account.

Investors should also be aware of the costs of owning certain funds. In terms of fees, index funds cannot be beat. Actively managed mutual funds tend to charge more in fees. Actively managed mutual funds are funds that seek to achieve a certain goal by investing in a wide variety of stocks. Fees tend to be higher for this type of fund.

Not all funds or fund families are the same. Fortunately, a single fund family often manages the funds offered to you within a retirement account. Unfortunately, not all of the funds that are generally available to investors will be accessible through your company's plan. When talking with your fund administrator—and by all means, do call (there is no need to use the Internet for anything other than information or to update your percentages), ask about the fees first. Even if you think that a particular fund is right for you, if it is too expensive (over 1.5 percent for an actively managed fund), opt for an index fund. If the fund choices are too limited, tell this to your human resource contact and request a broader amount of choices.

Fees play a major role in how much return you actually receive. Looking for low fees is a lot like searching for the cheapest gas station. Since all gas is basically the same, the cost of the fuel should be your only consideration. In the world of mutual funds, finding the fund that is cheapest in terms of fees means looking at different funds' similarities in a side-by-side comparison.

When comparing funds that offer balance, fees may be the best way to determine which one to invest in. Fees are usually charged based on the amount of invested assets. A fund with a fee of 0.50 percent would skim $50 off of a $10,000 balance.

You should be looking for funds that offer diversity and asset allocation with the least amount of fees for the effort. While the Fidelity Balanced Fund, mentioned previously, offers the investor good allocation, there are major funds that charge far less for virtually the same allocation between equities and fixed income (bonds), the same five-star rating, and nearly identical performance.

For example, the Goldman Sachs Growth & Inc Strategy Inst (ticker symbol: GOIIX, 4900 Sears Tower, c/o Goldman Sachs & Co., Chicago, IL 60606, 800–526–7384), with its 0.17 percent expense ratio, offers an even better opportunity for the long-term investor. The expense ratio eats away at potential returns, charging investors for managing their money. A fee of 0.17 percent on a $10,000 balance would amount to $17—far less than a fund doing a similar allocation at a higher fee. The more money left invested, the closer you will be to your retirement goals.

This fund employs a clever strategy to achieve those low fees; it uses a fund-of-funds strategy that incorporates holdings in a variety of index funds. (If this is offered inside your plan, beware the crossover investment.) This fund invests in the CORE Large Cap Growth, the CORE Large Cap Value, the Core International Equity Funds, CORE Fixed Income Funds, and the Global Fixed Income Fund. With a truly diversified offering such as this, the young investor can spread his or her wings in the rest of the portfolio.

The remaining 75 percent of the investment should go to a more aggressive approach, such as mid-cap indexes, small-cap indexes, emerging markets, or international equities. Beware of the last two; they often have higher expense ratios even in an index fund.

When you are screening for mid-cap and small-cap index funds, look for expense ratios lower than 1 percent. Expenses should play a major role in your selection of overseas index funds as well. This group tends to charge more for exposure to international markets. While some exposure to overseas investments is acceptable for this age range, you should limit your allocation to 10 percent or less. Using Yahoo's fund screener to find the best foreign index funds based on only two qualifiers turned up two funds. Our fund requirements were simple: top 10 percent of all international funds with fees of less than 1 percent. This search turned up two world funds:

American Funds Smallcap World R5 (RSLFX), with expenses of 0.79 percent

Oppenheimer Global Opportunities (YOGIYX), with expenses of 0.82 percent

Investors between Age 35 and Age 50

For the investor aged *35 to 50 years old*, a change in allocation is in order. People in this age group should allocate at least 50 percent of their pretax investment dollars to a lifestyle fund that balances equities with fixed income. The remaining 50 percent can be invested more aggressively in index funds that track the other 4,500 companies too small to be included in the S&P 500, with some (albeit minimal) exposure to international indexes.

Investors Older than Age 50

If you are *50 years old or older*, you should keep 75 percent of your pretax investment dollars in some sort of balanced or asset allocation fund. Exposure to riskier indexes should be limited to the remaining 25 percent.

In the absence of a good balanced fund, use an index of the top 500 companies or an index fund that offers exposure to the total market. Balance that index fund with a bond index fund. Use the same percentages—a ratio of 75–25 percent aggressive to conservative when you are young, moving gradually to the reverse, 25–75 percent, as you age.

If your plan offers age allocation funds or, as they have come to be known, lifestyle funds, jump at the chance at using these for balance, diversity, and low fees. These funds are readjusted to keep the right exposure of stocks and bonds for the targeted age group.

It has recently been discovered that these types of funds have actually done better for investors than portfolios that needed to be readjusted by their owners. Lifestyle funds seek to blend conservative, moderate, and aggressive investment strategies and make them age-appropriate. For the youngest investors, the fund would be tipped heavily toward risk. Such funds try to diminish risk as the investor ages.

A recent study published by Hewitt Associates, the employee benefits research firm, discovered that not only do far too few people readjust their portfolios to keep them balanced, but those who did still underperformed, if only slightly, those who used a fund that allocated the balance automatically.

The idea behind accepting more risk when you are young is the length of time you will be involved in the market. Simply put, younger people have time on their side. In a down market, they can ride out a longer period waiting for the next new high. Older investors, on the other hand, have a shorter time horizon and cannot afford to go through long periods of underperforming markets.

A lifestyle fund caters to age. For the older investor, these funds would allocate a slightly larger portion of the investor's money to more stable investments, such as bonds. As investors approach middle age, the amount of time they have to "ride out" market lows—and there will be lows—is much smaller than the amount their youthful counterparts have. A lifestyle fund will automatically change the way the money is allocated across stocks and bonds. This is called *rebalancing*.

The late Benjamin Graham, author of *Intelligent Investor*, was firm in his belief that all investors should hold an asset mix of 75–25 stocks to bonds. Those percentages change as an investor ages, but at all times, no matter how young or old he or she is, the prudent investor owns not only stocks but bonds as well. Younger investors should hold 25 percent in bonds (funds) and 75 percent in stocks (funds, either indexed or actively managed). As the investor nears retirement, those percentages are gradually reversed. Lifestyle funds do this for you automatically.

With a lifestyle fund, investors need to decide only the age at which they want to retire to determine which fund is right for them. The key to any plan's success remains simple: invest frequently and evenly, and diversify.

The Skill to Invest

You should now have a clear understanding of how time and risk are not only complementary, but forever intertwined. The longer the time period you have to invest, the greater the risk that you can take with your investments. With a limited time frame, your investments must balance your rewards and risk more carefully.

Successful investing will always involve some risk, but using diversity as a way to reduce that risk is extremely important. Use index funds whenever possible to spread your investment dollars around. This gives you a better chance at avoiding sudden changes in the markets.

Starting late is not an excuse for not starting saving for retirement. In many instances, you will work longer than you anticipate. Take your age into consideration. A 30-year-old can probably plan on a retirement life equal to the number of years spent working. Starting to invest at an early age allows the investor to assume more risk (and grow his or her money more quickly) and allows compounding to work its magic.

A 50-year old may actually have more than 20 viable years left in the workforce. Late savers may need to increase their payroll deductions to meet the same goals as the younger worker. Starting late does not mean that you should take additional risks.

Part II will take a look at mutual funds and discuss which ones are right for your tax-deferred retirement plan and which ones should be held outside of such plans.

PART II

◆◆◆◆◆◆◆◆◆◆◆◆◆◆◆◆◆◆◆◆◆◆◆◆◆◆◆◆◆◆

Profiting from Groupthink Using Mutual Funds

CHAPTER 7
Behind the Wheel

◆◆◆

Before we move on to the next leg of this financial journey, I want to take a few moments to address a few things that you need to know about yourself and the skills you will develop in this segment of the book, some of which you may not have known before.

First of all, while a good many of you are indeed utterly confused about investing and want to learn the skills you need to do it right, with the minimum number of mistakes and the maximum amount of profit, not all of you are reading your first financial book. That's okay. You can be utterly confused about a lot of financial matters after reading a lot of different philosophies.

There are numerous approaches to investing. Some people are market timers, while other use charts. Some books act as entrepreneurial coaches, prodding you on to millionaire status; on the same shelf are books that harangue, demand frugality, or try to coax you to think in a commonsense way. To those of my fellow authors who have had the opportunity to publish, congratulations. The trouble is that you, the reader, have often missed the point.

You are, if you are like me, somewhat cynical, eternally curious, and able to walk and chew gum at the same time. Yet when it finally comes to making any financial decision, we are on our own. Much as in driving—and hence the analogy I have been exploiting so far—it is the personality that you bring to your investing as well as the skills that you know you need that make the investment equation work.

In Part I, I did not discuss taxes or inflation, the structure of the funds you will be investing in, or the problems that have befallen those funds in recent years. I simply wanted you to develop the skills that would enable you to understand what you have begun by starting a 401(k) plan. This is quite possibly the best investment move available and the one that involves the least initial effort. We will revisit your retirement plan throughout the remainder of the book, and the focus will be, at least in part, on taxes and inflation.

Henry David Thoreau once said, "The heart is forever inexperienced." But common sense seldom is. There are only a few investors who are able to bring their financial savvy, their street smarts, and their market cunning to the markets and use them with any skill. Most investors, alas, still wear their hearts on their sleeves. They have common sense, but they have little will to listen to it.

You have to ask yourself why. Why do experienced investors act irrationally? Why do they follow the herd, buying into an upswing and selling when things turn sour? Why don't they use common sense?

Why do investors buy stocks when they are expensive and sell them when they are seemingly cheap? Why does emotion enter into the process at all? Isn't investing supposed to be coldly calculating, rational and straightforward, a win/lose situation with measurable consequences and possibly even predictable outcomes?

Why Do Investors Abandon Common Sense?

 There is nothing more uncommon than common sense.

Frank Lloyd Wright

Common sense is not so much learning from experience as listening to it. You will often find that the people who preach the loudest about common sense use it as a tool of doom. They treat it like an ominous warning, a singular understanding of not only what lies ahead but the fact that past failures are supposed to be your template for future actions. They would have you believe that you should move forward with great care. It's better not to take chances than to be forced to learn from your mistakes.

In truth, nothing could be further from the definition of common sense. Common sense, unfortunately, is not necessarily wisdom. It is not necessarily conservative, either. Furthermore, it is not meant to be a stand-alone approach to either life or investing.

Common sense on its own tends to create more fear than is necessary, and in so doing, it can slow the decision-making process to a crawl. Consider the investors who lost most of their portfolio in the market collapse back in January 2000. After having lost enormous amounts of money, if not all of their entire portfolios, many investors fled the stock market for the sidelines. Who could blame them? Their losses were very real and very emotional. It was that very emotional involvement in the stock market that hurt the most.

Investors, it seems, have very short-term memories. Here is a look back at some of the major crashes:

On September 1, 2000, the Nasdaq traded at 4233. Between September 2000 and January 2, 2001, the Nasdaq dropped 45.9 percent. By October 2002, the Nasdaq completed its descent, having dropped lost 78.4 percent from its all-time high of 5133. Eight trillion dollars in wealth was lost.

On August 25, 1987, the DJIA posted a record close of 2722. By October 19, 1987, after a single-day drop of 508 points, the Dow had lost 36.7 percent; 500 million of wealth was lost in the process.

The last high posted by the Dow before the fabled crash of 1929 occurred on September 4, 1929. When the markets closed on October 29, 1929, the overall stock market had lost 11.5 percent of its value. Because of the concentration of large company names in the Dow, it posted a much larger loss of 40 percent. A slow rebound followed, only to be derailed again in July of 1932. By then, the Dow had lost almost 89 percent of its September 1929 value.

While most investors admit that they were stung by the reality of their losses, they will all admit that the markets were infectious. It was easy to get caught up in the hype.

Most of them were stung by the fact that this was real money and real losses. Many investors didn't realize how bad things had gotten until the margin calls began arriving. With a margin account, which we will go into more detail about in Part IV, the brokerage basically loans the investor the money to buy stocks. Should the value of the investor's portfolio fall below a certain threshold, the broker will ask the investor to put up additional money; if the investor fails to do so, the broker can sell some or all of the stocks in the account to pay down the outstanding balance of the loan and, if that is not adequate, ask for a cash settlement.

Guided by optimism, few investors made contingent plans for just such a collapse. Even in the real world, optimism blinds us to the obvious perils that may lie ahead. When it comes to investing, optimism turns into invincibility.

Common sense would have given them some caution, which might have cushioned the fall. Even when the markets finally hit bottom, many investors, had they used common sense the way it was meant to be used, would have seen markets for what they were: an opportunity collapse.

While Common Sense Is Good, It Is Nothing without Intuition

 I feel there are two people inside me—me and my intuition. If I go against her, she'll screw me every time, and if I follow her, we get along quite nicely.

Kim Basinger

Intuition is basically the brain's way of calculating risk. By running numerous scenarios on the possibilities of success and the probability of failure, intuition can guide the investor, but only so far. Intuition alone, I'm afraid, is not enough. Add common sense to intuition and you will have created the perfect combination of emotional seasonings to become a good investor. They are the salt and pepper on your investment table.

So with common sense, which provides the experience, the understanding of what could be potential failure or success, added to intuition, the forward-looking ability to size up the danger and quickly determining the skill level needed to handle it, the investor possesses all of the tools that he or she needs to make the right financial choices. It is the balance between those attributes that will determine how successful we will be.

The Buddy System

Mutual funds exist for the utterly confused investor. They are, however, the kind of investment that takes some diligence. Be forewarned: they will need to be revisited quarterly, if only to ensure that everything is still on the course we have set—an occasional check to make sure that the driver of this financial vehicle, the money manager(s) we've hired to protect and grow our money, is not asleep at the wheel.

When did investors begin to use mutual funds as an investment?

The first mutual fund was created in Belgium in 1822. Originally called investment trusts, these structures were created at a time when banking was first developing. Boston was the birthplace of the first American mutual fund in 1920. Today, mutual funds (along with exchange-traded funds, or ETFs) offer thousands of choices for investors of every discipline.

Mutual funds are sort of like financial group hugs: a sharing of a similar emotion, a like goal, and an agreement that you will go it together rather than go it alone. They are a sort of buddy system for investors writ large. They are at once elegantly simple to understand and inherently complicated. They seem so logical, but they are hopelessly tethered to illogical circumstances, unpredictable outcomes, and, in a great many instances, the problems associated with the unfortunate involvement of humans.

(*Note*: Some mutual funds are now run solely by computers, and funds that track popular indexes are as close to investing on autopilot as you can get.)

And in keeping with the conundrum that is mutual funds, the pros do outweigh the cons—if you are careful.

Good versus *Necessary* Evil

Comparing the pros and cons is difficult when it comes to mutual funds. On the *pro* side of the equation, they are simply a great idea. They bring investors together with hired money managers, who come to the group with a philosophy in the form of a fund charter.

The fund charter is a commitment to invest a certain way. It would be similar to the fund manager actually saying, "I swear that I will buy growth stocks" or " I believe that a balanced approach is key"; another might profess "buying internationally," and yet another might suggest that "bargain hunting for value is essential for financial success." Whatever their approach, they are looking for like investors to join them.

Then investors look at these commitments and entrust those managers with their money. The managers, in turn, do what they were hired to do. They research and analyze, schmooze with CEOs and other corporate chiefs, sift through research, read financial statements, and consult with analysts and experts, all the while balancing the investors' best interests with the announced strategy.

I am not lionizing these professionals' efforts, but their task can require a good deal of intestinal fortitude. It is a difficult job. They get paid well, and if they do the job they were hired to do, investors will flock to their funds.

It wasn't always this tough a job. At one time, mutual fund managers were revered for their skills at making huge sums of investors' money grow. In those days, they could do so with very little effort.

Owning a piece of a mutual fund makes us shareholders. Being a shareholder of a mutual fund makes you, by proxy, a shareholder in every company held by the mutual fund. Some mutual funds have gathered so much stock in some companies that they are not only investing for us, but voting for us as major shareholders as well.

(Later on we will discuss shareholder advocacy, a way to make your ownership share in the company heard. Mutual fund managers act as our advocates. As major shareholders, though, their advocacy can change the way companies are run.)

A proxy is essentially an authorization. Because you have invested in a mutual fund, you also, at least in part, own the companies that the fund has invested in. Often, these companies will turn to their shareholders and ask for permission to do something, such as replace a board member. Your mutual fund manager will vote for you as your representative, or proxy.

The makeup of the fund, or what it is trying to achieve, can be determined by looking at the companies it invests in. For instance, a fund that considers itself conservative would probably hold household names such as General Electric or Citigroup as its primary investments.

A good way to judge a mutual fund is to look at its top 10 holdings. The best place to see a fund's top 10 investments at a glance is on such Web sites as finance.yahoo.com. This can help to give the investor some guidance as to the fund manager's thinking or the direction of the fund. In many instances, those top 10 holdings are only the tip of the iceberg, so to speak, when it comes to understanding exactly how the fund operates, but looking at them is a good place to start.

What is market dynamics and how does it affect the holdings in my mutual fund?

The role of a mutual fund as a major shareholder in specific companies is best exhibited by the holdings of one of the largest funds in the nation, American Funds Growth Fund of America A (ticker: AGTHX). As of the end of the first quarter of 2006, this fund had over $136.75 billion under management and owned more than 12 percent of the following companies, which made it the largest shareholder: Lowe's (14.9 percent), Target (14.2 percent), Fannie Mae (13.6 percent), and BellSouth (12.1 percent). It also had a very healthy stake in the other companies among its top 10 holdings: Altria Group (7.8 percent), Microsoft (3.6 percent), General Electric (2.4 percent), AT&T (7.9 percent), Citigroup (3.3 percent), and Google (5.6 percent). Positions of this size can make it difficult to sell a holding without hurting the fund in the process.

It works like this: as a fund reduces its position by selling shares, the price falls. This happens because of market dynamics. In the open market, the owners of shares determine the price at which they are willing to sell those shares, and buyers determine the price at which they are willing to purchase them. When investors want to buy and sell the same amount of shares, the stock would be considered fairly priced (more on that later in the book). When a mutual fund tries to sell off a very large stake in a single company, the share price falls because there are so many more shares available to buy. In addition, other investors, regulatory agencies like the SEC, and the company itself will want to know why the mutual fund is selling, and other investors may decide to follow suit. Thus, a mutual fund that tries to sell a large position may end up hurting itself somewhat in the process.

Mutual fund managers are no exception. In the next chapter we will look at the human element involved in investing and how it affects mutual funds. Because of their size, mutual funds exert a great deal of influence on the markets. And because of the investors in those funds, certain dynamics take place when we forget that we are in it together.

To help you really understand how investments work, we will continue to bring up the past. There is a good reason for this. True market historians will tell you that the only thing that remains the same is the investors. They are an anxious lot, prone to make the same mistakes over and over again. The markets, although they are referred to frequently as if they were actually alive, are driven by the emotions of investors big and small. Those same market historians will suggest that there are such things as the "January barometer," the "Santa Claus rally," "sell in May and go away," and "September is a month of doom." But the emotions of the market, even if they are cyclical and chartable and seem predictable, are still centered around the people involved.

CHAPTER 8
The Laid-Back Approach

I remember summer vacations when I was a kid. They revolved around a ritual drive in the family sedan north by northwest from Philadelphia to Syracuse, New York. What awaited us at the other end of that journey was fishing with my uncle in the Thousand Islands, swimming in an assortment of upstate lakes, and generally being led far afield by older cousins.

Those treks took place along turnpikes and highways that were served by the familiar Howard Johnson restaurants. Their colonial-style buildings offered everything a traveler could want. Howard Johnson's (or, as it came to be known in those early days of highway travel, HoJo's) was to a traveler's convenience what mutual funds are to investors.

Howard Johnson developed the first premium ice cream of his era, using dairy fat in increased quantities. People loved it. Opportunist that he was, he kept adding flavors and establishments to sell it. When the Pennsylvania Turnpike opened, Johnson negotiated a deal to put his restaurants between exits and usually between the traffic lanes as well.

 According to Hojo.com, Howard Johnson came up with a "secret formula" for vanilla and chocolate ice cream. The secret was, in fact, based on his mother's recipe for ice cream—all natural ingredients and twice the normal butterfat content. It was an immediate sensation, so he quickly added other flavors. He had invented a super premium ice cream.

Howard Johnson's offered something for everyone in a place that was familiar and expected. It came to symbolize vacation and hominess, risk and reward. Mutual funds, up until about 10 years ago, had largely and willingly fallen into that type of comfort zone. Investors knew what to expect, the managers knew how to deliver it, and the markets hummed along smoothly.

Those markets, like all places where commerce is carried on, were influenced by external forces, both economic and otherwise. Mutual funds, however, were mostly along for the ride.

There were ups and downs; fortunes were made, lost, and grown. But the staid mutual fund seemed best designed for widows and orphans; it was a place to park money that was meant to be kept safe, growing at a predictable rate over a long period using a broad range of investments to keep everything all nice and even. Mutual funds were *the* buy-and-hold investment.

They became a natural investment for the newly created 401(k) plans we discussed earlier. They protected our hard-earned money and could be left alone for long periods of time without much worry. With mutual funds, you could put your investments on cruise control and they would move forward, steady as she goes, predictably.

Then things changed. The market dynamic was changing because business was changing. Companies were beginning to recognize their need to evolve into leaner operations as competition from other countries increased. The United States, which, while always involved globally, had previously used the biggest dog on the block approach to capitalism, was facing increasing challenges from around the world.

When investors were finally coaxed back into the market after the crash of 1987, they appeared tentative, unwilling to take too much risk. The recession that followed that crash didn't help investor sentiment.

The only thing that saved the country from a deeper slide was the protection of the banks and financial institutions by the Federal Reserve Board.

What was Black Monday?

Black Monday was October 28, 1987. On that day, the Dow lost 22.6 percent of its value. What happened that day was the result of a series of events. The Securities and Exchange Commission, which was created to protect investors, began a series of investigations that led to a sudden uneasiness about the markets. The existence of insider trading was generally acknowledged, but the combination of some cleverly packaged IPOs (initial public offerings) and the sheer number of SEC accusations caused investor alarm. By October, the selling had begun.

The financial losses were devastating. But as I have warned you, investors are very emotional in the beginning. Then they become a forgetful lot.

Investors dragged their emotions into the mix (in the chart in Figure 8.1, the top section shows the prices and the bottom section shows the volume), but when the selling began, there was little they could do but watch.

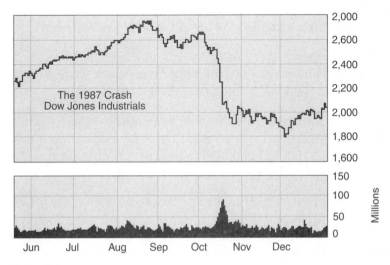

Figure 8.1

Markets will fall and markets will rise. The stock market in particular has a way of doing that. If you are not careful, it can take you along for the ride. The idea is to protect yourself from the fall and control your enthusiasm when it escalates. That sounds easy enough, doesn't it?

It didn't take long for the enthusiasm to come back. The 1990s brought new technologies and exciting new products, and those innovations and good news about the economy brought with them another round of investor amnesia. When IPOs became hot again, many of them touting products and promises of profits that had not yet been realized in the market, let alone in the market-place, investors ignored the similarities to the late 1980s and began to push markets higher on news of these innovations.

That is a very short version of what happened up until January 2000, when the market began its decline from its all-time highs. I mention this only to illustrate how short-term investors' thinking can be when they are searching for increased rewards, are willing to take unnecessary risks, and invest with their "hearts on their sleeves."

During the period between Black Monday and the late 1990s, the mutual fund industry began to expand as a result of this renewed investor enthusiasm. Understanding that the mutual fund shareholder was also a fee-paying customer, funds began inviting new investors into their fold. Mutual funds were no longer just the HoJo's on the highway; they were the highway.

They had become what every ordinary investor needed: a way to get to the same place that only more seasoned investors, more savvy professionals, and far more experienced individuals would otherwise be able to go.

Their advertising campaigns suggested this, and the average investor bought the message. Investors were first exposed to mutual funds in the workplace as pensions changed to defined-contribution plans. Owning mutual funds had become the best way for the average investor to be involved.

This came with a cost. Just as highways charged tolls for their use in those early days, mutual funds charged fees to cover expenses. The more cars there are on the road, the more tolls are paid; the more investors there are in a mutual fund, the more assets the fund will hold, and the more fees it can charge on those assets. In some cases, these tolls were paid as you entered the highway (these are called front-loaded funds); in others, they were paid as you exited (these are called closed-end funds).

Roads with no tolls offered what appeared to be a free ride (no-load funds do not charge an initial up-front fee to invest or levy an exit charge), yet they received money for their skills via fees. In this case, mutual fund fees acted like a road tax.

With people flocking to invest in mutual funds as never before, fund managers and the fund families they worked for began opening a large number of boutique funds, designed to lure each and every investor. Funds were opened with more investment-specific charters. Index funds, the ones that mimic the entire market or a certain sector, were your father's investment. Funds focusing on specific hot spots like the Internet, technology, or telecommunications were attracting thousands of new investors.

As mutual funds began offering shares in these new funds, investors were drawn to these funds like so many insects to the evening porch light. But it was the stock market that got all of the attention.

The wild rise of the stock market made the evening news. Everyone was talking about it. The hype, the speed, the trajectory was infectious. Investors wanted in, and they wanted more than just an index fund. They wanted excitement, high returns, and all the promises of wealth that individual shareholders had—but without the individual risk.

Mutual fund managers jumped in with both feet. Fund families created new funds chasing hot stocks and overheated sectors. Funds inside 401(k) plans soared in value, and folks who were no more than middle-aged began thinking about and calculating their chances of taking an early retirement.

Looking back, it was a really good time while it lasted.

One Step Forward, Two Steps Back

With so many mutual fund investors and so much retirement money tied up in speculative companies, bought by fund managers who had been hired to be market mavericks, the end seemed doubly bad. And when it arrived in January 2000, it seemed to happen all at once.

(My apologies in advance if I continue to mention that one particular crash repeatedly. I have my reasons. Investors, as I have also mentioned before, have notoriously short memories. In fact, most investors can barely remember just two years ago. The market offers us daily lessons in history, many of which fall on deaf ears. If I repeat myself, it is because it is important. Seven years ago is a long time.)

Mutual funds, once a drift-along investment for measured returns and conservative yields, were now giving investors double-, sometimes triple-digit returns on their money. The combination of unheard-of returns and a whole new group of investors played a major part in the continued fall of the stock market.

Here are some numbers on how the mutual fund industry grew from 1984 to 2004 as published by the Investment Company Institute.

Year	Total Net Assets ($ billions)	Number of Funds	Number of Shareholder Accounts
1985	$495.39	1,528	34,098
1990	1,065.1	3,079	61,948
1995	2,811.29	5,725	131,219
1997	4,468.20	6,684	170,363
1998	5,525.21	7,314	194,078
1999	6,846.34	7,791	226,346
2000	6,964.67	8,155	244,839
2001	6,974.95	8,305	248,816
2002	6,390.3	8,244	251,224
2003	7,414.40	8,126	260,882
2004	8,106.87	8,044	267,363

Investing Defensively

When you buy into a mutual fund, you agree to certain things. You agree to pay the fees. Having paid the toll, you take to the road with numerous other investors. The direction you have chosen is all you have in common with these other face-less passengers, your fellow shareholders.

This is fine as long as traffic is moving. A stock market crash acts much the same way a jackknifed truck does. Traffic stops. It begins to back up. As the first drivers stop and begin to wait, and the line begins to form behind them, other drivers start looking for an exit, a detour, anything to keep them moving. The accident is starting to have a ripple effect. The line eventually becomes long enough that traffic approaching the mishap sees it, finds an exit, and leaves. More do the same.

In their rearview mirrors, those who are stuck try to escape as well. Soon both approaching traffic and waiting cars are trying to get out from behind the obstruction. Chaos breaks out as surface roads begin to back up.

When you buy shares in a mutual fund, the manager buys stock with the cash you have just invested. Because funds keep little cash on hand—the more money invested, the more money at work—redemptions can be difficult if everyone wants theirs at the same time. When someone wants to sell her shares in the mutual fund, the manager must sell some of the fund's investments to pay her. This is a good arrangement as long as it happens only occasionally.

What happens when an investor leaves a mutual fund and sells his shares?

Redemptions create all sorts of problems for the fund. Not only does the fund manager have to find the money to pay the shareholder who wants to leave, but she must also make some important tax decisions (will the sale result in a profit or a loss?) and deal with transaction considerations (the cost of buying and selling have a very real impact). The manager will also wonder why the shareholder is heading for the door. A large number of shareholders selling all at once can be devastating both for a fund and for the returns of the shareholders who are still in the fund.

When a fund performs as expected, shareholders stay with the fund. It is a good idea to set performance expectations for your fund. You should be able to stomach a small setback in performance on occasion. If your fund fails by more than 5 percent relative to the index that it should be compared to for more than two quarters, it is time to consider a change.

This can happen for a variety of reasons. The fund may have a new manager or a new management team. When this happens, there are usually some changes in the structure of the holdings. The new managers, in essence, clean house. They may be simply jettisoning holdings that do not fit the profile or charter of the fund. Sometimes there are large redemptions because of this.

Just a side note: because mutual funds are run by people, and those people are paid out of the fees collected, they want to keep the fund inflows—the money coming in to be invested—constant. Remember, the fund managers have to buy stocks with that money. But mutual fund managers with great reputations and track records can be lured away from their jobs with the promise of greener pastures.

Hedge funds have been actively recruiting mutual fund stars with the promise of not only better money (hedge funds usually pay these investment stars 2 percent of the total assets under management *plus* 20 percent of the profits), but also the ability to spread their wings and do some market trickery that is currently not allowed by mutual funds.

What are hedge funds?

In Chapter 12, we will discuss these funds in more detail. Hedge funds are important to all investors, even those who do not have the million dollars or more required to join this exclusive "club." They are a primary vehicle for private and public pension funds and retirement accounts.

Since 2004, the SEC has sought to regulate this industry and has been repeatedly rebuked by the D.C. Court of Appeals. Hedge funds fall neatly between two existing regulations: the Investment Advisers Act of 1940 requires broker registration when more than 15 clients are involved, but as the fund has less than 100 investors, it need not meet the demanding requirements of the Investment Company Act of 1940. The SEC, with Wall Street in opposition and without the help of the courts or Congress, has sought to redefine the word *client* in order to broaden its regulatory powers.

Other reasons for a streak of minor losses involve outside forces pulling the fund down with it. The markets may have declined unevenly, leaving some of the fund's holdings in a losing position. After two quarters of losses, you will need to investigate on your own.

Sites like finance.yahoo.com can help. You can enter the fund's ticker symbol and click through each of the selections, from holdings to performance to news. When the quarterly returns arrive, read the letter from the fund manager.

If you have questions, call the fund and ask.

People call fund managers to ask questions more frequently than you might imagine. The usual questions asked range from fund holdings to information on late-breaking news that might affect the fund. But the real question that needs to be asked is often ignored. In 10 years, baby boomers like me will begin to retire. How is the fund manager planning today for that onslaught? The answer will probably disappoint you. Chances are that the manager has done very little planning for the future. Chances are that your fund manager is more concerned with finding the right fee level to attract new investors and keep the old ones from fleeing, maintaining better than average asset growth, and of course, posting better than mediocre returns. Chances are that your fund manager lives for the here and now. But this is a great first question to ask. It just needs to be asked more often.

Just as a shareholder in a company becomes a partner in the business, a mutual fund shareholder becomes a member of a group, each of whom has the same desires and goals. You have a right to ask questions.

Start researching other funds with similar investing disciplines. If your mid-cap growth fund does poorly, look for a better fund in the same category. We'll discuss balance and rebalancing a little further on. For now, though, if you have built a diversified portfolio, one that invests in a number of different parts of the market, stay with the strategy. If you need to sell a fund, buy another of the same type.

On the other hand, when a fund begins to perform very well, it attracts additional investors who are looking to share in the wealth that the fund's manager is generating. When the fund performs exceptionally well, folks start hammering on the door for access.

However, when a fund performs badly and this is a surprise to the shareholders, this taps into investor emotion and folks head for the exits en masse. This forces the fund manager to sell and keep selling to pay all of those who want their money.

This creates a sort of black hole that everyone unwittingly falls into. Fund managers and individual investors all begin to sell at the same time, leading prices to fall and continue falling. That's the way the market works. Sellers need buyers, and vice versa. When everyone is selling and there are no buyers, markets and, more importantly, prices tumble.

All of that activity is based solely on investor emotion. Sure, there is always the possibility that some shady activity prompted the change in investor sentiment. There is always the chance that the sudden rash of sellers is based on some sort of rampant speculation associated with those shady companies. Selling always accompanies the resulting investigations before, during, and after the fact.

What the Experts Say The degree of one's emotions varies inversely with one's knowledge of the facts.

Bertrand Russell

But it was the emotion of the investors, the return-driven money managers, and all of the participants on or near Wall Street whose reputations and pay-checks depended on ever-higher markets that, in hindsight, led to the spectac-ular drop in prices in 2000. Similarly, it was the emotion of the investors, the money managers who should have known better, and all of the participants on or near Wall Street who acted like cheerleaders until the bottom began to drop out that drove those prices higher in the first place.

Unlike Black Monday, when the markets lost 22.6 percent in a single day, the 2000 crash lasted an agonizingly long time and took years to recover from emotionally. The participation of so many mutual funds was what made the eventual crash more dramatic and personal.

All of those hapless 401(k) investors who changed their retirement plans from a conservative approach to much more risky mutual funds not only lost huge amounts of gains but also lost any chance of a timely retirement. Enthusi-asm was so high that many 401(k) investors actually were eyeing the possibility of an early retirement.

All that suffering came about because emotions entered into the marketplace and those who should have known better didn't act as if they did. Those who should have known better encouraged those who didn't know much to join in the free-for-all of riches and profits. Those who knew very little joined in and were hurt the worst.

What you will learn in the following chapters are timeless skills. You will learn to evaluate performance, build yourself a solid criterion for selecting mutual funds now and in the future, and, if we are fortunate, find the investor in you.

CHAPTER 9

Picking the Road Better Traveled

◆◆◆

New drivers always have a certain amount of nervousness. They lack the experience, the confidence in their new skill. Their fears make them apprehensive.

Older drivers are often more apt to take those fears into consideration. They will purposely avoid roads that have heavy traffic, are known for their crazy drivers, or simply move at a pace that is not acceptable. Experience has taught them what they will tolerate, and they adjust to those memories.

The same sort of apprehension can be found in new investors. Older investors know their tolerance; they know what they can accept in terms of risk and returns. Experience has taught them not only something about the markets but also something about themselves.

It doesn't matter whether you are sitting behind the wheel for the first time or the millionth; each new road traveled offers something that the previous road did not.

The old Chinese curse wishes, "May you live in interesting times"; these are interesting times. Consider yourself lucky. Being utterly confused means starting with a fresh perspective.

The utterly confused do not need to relearn techniques such as how to determine performance, which fund manager is right for the job, and, even worse, given that there are so many funds available, which one is right for them. This is a new road for them, a road that has been traveled by investors who understood their emotions, harnessed their fears, understood the dynamics of investing, and arrived at point B safely.

Mutual funds are divided into two categories: active and indexed. All funds can be boiled down to these two very broad categories. Think of mutual funds as a two-lane highway encased within solid white lines, separated by a broken line down the middle. All traffic moves in the same direction, governed by the same speed limit and road rules. All traffic begins at a certain point, and throughout the journey, new travelers merge onto the highway while others are exiting.

Index fund investors occupy the right lane, with active funds driving in the passing lane.

In active mutual funds, the manager of the fund buys and sells stocks using a number of formulas and computer models, hunches and skills, and so on. This type of fund occupies the passing lane with good reason. Traffic in that lane will—or at least should—always move faster than the more conservative indexed drivers.

Indexed funds differ from actively managed funds in that they buy and sell stocks only when the index that they mimic is changing the companies in its roster. There are mathematical equations by the bucketload governing these transactions, many of which will not be covered in this book.

So active mutual funds are moving and shifting entities, while indexes are static for the most part. As a general rule, that is true. That explanation, though, is far too simple.

What to Ask?

What is the efficient market hypothesis?

The efficient market hypothesis is the cornerstone of index investing. Controversially, it suggests that all stocks are priced at fair value, so it is not possible to beat the market. There is plenty of evidence suggesting that the S&P 500 index will beat an actively managed fund over a period longer than 20 years. Be careful about wrapping yourself around such theories too soon. We have a lot more to talk about when it comes to investing.

If all index funds were truly static, their performance would be relatively easy to determine. One S&P 500 index fund would be basically the same as any other. While there might be slight differences in fees, they would be essentially the same. They all track the largest 500 companies on the open market. They all carry the same companies in the same ratio. This is a true index. It is a widely diversified opportunity for investors to own a broad swath of the market.

Indexes, however, are evolving. They are being forced to do so by the increasing popularity of exchange-traded funds (ETFs). This new breed of funds has some distinct differences from their mutual fund counterpart, but they are essentially index funds that are traded actively on the open market.

We'll discuss ETFs in more detail in subsequent chapters. For now, it is enough to know that ETFs have piqued investors' interest. And while their impact is still small compared to the much larger, more established mutual fund market, their impact has been felt. Fund families have taken notice. Investors' interest in indexes that track ever-smaller groups of stocks in increasingly narrower sectors has forced the industry to sit up and take notice.

Indexes are more than what they were just 10 years ago as they seek to attract additional investors who are interested in those somewhat riskier opportunities.

The Not-So-Vanilla Index

So instead of tracking 500 of the largest companies, these new indexes offer something different. They might track just the financial companies in the index, or perhaps just the companies whose business is health care.

With ETFs offering indexes in increasingly specific categories, mutual funds have had to react and offer a wider variety of products, all the while retaining their passive status.

To some more experienced investors, ETFs may sound like sector funds. Sector funds specialize in buying companies in a certain category, such as technology, energy, health, and so on. However, sector funds are not index funds. They are usually actively managed, with no set index to follow.

ETFs have given investors a new type of index fund that tracks a more specific category, providing the investors with a chance to increase their risk without adding to their costs.

Intellidexes are hybrid index funds sold as ETFs on the American Stock Exchange (amex.com, click on ETF). They are designed to sort out the winners in an index and create a new index based on 25 different criteria. They do, however, mirror the weighting of the index. That means that if an index has 30 percent technology, then so does the Intellidex.

Rethinking indexes has become more than just a fad. Some major mutual fund families are looking at the indexes from a different angle. Suppose an index was more than just a group of similarly sized companies?

If the best index was based on footprint and not share price, would the index outperform the total market? The term *footprint* refers to a company's overall contribution to the index. Indexing by share price, on the other hand, allows fair value to creep into the equation. A company that has a high fair value or is considered of higher value in the index could actually be overrepresented. Conversely, a good company with a low share value might not be well represented in the index. This is a missed opportunity to some.

Robert D. Arnott, a subadvisor to two new PIMCO funds that hope to beat the standard indexes, believes that the top 1,000 companies in his index will do better than the S&P 500.

If Mr. Arnott's idea proves to be a better tool for measuring actively managed funds, it would be welcomed with open arms by investors. Actively managed funds are often compared to the indexes they most closely resemble. However, this is often an unfair comparison and can confuse investors. How can you compare a mutual fund that is actively traded and holds only a hundred or so companies to an index of 500, and why do fund managers continue to do it?

The simple answer is that it makes them look better. Managers of actively managed funds can pick and choose from among the stocks represented in the index. If they pick well, they will beat the index and will attempt to attract new investors by using this feat. If they pick poorly, they will downplay the comparison. Which lead us to the next question: "Why don't all actively managed funds beat the index?"

Managers of actively managed funds, however, may not be too keen on the idea of these new indexes. You will find that fund managers like to shine the brightest possible light on themselves and their work. A new hybrid index, one that would mimic some actively managed funds more closely, would not be welcomed with open arms.

Investors, however, should pay attention. Suppose for a moment that you have an actively managed fund—one that does not follow any specific index, but instead invests in growth stocks. When the quarter ends—the investment year is cleanly divided into four separate segments—the actively managed portfolio produced better returns than the S&P 500 index did in the same quarter. But the basket of stocks that the fund manager invested in may not have included many of those 500 companies. There may have been some undervalued companies in the fund's portfolio that did exceptionally well. This made the performance numbers go up. So comparing a fund that is actively managed, a fund where the manager can tweak the portfolio, to an index fund does not give the investor a clear picture of how well the fund did. It happens. This is why the search for the be-all and end-all comparison tool continues.

But the question that begs to be asked is, what exactly will this new type of index fund be better at doing? Better returns are definitely a possibility. It may provide a better tool for comparing funds. It remains to be seen.

Whatever happens, the new PIMCO index fund will be too expensive for individuals—at least most individuals—to join. The $5 million initial investment would probably stop us cold. Here are the ticker symbols for the funds: PIMCO Fundamental Index PLUS (PFPAX) and PIMCO Fundamental Index PLUS Total Return (PFPIX), in case I am wrong about what you can afford.

What is performance?

Performance will always involve some sort of judgment call on the part of the investor. Funds want to appear better than they are, and in many cases they will not provide you with the best way of determining how well they did. When an actively managed fund or a new hybrid index compares its returns to those of an index like the S&P 500, beware. Few funds have 500 holdings, and over the long term, the larger the number of holdings, the more diversified. Still fewer funds have so many dividend-paying companies (roughly two-thirds of the companies in the S&P 500 pay a dividend) among their holdings. And fewer still can match this without offsetting their holdings with some sort of fixed-income debt holding, much as the PIMCO funds are doing. Read through the hype and look at the top holdings. Comparing mutual funds can be done, though.

There is a fine line between indexed funds and actively managed funds. While some of these new funds and ETFs walk that line, it is always important to know that promises of increased returns by beating large market indexes have the same downside risk as the rest of the markets. For instance, holding a basket of stocks that were narrowly picked to meet all of the criteria set forth by a new index doesn't necessarily guarantee great returns.

When a mutual fund suggests that its model of success—in this case, a new index—is better than what is currently available, it doesn't want you to take the following into consideration: markets go up and markets go down.

The PIMCO funds, using Mr. Arnott's index model, would target a company's market footprint. That's just a fancy way of saying sales or revenues. This differs from the current method employed by the S&P 500 index, which is weighted based on market capitalization.

 How is "cap" or capitalization calculated?

Capitalization is the amount of stock that is available in the open market multiplied by the price per share. Simply, if a company has a thousand shares selling at $5 a share, its capitalization would be $5,000.

Calling themselves fundamentalists, advisors like Mr. Arnott find structural faults with the current index offerings. Perhaps they are correct. Time will certainly tell.

What makes companies thrive is as much the vote of Wall Street (which is determined by the share price) as it is the customers who buy the products or services (which Mr. Arnott would suggest are more important).

Diversification, which is a key factor in investing the right way, is best achieved without simply picking the winners. Herein lies the problem with some of the newer indexes: they tend to be winner-heavy. It is important to note that the conditions that have made the top 1,000 companies what they are today are not by any means guaranteed to exist in the future.

It is too early to tell whether these funds will perform well. It is too early to tell whether investors will embrace them as the new way to judge their actively managed fund's performance. These new types of index-tracking funds like PIMCO's new offerings may prove to be better as a tool than as an investment.

One of the first tests of your investing skills will be the top 10 performer lists published in many major newspapers at the end of each quarter. Newspapers like the *New York Times*, the *Wall Street Journal*, and *Barron's* have special pullout sections filled with a mind-boggling array of statistics and performance charts. These fact sheets can entice you with the spectacular returns of the winners and force you to scan the list of losers. If you find yourself in the market for a fund or you want to add to your portfolio, be cautious of fawning over the short-term winners. Avoid focusing on funds that have made it to the top of the list for the previous quarter, the year to date, or previous one year. Look instead at the top 10 performers for a five- or ten-year period. Why? The factors that lead certain funds to perform exceptionally well in the short term often do not last more than a quarter or two. Tastes change. Always look for the longest-term performer and begin your search there.

So far, we have spoken of only one index, the Standard & Poor's 500 index of the largest capitalization companies. The following is a partial list of other indexes published by Standard & Poor's that are widely used by investors and mutual funds.

S&P U.S. Indexes

S&P 500

This index is so widely used for three simple reasons: it tracks 500 leading companies, these companies cover the leading industries in the U.S. economy, and, last but not least, because of the size of these companies, this index covers over 80 percent of U.S. equities by market capitalization. It remains one of the best comparison tools for the total market.

S&P MidCap 400

Mid-cap companies have come into their own as a separate asset class. They provide diversification with regard to risk and offer some additional reward to investors who are looking to spread their investments farther afield than just the largest companies. The S&P MidCap 400 covers approximately 7 percent of the U.S. equities market.

S&P SmallCap 600

As companies get smaller, their risk increases. It is often considered more difficult to run a small company, and for that reason, the S&P has set forth specific criteria (the companies must be financially fit and investable). This small-cap index covers approximately 3 percent of the U.S. equities market.

S&P Composite 1500

This index combines the S&P 500, the S&P MidCap 400, and the S&P Small-Cap 600.

S&P 1000

The S&P 1000 is a combination of the S&P MidCap 400 and the S&P Small-Cap 600.

S&P Total Market Index

The S&P Total Market Index (TMI) covers more than 4,500 companies, extending beyond exposure to large-, mid-, and small-cap companies to include an even smaller group, the micro-cap companies. The S&P TMI provides investors exposure to the entire U.S. stock market, including all common equities listed on the NYSE, the American Stock Exchange, the Nasdaq National Market, and the Nasdaq Small Cap.

The Russell Indexes

The Russell indexes provide another look at indexing the markets. Based in Tacoma, Washington, this company, referred to as a "manager of managers," offers indexes that run the gamut. This section gives a few examples of the wide variety of indexes that Russell offers.

Russell 3000

This index was designed to measure the performance of the 3,000 largest U.S. companies based on total market capitalization. Spreading the net this wide encompasses approximately 98 percent of the U.S. equity market deemed investment-worthy. The Russell 3000E extends that net even further to include the micro-cap companies in the firm's Micro-Cap Index.

Russell 1000

This index identifies a large segment of the market (92 percent) on the basis of its performance. Like PIMCO's Arnott, mentioned earlier, it charts the top 1,000 largest companies.

Russell 2000

This is the most commonly used index published by the Russell Company. It offers a broad look at small-cap companies. Over the last several years, this volatile group, representing only 8 percent of the marketplace, has produced enormous returns for investors. There is a good deal of risk in attempting to find individual companies within this segment that are worthy of your individual investment dollars, but using an index such as this can spread that risk very far. If you own a small-cap mutual fund, this is the comparison tool that is most likely used by your fund manager.

Wilshire Indexes

The Wilshire Company publishes two of the most comprehensive indexes available. Its total market index, the Wilshire 5000, actually contains more than 5,000 U.S. companies. At its inception, there were less than 5,000, yet the all-inclusive nature of the index allowed investors to see the big picture. This section gives a profile of the two most identifiable indexes that the company offers its clients. (*Note*: A disclaimer on the Wilshire Company's Web site states: *The Dow Jones Wilshire Indexes are calculated, distributed, and marketed by Dow Jones Indexes pursuant to an agreement with Wilshire Associates*.) The Indexes were created in 1974 and first appeared in *Barron's* on January 13, 1975.

Dow Jones Wilshire 5000

Companies listed in this index must be based in the United States and use a U.S. exchange as their primary listing. They can be companies that have issued common stock, act as a REIT (real estate investment trust—more on this interesting investment later on), or be a limited partnership with available equity offerings. How the index is valued is based on certain criteria, such as market capitalization and trading volume. The index is rebalanced on the third Friday of each month, when all the companies in the index are reexamined, new ones are added, and any adjustments are made.

Dow Jones Wilshire 4500

Created in 1983, this index simply removes the 500 largest companies, leaving an index that includes all investment-worthy mid-cap and small-cap companies. Removing the largest companies, or 92 percent of the market capitalization, increases the risk and volatility of the index. Consequently, this is a much better comparison of the total market other than the big players.

Morningstar

Morningstar uses a wholly different approach to measuring the markets. Using what the company refers to as "style boxes," it breaks down the market according to size and methodology and offers a closer glimpse at the composition of the markets.

For instance, Morningstar's broad market style box, which includes 97 percent of the equity offerings traded would look something like this: ▓

To accommodate the largest companies in this type of grid, its index for 70 percent of the traded markets would look like this: ▦

Mid-cap indexes, making up 20 percent of the markets, would appear on Morningstar as: ▅

The remaining companies, listed as small caps and occupying only 7 percent of the investment-worthy markets, are charted as: ▄

Morningstar takes this methodology several steps further to include value (▐), core (▐), and growth (▐) companies within the fund. This allows the investor to determine a fund's discipline much more easily. When Morningstar refers to value, it means companies whose worth may not be recognized by the markets because their growth is slower and more stable, and therefore are likely to be undervalued. Core simply refers to funds that invest in a wider group of stocks that fit into a specific size bracket (large, mid, or small) and may contain both value and growth stocks depending on the fund manager's charter. Growth is often defined or characterized as actively engaged companies that may or may not pay a dividend, that may or may not be finished expanding, and that may or may not be considered risky.

Morningstar uses 10 variables to determine inclusion into each category, with each of the indexes representing a third of the overall market that the company tracks.

Large value: ⊞

Large core: ⊞

Large growth: ⊞

Mid-cap value: ⊞

Mid-cap core: ⊞

Mid-cap growth: ⊞

Small-cap value: ⊞

Small-cap core: ⊞

Small-cap growth: ⊞

Because Morningstar style boxes are so easy to use—just a glance at the graphics can tell you a good deal before you actually begin any more research—it is probably a good time to outline some of the holdings that these indexes consider to be value, core, or growth.

For the sake of space, we will just look at the top holdings in the largest-capitalization indexes. Remember, these indexes will be rebalanced before this book gets into print, so this will be a snapshot in time, but it is a fairly reliable indication of how these indexes are built.

For instance, the large-cap value index, as of this writing, contains the following holdings (keep in mind that these stocks represent over 46 percent of the index based on weight in an index that only lists 93 companies, as shown on the next page).

The Morningstar large-cap core index contains 98 companies, of which the top 10 holdings make up 40 percent of the index—once again, this is a snapshot at the time of this writing.

And finally, the large-cap growth index includes 104 companies, with the top 10 holdings representing about 34 percent of the total group.

	Percentage of the Index
ExxonMobil	9.78
Citigroup	6.41
Bank of America	5.91
Pfizer	4.78
J.P. Morgan Chase & Co.	4.05
Altria Group	3.85
Chevron	3.49
ConocoPhillips	2.83
AT&T	2.61
Wachovia	2.48

	Percentage of the Index
General Electric	9.85
Procter & Gamble	5.14
Wal-Mart Stores	5.06
American International Group	4.55
IBM	3.49
Wells Fargo	3.08
Coca-Cola	2.68
Home Depot	2.28
Time Warner	2.14
Goldman Sachs Group	1.88

	Percentage of the Index
Microsoft	7.22
Johnson & Johnson	5.04
Cisco Systems	3.73
Intel	3.40
PepsiCo	2.80
Qualcomm	2.44
Amgen	2.42
Genentech	2.41
Google	2.41
Schlumberger	2.36

Other Indexes

There are numerous other indexes that can be used. The ones discussed in this chapter are the ones that are used most commonly. Here is a short list of some additional indexes that your mutual fund manager may use to help you compare the manager's performance.

Dow Jones Indexes

Barra Indexes

Bloomberg Index Data

MSCI Indexes (often used by ETFs)

Compare International Funds

Compare Small Cap Fund

Compare Large Value

Compare Emerging Markets

Chapter 12 provides some additional information concerning the tax implications of an index fund. You will also find some not-so frequently asked questions as well. If knowledge is power, as they say, understanding how to be a little bit cynical when it comes to investing can save you thousands of dollars over the long term. This section will, if anything, add to your understanding and, with any luck, give you the ability to make better decisions.

Index funds trade on a regular basis, usually at specified intervals or when one company in the index has fallen so far out of favor that continuing to include it in the index is inappropriate. The tax advantages of not trading are huge. Once a fund, whether it is an index fund or an actively managed one, must trade a stock, the taxes levied on the profits are essentially yours.

What the Experts Say

I'm proud to be paying taxes in the United States. The only thing is—I could be just as proud for half the money.

Arthur Godfrey

If there is a loss, the fund must use that to offset profits and, with any luck, break even—an equal loss will cancel out an equal profit, at least based on the roughest of calculations.

In Part I, I suggested that when you invested in your 401(k), you should include a S&P 500 index fund as your core investment. I did this for two reasons. First, it is the best index available overall. It should be at the heart of every portfolio them.

The second reason is based on a bet that tax rates in the future will not be as favorable as they are right now. Inflation will take its toll, but taxes will not get lower than the 15 percent currently being charged on capital gains. What that means, and this is strictly an opinion, is that personal income tax rates 10, 15, or even 30 years down the road are bound to be higher. Using this sort of "worse-case-scenario" to plan for the future becomes a win-win opportunity. If personal taxes on capital gains are *not* higher when you retire, you win. If they are higher, as I believe, then you are at least prepared.

What is a capital gain?

A capital gain is the difference between what you paid for a security or property and what you receive when you sell it at a profit. A capital loss is the difference when you sell it at a loss. Both have tax consequences. Profit is taxed at the going rate; losses can be deducted against earned income.

Most companies in the S&P 500 pay dividends. A full two-thirds of these companies offer their shareholders a tangible and real piece of their success. Dividends are a way for the company to give back a portion of the profits it made during the course of its fiscal year to the shareholders. These payouts to shareholders can be handled in a couple of ways.

In a 401(k) or an IRA, be sure to check the box that allows the mutual fund manager to reinvest your dividends by buying you more shares of the fund. We will discuss the nature of dividends further on, but in retirement accounts, these profit windfalls should be reinvested.

In mutual funds owned outside the tax-deferred arena, dividends can sometimes be drawn on as a source of additional income. That means that when your mutual fund gets a huge dividend check from a company that the fund that has invested in, all the shareholders get their share as a form of taxable income.

Dividends can have an impact on how well a fund performs. That can affect returns, which is one of the first comparison tools we reach for when judging a fund. Index funds may be referred to as passively managed, but the underlying investments are very much alive, with each company striving for success, and in an index like the S&P 500, a full two-thirds of them pay some sort of dividend.

While indexing provides the most comfortable ride for the average investor, the actively managed mutual fund provides the thrill. In the next chapter we will take a look at this type of investment, where theories are tested, chartists roam free and wild, and fund managers become stars among their peers. This is where investors can find the thrill of owning individual stocks while retaining the comfort of being with like-minded individuals.

This is a good time to begin to remind you that as you continue to progress as an investor, keeping a firm footing is important. That "footing" depends on your participation in any retirement account that is available, indexing what isn't tax deferred, and using money that is *not* earmarked for either of those two tools. Each time we add something to this process, your investment must come from sources that do not jeopardize your footing.

CHAPTER 10

The Active Approach

O nce you are traveling at the speed limit of the market indexes in vehicles such as the S&P 500, which has come very close to posting a solid 10 percent return over the last 10 years, changing lanes can seem just a little bit scary. The S&P 500 provides the investor with a certain amount of safety and comfort. It is, however, your grandfather's Buick.

It is our nature to want more. Once we have become fully invested in our retirement funds, building a portfolio of mutual funds, both indexed and actively managed, is the next step.

While investing in an actively managed fund can provide you with a different perspective on the markets, there is no guarantee that you will get better returns or improved performance. In many instances, you will have greater exposure to risk, a wider range of investment options, and, of course, higher fees than those charged by index funds.

The idea of pushing the pedal to the metal is almost irresistible. Actively managed mutual funds—the ones led by people with souped-up philosophies about investing, with unusual approaches to the facts and figures, with portfolios that reflect boutique notions for picking the winning basket of companies— exist for the thrill of doing better than the index and ultimately propelling the fund to the top of those lists I told you to ignore earlier.

Actively managed mutual funds are where the true mavericks of investing live and grow. They seek value; they seek growth; they seek outsized performance numbers; they seek as many investors as they can gather under their wing. Each will do whatever it takes to show the investment world that it is the best.

Once you are in the passing lane, the goal is to get ahead faster than those staid investors in the index lane.

Costs Worth Considering

This is where it gets to be fun. The top is down, the sun is shining, and every piston is firing in perfect sequence. Actively managed mutual funds are the thrill ride that cautious investors are looking for without the cost and the risk of doing it alone. Before we go too much further, I want to be clear: There is always risk in investing. Always, always, always.

We can try to grow our money with a minimum amount of exposure to risk by using index funds, or we can become more active and assume slightly more risk. But without risk, we would be opting for the "savings stuffed under the mattress" approach to investing. It's safe, yes, but by removing the risk, you remove any chance to grow your money.

Not only will your money fail to grow, but it will actually lose value over time because of inflation and, in some cases, taxes. Investing involves risk. What actively managed funds do, especially the successful ones, is take that risk and look more aggressively for the reward.

Ironically, the success of individual investors and institutional investors, the ones who pick stocks rather than index their shareholders' money, can actually increase the returns and performance of the very indexes they try to outperform.

Actively managed funds can do better than the indexes they compare themselves to, but the cost of that success can often be greater. In a car, the faster you go, the higher the likelihood that you will use more gas and the greater the chances that something mechanical will go wrong or that a mistake in judgment will be fatal. These are costs worth considering.

While actively managed mutual funds cost more and are prone to mechanical difficulties, the results are seldom fatal. Seldom, but not never.

How Actively Managed Funds Work

An actively managed mutual fund has either a single manager or a team of managers. Some managers use computer models, sector indexing, or any other combination of strategies that can be thought up by those clever people on Wall Street. Actively managed funds buy stocks, bonds, or a combination of both based on specified charters designed to draw investors with similar dispositions. The actively managed mutual fund is the driver who cannot be satisfied with an average journey from point A to point B.

So, is it all about who is driving? In a NASCAR competition, all the drivers start out with the same car. The winning team is made up of a driver with superior skills and good mechanics who execute their tasks with flawless timing and precision. Actively managed mutual funds have the same requirements. The stock market is a level playing field and even oval-shaped at times, so better than average performance may be brought about by the manager and his or her support staff of analysts and researchers.

So how do you pick a manager? A study published in April 2005 found that the sex of the manager might make a difference.

The study found that women investors make fewer mistakes when it comes to investing, and when they do make mistakes, they make them less frequently than their male counterparts. The reason seems to lie in the approach. Women see investing as a necessity rather than as the pursuit of the simple achievement. This study, whose sole purpose was to examine the financial differences between men and women, came to one basic conclusion: women are better at investing than men.

If that is the case, pick a woman for your fund manager. Here is what the study uncovered about women as individual investors compared with their male counterparts. Keep in mind that the following survey looked at the difference between men and women as investors. It doesn't, however, suggest that money managers who are female will do a better job than their male counterparts. When you consider that the same investment tools are available to both sexes, how they use them to achieve their goals can be quite telling.

A new study also suggests that women are better fund managers, and for many of the same reasons uncovered in the earlier Merrill Lynch study. Using only actively managed domestic equity funds, an assistant professor of finance at the University of Cologne, Stefan Ruenzi, found that women were less likely to engage in a practice that plagues actively managed funds called *style drift*.

This is probably as good a time as any to explain what this is. Style drift occurs when the fund, led by the fund manager, changes course ever so slightly from what it was intended to do. The temptation to do this is always there. The sole reason that a fund manager drifts off course is performance.

Who are better investors: women or men?

The Merrill Lynch Investment Managers survey conducted by Mathew Greenwald & Associates Inc. found the following:

Women	Men
When they had a losing investment:	
Sell rather than hold (35%)	Hold rather than sell (47%)
When they had a winning investment:	
Sell rather than hold (28%)	Hold rather than sell (43%)
Women, the study found, approached diversification differently:	
Apt to allocate (23%)	Apt to focus investments (32%)
When it came to choosing stocks, women approached hot picks differently:	
Prone to do research (88%)	Prone to do research (76%)
Women learned from their mistakes. The study found a difference in who was prone to repeat their mistakes:	
Bought stock w/o research (47%)	Bought stock w/o research (63%)

The reasons for those mistakes were also telling:

Overconfident	20%	33%
Greedy	16%	32%
Impatient	19%	28%

There were some nuances of the markets that women did not fully grasp. Some did not use dollar cost averaging:

	39%	65%

Some did not factor in the cost of inflation:

	43%	67%

Performance can be quite an unforgiving master. Your results, or how well your fund performed, will be widely scrutinized and dissected, not only by your own shareholders, but by those who track such doings in the media.

Style drift is simply a desperate attempt to outshine your peer group.

Suppose your fund manager is a machine. Wells Fargo created the first machine-run mutual fund based on quantitative research. Its index fund of 1,500 New York Stock Exchange (NYSE) stocks made its debut in 1971. So how do you ask a machine a question? While we are mostly suspicious of artificial intelligence, these computers are designed to react in a certain way, and as a result, they take the human element out of the equation. No stars, no celebrity, no chance for style drift. And in many instances, you will find its performance as measured against its peer group of active managers consistently better. So what do you say to the machine running your fund? Thanks expressed as zeros and ones!

Style is knowing who you are, what you want to say, and not giving a damn.

Gore Vidal

For example, if your fund is one that sets out to find companies whose value is not recognized by the markets—in other words, stocks that are selling for less than they should because the overall market does not appreciate their value—and you buy a growth stock whose price is likely to appreciate quickly, your style has drifted.

If you are a fund manager who is required to hold a certain percentage of bonds to keep the fund balanced, and you hold less than the agreed-upon amount, your style has drifted.

If your fund is focused on mid-cap stocks and you buy a hot small-cap stock that comes along, your style has drifted.

Women are much less likely to have style drift, the study found, and that can be a big plus for investors. When we get to the discussion of diversification, I'll explain this further, but for the present, style drift changes the product you are buying. It is a sort of bait and switch.

But what exactly did women do differently as managers that separated them from their male counterparts? Women managers tended to be more conservative, protected their shareholders better, traded less often, and were generally more stable. Men tended to make outsized gambles without much in the way of noticeably increased returns.

Managers are always grappling with new ways to compare their performance. Unfortunately for them, they will always be judged by the index closest to their type of investing. They understand that beating the index time after time is very difficult (which only adds to the argument for index fund investing), but they continue to try.

Beneath the Attractive Exterior...

I have made the argument that putting your entire holdings in index will give you a good and inexpensive way to participate in the stock market. That may not be enough, though. Assuming some additional risk can increase your returns, improve your performance, and grow your portfolio. But what, other than the sex of the manager, is a good criterion for picking a long-term winner?

 Investing should be more like watching paint dry or watching grass grow. If you want excitement, take $800 and go to Las Vegas.

Paul Samuelson

One of the most successful managers in the world of active managers works for Legg Mason. He has methodically beaten the S&P 500 for 15 years running, and with his current investment style still focused, he looks as if he could go on for 15 more. Bill Miller runs the Legg Mason Value Trust (ticker: LMNVX), a fund whose performance numbers often make finding something similar very difficult.

(Mr. Miller's fund requires an initial investment of $1,000,000—ouch! While this is too rich for many investors, the following research was done with one thing in mind: to find a fund that does the same thing, has similar returns, and does not cost a lifetime's worth of savings to join.)

So I turned to the Yahoo.com fund screener to see if I could find something comparable in style, if not in returns. I'll admit that I didn't have much luck. I looked for some of the things that make Mr. Miller's fund special.

The Legg Mason Value Trust is a large blend fund, meaning that there are no speculative stocks from the world of smaller companies. (Remember, smaller companies occupy a much more narrow universe. Some of the obstacles to

What is value?

A value fund seeks investments that Wall Street has overlooked or that have fallen out of favor. Stocks held by funds such as the Legg Mason Value Trust are essentially good companies; there are surprisingly familiar names among the top 10 holdings. The following information is as of May 1, 2006.

Top 10 Holdings (45.24% of Total Assets)

Company	Symbol	% Assets
Sprint Nextel Corp.	S	6.43
United Health Group	UNH	5.69
Amazon.com Inc.	AMZN	5.58
Tyco Intl. Ltd.	TYC	5.29
Google	GOOG	4.39
AES Corp.	AES	4.15
JP Morgan Chase Co.	JPM	3.80
eBay Inc.	EBAY	3.42
Aetna Inc. New	AET	3.28
Qwest Comm Intl. Inc.	Q	3.21

their success include competition, the economy, and any number of other headwinds. In other words, they carry a good deal of additional risk.) A large blend fund, and specifically one that considers itself a value fund, focuses only on large, established companies.

Perhaps one of the keys to the success of Mr. Miller's fund lies in the fact that he very rarely sells stocks. His turnover ratio is one of the lowest among actively managed funds. With a ratio of just 9 percent (the category averages more than 75 percent) he is a true buy-and-hold manager. This, of course, has a positive influence on his taxes and allows him to charge exceptionally low, almost indexlike fees for his management.

Turnover refers to the number of times a fund's holdings change during a given period. Lack of turnover usually means lower taxes. A fund is taxed only when it sells its winners.

Using tools like fund screeners requires some compromise on the part of the user. The online screener at Yahoo.com failed in several ways and succeeded in others, but was able to find something very similar to Mr. Miller's fund.

For instance, the fund screener was unable to find an inexpensive fund that had as low a turnover ratio as Mr. Miller's. By inexpensive, I mean a fund with low fees and low initial minimums for both IRA and non-IRA investing. I wanted the screener to find a manager with tenure similar to that of Mr. Miller, and I wanted a fund that had a similar charter. And I wanted returns that beat the S&P 500. What I found was surprising.

The American Funds Fundamental Invs F (AFIFX) fit the bill nicely. The only difference was a slightly higher turnover ratio of 24 percent. Otherwise, this fund had a healthier five-year return than the more costly Legg Mason fund, similar expenses, and an equally long-tenured manager.

Among the holding in the American Funds Fundamental Invs F (AFIFX), managed by James Drasdro, are some equally recognizable names.

Company	Symbol	% Assets
Suncor Energy Inc.	SU	4.28
Altria Group Inc.	MO	2.26
Microsoft Corp.	MSFT	2.08
Royal Dutch Shell PLC ADR	N/A	1.68
Roche Holding	N/A	1.63
AT&T Inc.	T	1.57
Lowe's Companies	LOW	1.47
Texas Instruments	TXN	1.38
Deere Co.	DE	1.37
Washington Mutual	WM	1.37

The criteria used on finance.yahoo.com were as follows:

Overview

Category	Large Value
Fund Family:	Any
Rank in Category: (1-Year Performance)	Top 10%
Manager Tenure:	Longer than 10 years

Ratings

Morningstar Rating:	Min: 3 stars	Max: any
Return Rating:	Min: average	Max: any
Risk Rating:	Min: average	Max: any

Performance Returns

YTD Return:	Any
1-Year Return:	Any
3-Year Return (Annualized):	Any
5-Year Return (Annualized):	Up more than 5%

Purchasing & Fees

Min. Initial Investment:	Less than $5,000
Front Load:	No load
Total Expense Ratio:	Less than 2%

Holdings

Net Assets:	Min: Any	Max: Any
Turnover:	Min: 10%	Max: Any
Median Mkt Cap:	Min: Any	Max: Any

Other funds meeting the screening:

Symbol	Fund Name	Category	Rank %
AFIBX	American Funds Fundamental Invs B	Large Value	4
AFICX	American Funds Fundamental Invs C	Large Value	4
AFIFX	American Funds Fundamental Invs F	Large Value	2
CLVFX	Croft-Leominster Value	Large Value	5
HIEQX	Harris Insight Equity N	Large Value	6
ICAEX	ICAP Equity	Large Value	10
MAPNX	Merrill Lynch Focus Value I	Large Value	10

Fund screeners like those at Yahoo.com or Morningstar.com can prove to be an invaluable tool when trying to crunch hard facts. Performance, that feeling of getting into the passing lane with enough power to accelerate, is not the only consideration for a mutual fund. On our two-lane highway, you are a danger to other investors if you move into that passing lane and are unable to go fast enough.

 Actively managed funds come with a cost. While fees are usually what pops into your mind first, investing requires as much due diligence on your part as anything you are likely to do—except raising a family, of course. But like rearing kids, your investments require that you stay focused on the road ahead.

In the next chapter we will take a look at the prospectus and delve into diversity a little further with a look at not only equity mutual funds, but those that offer fixed-income solutions to your investment needs and funds that take the guesswork out of investing based on your age.

CHAPTER 11
The Cost of Speed

I spent my formative years on the East Coast, so I am most familiar with the Pennsylvania Turnpike. When I think of toll roads, highways that charge a fee for access, I think of this ribbon of highway, particularly a stretch that takes you from Valley Forge to Scranton. While toll roads seem to be mostly concentrated east of the Rockies, the reason for charging users a fee was simple: maintenance costs for the highway would be paid for directly by the drivers that used it.

The trouble with the system was that it provided no way to comparison-shop. You could either take more antiquated surface roads or use the highway and pay the toll. Mutual funds charge fees for the same reason: the shareholders pay the costs of running a mutual fund.

The question is, how much should those costs affect our choice of funds? To what extent should fees come into play when we are using tools like fund screeners? Are we passing up the possibility of better returns if we bypass all funds that are burdened with potentially higher fees?

As well as providing diversification, which is a selling point that is hard to ignore, index funds have incredibly low fees. The cost of doing business is so extraordinarily low for index funds because of the funds' autopilot feature. Add to that the fact that index funds trade infrequently, which leads to low turnover. This makes managing an index fund a simple and inexpensive matter.

(Never assume, though, that every index fund has the same costs. While index funds are created equal, any fund that claims to mimic an index should be bought directly from the fund family. Tenths and hundredths of a percentage point in fees can really make a difference over a long period of time. Avoid buying index funds from a broker. Ultimately, the broker will receive a fee for this service, and you will pay for it. Shop around.)

Understanding Fees

When it comes to fees, actively managed mutual funds are a different story.

Jack Bogle, former chairman of Vanguard Funds and head of the Bogle Financial Research Center, believes in performance-based fees for managers—except in index funds. Performance-based fees, which some funds like Fidelity Windsor, a large value fund, use, are called incentive fees. The managers of funds using this technique receive a bonus for beating the benchmark along with a base fee of 0.12 percent of assets. Incentives such as these are great when the manager is beating the index, but the penalty for not making that benchmark can show up as a pay cut. For several years, the fund did not beat the S&P 500 and the managers received a fee of only 0.04 percent.

Fees abound in mutual funds, and even if they have gotten less intrusive, they still play a major role in how much money we will actually make.

Each time a trade is executed, fees are charged. While this kind of straightforward pricing is why folks like individual stocks, in mutual funds, those costs can be less clear. When the individual investor buys a stock, he or she can coolly calculate how much the trade really costs and how much he or she will make if it rises to a given level. When mutual funds buy stock, the fee for the trade, the cost of the research supporting the trade, and the price of the fund's maintenance often get bundled together.

It is a hard fact the mutual funds will charge fees. Actively managed mutual funds will charge higher fees than their passive counterparts. But how do you strike a balance between what is too much and what is needed to get the job done?

What is meant by load?

No-load funds can be described as funds that do not charge either an up-front fee or a back-end fee, both of which are called a load. Front-end-loaded funds charge you a set percentage when they sell you a share in the fund. A back-loaded fund or closed-end fund will charge you a percentage of your assets when you withdraw or move your money. With a no-load fund, an investment of $1,000 will cost you no money, and if the fund gains 10 percent in your first year, you will have gained $100, increasing your fund balance to $1,100. A front-loaded fund charging 5 percent will take $50 out of your investment right at the beginning. A 10 percent increase on the remaining $950 would amount to $95, or a net of only $45 over your initial investment, bringing your balance to $1,045. In a closed-end fund charging 3 percent, if you withdraw your funds at the end of a year in which the gain was 10 percent, you will be able to take out a balance of only $1,067.

Estimates of exactly how much shareholders pay mutual funds abound, but educated guessing suggests that the industry charges over $60 billion in fees annually. Almost half of that money pays for marketing, administration, and portfolio management. The remaining money is profit for the fund family.

Why are fees so important?

Mutual fund management fees and other so-called expenses for operations can add up to as much as 75 percent of the total cost (the fee paid) for an investor in a stock fund. The remaining money is usually allotted for such expenses as distribution, with half of those fees being spent on 12b–1 charges. (See Chapter 12 for a full description of 12b–1 fees.)

These costs have raised some eyebrows over the last several years. The industry hummed along quite nicely for the first 80 years of its existence. Then scandal hit, SEC investigations were begun, and mutual funds became the target of investors' ire over abuses and costs. Some of those problems have been addressed, and many are being fixed. (See Chapter 12 for complete explanations of terms such as soft money, market timing, and hard closes.) In some instances, the knee-jerk protection against these abuses that many mutual funds offer has actually raised fees. Go figure.

On the other hand, index funds, which have always been seen as the benchmark for the lowest fees available, have continued to slice what little they charge in the hopes of attracting more investors. Fees have become an "economy of scale." When mutual funds were posting double-digit gains, the fees that these funds charged seemed almost irrelevant. But when the average annual return has fallen to, in many cases, below 9 percent, any additional charge levied by the fund company appears to be too much, eating away at what little profit or return you have received. Investors seem to be answering the question of how much is too much, but only when the fund's returns fail to beat the inexpensive index.

Ask yourself, what do you have? Do you have a broker, an advisor, or a planner? They are not the same, especially when it comes to advice. A broker is basically a securities dealer providing nondiscretionary advice. Those tidbits of information you get from a broker, stuff that is solely incidental to its brokerage services, are exempted from the Investment Advisers Act. It doesn't matter whether your broker charges an asset-based or fixed fee (rather than commissions, mark-ups, or mark-downs) for its services.

The Investment Advisers Act of 1940, however, clearly outlines the role that an advisor can play for a client. Under that act, an advisor should always put the needs of the client first by offering the client the products best suited to his or her needs. The problem with brokers, advisors claim, is the way they traditionally conduct business. Brokerage houses charge commissions, which can skew brokers' investment "suggestions" somewhat to the advantage of their employer. And many investors understand this. But clients of brokerage houses often assume that they will receive advice that is focused on their own investment welfare.

Planners work their magic through a series of goal-setting techniques designed to engage your whole financial picture. Financial planners should act as mentors. What they are not is almost as important to note as what they are. According to the Certified Financial Planners Board of Standards, financial planning should not be confused with investing, nor should planners make any guarantees on investment returns.

Do you know what you have?

Surprisingly, many people continue to buy mutual funds from brokers. It could be because of the convenience or because they feel overwhelmed by the more than eight thousand choices. Be warned: this lack of initiative on your part comes with a cost, one that you could have avoided had you shopped around and bought the fund on your own.

Many brokerage houses offer several funds in different classes. In many instances, it breaks down this way: A fund will offer class A shares, which are front-end-loaded; class B shares, which are often saddled with a redemption fee, making them closed-end funds, and class C shares, which are the no-load variety.

If you find that you have to make a decision about buying a mutual fund from a broker, be sure to ask the following question: does the broker's sales commission come from the employer or from the mutual fund itself? If the fund is paying the broker, that money is coming from the assets of the fund. Get up and leave. Buy the fund on your own.

 What the Experts Say   I feel that luck is preparation meeting opportunity.

Oprah Winfrey

Fees are a very sensitive issue. Fund families like American Funds have taken the concept of economies of scale to heart and, as a result, have offered some of the fastest-growing funds. By creating a breakpoint in their funds, they are able to reduce the amount of fees the fund charges as the portfolio grows.

A breakpoint acts like a threshold. Once the fund reaches a certain size, the need to charge standard fees is reduced. This is not only an example of how funds can fix their own problems, but yet another reason why some funds are better than others. (This is not a recommendation to buy funds from American. I use this fund family only as an example.)

Some funds will wait for the Securities and Exchange Commission to force the issue and require change. When funds control themselves for the betterment of their shareholders, news travels fast, and investors flock to those funds that offer a proactive approach to management. Yet in many cases fees are still too high.

For a mutual fund, one of the key elements of success is in the hands of the fund's board of directors. Think of them as the tires on the car you are driving. They act as the go-between for your car and where you are going, and with any luck, they provide each shareholder a smooth investment ride without the bumps.

But wait. As an investor in an actively managed fund, you might ask, not only do you need to be concerned about the fees charged, the manager's experience, and the focus of the fund, but you also need to be conscious of who is on the board of directors? Yes, yes, and yes.

The board of directors of a mutual fund should act like shareholder advocates. This is not really possible if the board members have a vested interest in the company. They need to be watchful, using their experience to steer the fund along its predetermined course with a certain level of honesty and integrity. The best way to achieve this is to have independent board members from outside the company. You can find information about the board of directors in the prospectus. That booklet issued by the fund company describing the inner goings-on of the fund is an important source of information.

The prospectus contains not only information about who is running the fund company, but who the manager is, what philosophy he or she will employ, and some explanation about where the fund has been—and where it is headed. Fund managers understand the importance of enticing you to invest with them—their paycheck depends on it—and a prospectus can be a wonderful tool to use. One might even call it your fund's owner's manual. Don't treat it like one, though.

We all know what happens to owner's manuals. They get read once, if only for the quick tour around the instrument panel or if you can't figure out how to turn off the dome light. Otherwise, they sit in the glove box, encased in the same plastic they arrived in and never referred to again.

Prospectuses and quarterly statements contain important, vital, and often timely information. While mutual fund investing has always made the assumption that we are nothing more than back-seat passengers, with the real driving being done by the stock market (and to a certain degree that may be true), letting your money ride without at least a passing glance at your statement is just not right.

In a 401(k), you want to make sure that your allocations are correct and that the money you think is being deposited actually is. Ask your fund administrator for prospectuses if they aren't issued on at least an annual basis.

In a mutual fund outside of a 401(k) plan, whether you own it as part of an IRA or not, always take the time to look for any evidence that the fund is changing course. Are mid-caps being replaced by small caps for a bump in the fund's returns? Remember style drift?

Smaller stocks are generally considered more risky. Mutual fund investors have found some real returns in portfolios that contained some exposure to these kinds of funds. The problem here is double exposure. If you already own a fund that holds small caps, you don't want your mid-cap fund owning them as well.

How is market capitalization determined?

Large cap refers to companies with large market capitalizations. A company's market capitalization is calculated by multiplying the share price by the number of shares outstanding, or available to trade on the open market. In simple terms, it works like this: if your company has issued a hundred shares of stock and that stock is trading at a price of $3, your firm has a market capitalization of $300. In the real world,

Large-cap companies have a capitalization of $5 billion or more.

Medium cap or mid-cap refers to companies with $1 billion to $5 billion capitalization.

Small-cap companies have a market worth between $250 million and $1 billion.

Micro-caps generally are everything smaller.

Later, when the discussion turns to the stock market and the purchase of individual stocks, we will look more specifically at how this works. The boundaries between the different business size categories can change rather rapidly. Buying a small-cap company and watching it grow to mid-cap or large-cap size in a short time is not what a small-cap fund manager wants. That means that the fund has to sell a winner because it has become too expensive to own.

That means taxes. That also means looking for another place to put your investment dollar. It is, at best, a profitable hassle.

The Price for Losing

While having winners in your portfolio is the good fortune that anyone, including a fund manager, might like to have, it is often the reverse that happens. If a company is being punished by the markets and is losing value quickly (remember that the stock market rewards companies with an elevated share price and punishes them with a decline in share price), some funds will be forced to sell that company as its capitalization changes.

(There are numerous reasons why a company is in favor or out of favor, including its earnings, scandal, or new products and services. But once the Street scorns a company, the road back to respectability is often long. In order to protect the fund, managers will sell their holdings along with everyone else.)

What fund investors need to look for when they are thinking about investing in one fund or another is much more complicated than that. Fund managers need strong returns to draw new investor money. The manager's reward (or, if you prefer, his or her compensation or paycheck) may be tied to the success of the fund. The problem is that in the short term, a fund's performance is likely to be below the benchmark, not above.

In the Real World... The mutual fund industry still has some changing to do. Without being forced to do so, funds should begin to fully disclose how much managers get paid. Managers' compensation package comes out of your assets and should be fully disclosed.

What was in favor last quarter might not be in favor next quarter. The fickle nature of the markets prevents one strategy from prevailing quarter after quarter, year after year. Only over the course of 5 to 10 years can a fund be truly judged on how it survived this fickleness and remained profitable as well.

When you do decide to be come one of the 95 million people who own mutual funds (more than twice the number of people who own individual stocks), you will want to concentrate on making sure that the stocks held in one fund that you own are not also held by another fund in your portfolio. This is called diversification.

Diversifying in index funds is a much simpler exercise. When you buy an S&P 500 index fund, you have bought into 92 percent of the investment-worthy companies. By purchasing an index like the Wilshire 4500, you can buy a piece of the rest of the market. Or you can use the style boxes created by Morningstar, buying nine different funds designed to cover each of the different sectors—large to small, value to core to growth. But with actively managed funds, diversity becomes much more of a chore and requires some diligence on your part.

A mutual fund portfolio, and we will have several suggestions for building one at the end of this discussion, should be diversified. Such sage investors as

Warren Buffett have called diversification an absolute must for someone who is unsure of what he or she is doing. This is actually good advice for all investors, no matter what their skill level. You need to make sure that your small-cap fund isn't holding onto any sizable companies that may now be regarded as mid-sized. This is especially important if you have diversified your holdings by also purchasing a mid-cap fund.

Those labels on your fund are very important. I have suggested using a fund screener to narrow down the list of mutual funds to those that you believe are right for you. However, this is a little like buying a car online. While you can do the research in your bathrobe, in most cases you still need to actually drive the car to complete the deal.

This is why there is increased reliance on rating services to provide you with a way to narrow your selection even further. The trouble is, most rating services are backward-looking. In fact, almost all of the financial information you receive is a rearview mirror experience.

Morningstar, ValuLine, and Lipper Analytical Services all employ a backward-looking system for rating a fund that they hope will provide you with a forward-looking picture of where the fund might be headed. The problem is understanding how to use these systems.

Morningstar uses a method that looks at downside risk when assigning a rating of one through five stars to a mutual fund. It also looks at expenses and loads and offers a look at the perceived style of the fund using the style box divided into nine squares that I mentioned earlier. Morningstar also uses a 10-year time horizon when analyzing a fund's performance.

ValuLine is all about performance and rewards a fund for consistency. As long as the fund does better than its peers, it receives accolades and is also assigned a numerical rank of one through five. The five-year window that it uses for performance may be too short for the best analysis of how a fund will perform long term.

It is an immutable law in business that words are words, explanations are explanations, promises are promises, but only performance is reality.

Harold S. Geneen

Lipper uses a slice-and-dice approach, breaking funds into ever-smaller style categories in the hope that investors can better compare how the fund they are researching has done.

The need to look forward, especially given the ever-present warning that "past performance is not a guarantee of future returns" makes shopping f or the right actively managed fund more difficult. Not impossible, just more trouble. But in many cases, it is worth it—once you find one.

Beneath the Glossy Veneer

Even seasoned investors would be opening themselves up to potential problems if they tried to use the a fund's top 10 holdings as a good method of predicting the fund's future performance. Far more brilliant economists and strategists than you or I will ever be are hard at work deciphering the inner workings of P/E ratios, hoping to unlock the secrets of performance. These financial explorers will be looking for clues in the performance of a fund's holdings by comparing them to a hypothetical model based on the holdings had the fund never traded. And still others researchers looking for the key to understanding performance will conduct scholarly exercises in search of truth, justice, and a clean, easy-to-use tool that can peer into our financial future using past results.

When they figure out how to help us determine the a mutual fund's future performance, we will be very grateful indeed. For now, though, we will use the tools we have at hand, use our blend of commonsense and intuition, and trust that although we may make mistakes, we will profit over the long term.

One of the initial ways to determine the performance of your fund is by using the net asset value (NAV). The NAV can be easily checked on a daily basis and is posted at the close of the markets on the East Coast (4 p.m.). The NAV is calculated using the following simple formula:

NAV = current value of fund holdings ÷ number of fund shares outstanding

The increasingly high cost of ink has forced many newspapers to stop running daily fund listings and to direct readers to their online counterparts, where the information can be updated almost instantaneously. But between you and me, even daily monitoring of your mutual fund's asset value is not worth the time or effort.

The NAV can change with an increase or decrease in the number of investors or investments. Increasing or decreasing the number of shares or the assets of the fund can alter the NAV.

Another way to evaluate performance is by using total return. When you purchase a fund, this is the backward-looking number provided to give the investor some idea of a fund's consistent performance. But total return is much more personal once you buy into a fund. It can be calculated like this:

Change in value

(what your account is worth, including dividends or distributions)

divided by the cost of the initial investment

(that number could be your account value at the beginning of the year, the beginning of the quarter, or when you first bought shares in the fund).

This will give you a total return.

For instance, suppose you invested the required $2,000 in a mutual fund and the fund performed incredibly well. The underlying shares in the fund increased dividends and the fund made distributions to your account. Suppose the added cash, wisely reinvested, was $500. This increased your fund balance and, as a result, your account's return was 25 percent.

Another method for determining fund performance is yield. This measure is often used when evaluating bonds, but mutual fund investors can use it to determine their income from funds when the dividends and distributions are not reinvested. The following formula shows you how to determine the yield of a share when dividends are paid. This can be used to calculate the yield on dividend-paying stocks when they are bought individually, outside of a mutual fund.

Distribution per share ÷ closing price (NAV) = share yield percentage

There are three things to keep in mind when trying to predict performance with any accuracy. First, active fund managers find it increasingly difficult to beat the indexes when the time frame for comparison is lengthened to 20 years or more. In fact, the number of funds that beat the indexes over that period rarely tops 10 percent. Second, and worse, the style that is most popular at any particular time, whether it be growth, value, or a blend of some kind, will not be fashionable for the long term. If a growth strategy posts the best short-term returns, for example, the chances are that indexes will beat growth funds when comparing performance over 20 years.

 The funds attract additional cash flows after the introduction of new share classes, which may in turn hurt fund performance due to increased fund size and higher cash-flow volatility.

Lu Zheng

And lastly, Lu Zheng, assistant professor of finance at the University of Michigan's Stephen M. Ross School of Business, has found that a fund's performance can be affected by the addition of new share classes. Funds often set up A, B, and C share classes to allow for different fee structures. Professor Zheng found that there was a two-year impact not only on the performance of funds that made these changes, but on their cash flow as well. The full text of the study can be found at http://webuser.bus.umich.edu/luzheng/web_page/lu_papers/ multipleclass.pdf.

Just the Right Balance

For the actively managed mutual fund, not all driving is done faster than the indexes.

We have discussed balanced funds as a way to limit the exposure your investments have to the stock market. The inclusion of age in an investment equation is as important as diversification, judging performance, or any of the other skills you will develop later on. While time is on your side when it comes to compounding and dollar cost averaging, the creeping specter of getting old works in reverse. Each day brings you a little closer to the end of your working career.

Using balanced funds in a portfolio makes sense if you are within a decade of your retirement date. Balanced funds can help you achieve a good mix of exposure to equities and fixed-income investments.

It is true that over the long term, stocks will make you money, but short-term occurrences can be portfolio-shaking at times. Balanced funds seek to avoid

What are the differences between a balanced fund and a lifestyle fund?

The differences between balanced funds and lifestyle funds are subtle at best. A *lifestyle* fund is designed with a specific retirement date in mind. A fund that is dubbed a "2040" will be investing with that expectation that you will begin to receive a distribution in that year. The fund managers attempt to take this into account by gradually limiting the investors' exposure to riskier investments such as stocks and moving into fixed-income investments. A *balanced* fund, on the other hand, has certain predetermined percentages for stocks and bonds (or other fixed-income securities). The investor knows exactly how the money is allocated.

those financial bumps by adjusting your speed limit ever so slightly. You will be moving faster than an index fund might, with any luck, but at a much more measured pace.

Balanced funds do not replace index funds, and because of that they do have some additional risk. Index funds, as I mentioned earlier, are not without risk. Although the risk in a balanced fund is offset because the fund manager hold bonds in the portfolio, these holdings can often become a drag on performance. This makes judging the performance of these funds somewhat harder.

The bond factor is the reason for this inability to accurately judge how well a balanced fund has done. Bonds tend to make up about 40 percent of the holdings in a balanced fund. Because bonds are sold with maturity dates, good fund managers will try to ladder these bonds.

I promise that we will devote quite a few pages to this subject. For the sake of this discussion, however, bonds are basically loans, and these loans have a due date (maturity). Savvy bond investors will buy bonds with different maturities (laddering).

Balanced funds are appropriate for those who are looking to protect some of their long-term gains. However, you can balance your own portfolio, and probably with better results. If you purchase two equity indexes, one that tracks the S&P 500 and one that captures the rest of the market, like the Wilshire 4500, your equity exposure is well taken care of—to a degree. You will still be fully exposed to the stock market, and as you age, you will want to shift into something a little more conservative.

A Conservative Approach

Funds that invest in bonds and other fixed-income securities can seem to be less actively managed than their stock market counterpart, and in some instances that's true, but not always.

Using a bond fund is hands down the best way for the average investor to buy bonds. The help you get from a bond fund manager is priceless.

Bonds are to investing what Volvos are to driving. Going further than just sweating the details, Volvo engineers worried all the risk out of their vehicles in the quest for the safest cars on the road.

Bonds buyers are focused on worry. Essentially a debt instrument, bonds are sold by companies and governments, big and small. They are used to finance projects and purchase equipment. They are a pledge by the borrower to repay the money it has been lent in a timely fashion, paying interest at an agreed-upon rate and at agreed-upon intervals, usually every six months.

 Individual bonds can be expensive to purchase, as they often have face values in the tens of thousands of dollars. The quality of a bond is determined by credit agencies. The better the credit rating a company has, the greater the chance that you will get repaid and the lower the risk; hence, the interest rate will be lower. If a company gets a bad credit rating, investors will see it as a risk. You know what happens then. Once the perceived risk increases, the cost of the loan goes up.

Bonds provide something that very few investments can claim: they provide a high current income and preservation of the money invested, the capital.

Bonds basically make you the lender in the financial transaction. As the lender, you of course would like to have the loan paid back on time and with interest. You would also like the best reward for your money possible, which is called the yield. While investing in bonds outside of a mutual fund is a complicated matter, it is still vital to remember two things.

First, the price of a bond moves in the opposite direction from the yield. This is not as difficult to understand as it first seems. If you as a company, a municipality, or a government are in need of cash, you need to attract money. You look for investors who are willing to lend it. But first, investors need to know whether you can pay them back in full. Failure to do so, called default, would have a negative effect on your efforts in the future. It isn't wholly unlike you and your creditors outside the world of bonds.

Once the borrower is rated by a credit agency, the interest rate is determined. The bonds are offered at a price that reflects that interest rate (or yield). Setting that yield is very important to fixed-income investors, and with good reason.

The higher the return on the investment, the greater the chance that a company or government will attract people who want to lend it the money it needs. But these investors will ask themselves why the company, municipality, or government is offering such a high yield. Perhaps they will wonder, is there a chance that the money might be used for a risky investment? Is there a chance that this risk might not pay off? Will I get paid?

On the opposite end of this example is a company, municipality, or government that uses bonds to raise money and, because of its good credit rating, is most assuredly able to pay you, the lender, back with interest.

What the Experts Say

A conservative is a man who has plenty of money and don't see any reason why he shouldn't always have plenty of money.

Will Rogers

So the safer the borrower, the higher the price for the bond and the lower the yield the issuer will offer. The riskier the investment, the lower the price will be (with the yield moving in the opposite direction from the price) in order to attract investors who are willing to take a high degree of risk.

One could argue the same idea this way: Two companies issue a bond valued a $1,000. Because company A is a very good credit risk and is likely to repay the bond in full (in the form of coupon payments every six months—in this case, the offered yield is 5 percent, so the payments would be $25), the market determines that this is good deal. The full price of the bond is determined to be worth the asking price and the market gladly pays.

But company B has problems and is issuing the bond to help resolve some other outstanding debt. Their credit rating isn't so good, either. The market (led by the credit agencies) discounts the bond driving the $1,000 face value down to $500. Because yield and price move in opposite directions, the interest rate rises to 10 percent. On the surface, this seems like a great deal. Better coupon payments (now $50 every six months) are simply an enticement for the investor to assume additional risk.

In bonds, you are rewarded for risk. Conversely, you can also be punished if the company defaults or calls the bonds in.

But that is, and most fixed-income aficionados would agree, an incredibly simplified explanation. There are many more elements involved in this investment that further complicate what seems to be a relatively straightforward transaction.

Bonds do play a part in a balanced portfolio. The best way to include them is through a mutual fund that specializes in bonds or through a balanced fund that invests in both bonds and stocks.

It is important that you use the same criteria for investing in bond funds as for equity funds. Always choose a no-load fund with low expenses. Choose a fund with a manager or management team that has been at the fund for some time. It is considered best if that experience spans at least a three- to five-year period or longer. Someone who is the helm of a bond fund will need time to develop his portfolio using techniques like laddering.

How does time affect bonds?

The very best funds use time as an ally. Bonds are sold with different maturities or due dates. The shorter the maturity, the more frequently the investor will need to reinvest the money. Laddering essentially always keeps money invested by purchasing many different bonds with different maturities. This is hard to do when investing individually unless you have huge amounts of money.

Be sure the bond fund is being compared to similar-type funds with comparable investing styles. Index when you can, and be sure that you look at performance results, once again, over a long period of time that includes at least one good market cycle (approximately five years, or perhaps longer).

The first bond index fund appeared in 1983 from the flagship fund company Vanguard. Such index funds don't necessarily own all of the available bonds.

Instead, they use a technique called sampling to get a good cross section of the bonds available.

Lehman Brothers is the premier fixed-income index company, much like Standard and Poor's in the equity markets. The Lehman Brothers Aggregate Bond Index is widely used by bond fund managers to measure their performance. Lehman offers a wide variety of indexes, both domestic and global.

Here is a sampling of Lehman's indexes.

U.S. Universal. This is the total U.S. bond market index. It contains almost 70 percent of what are considered Aaa-rated bonds; 90 percent of the index is included in the U.S. Aggregate holdings.

U.S. Aggregate. Fixed-income holdings in this index are more or less evenly divided between Treasuries (fixed-income securities issued by the U.S. government), government-related, corporates (corporate bonds are how businesses borrow money; issuing shares creates a partnership between the shareholder and the company, but bondholders are interested in only one thing: getting their money paid back with interest), and mortgage-backed securities (MBSs). (When you borrow money to buy a house, a mortgage is created. The mortgage is then bundled with a bunch of other mortgages and sold as an MBS so that banks and lenders can use the funds to create more mortgages.)

U.S. High-Yield. This index tracks corporate borrowing and, to a lesser degree, utility offerings. High yield is basically a reference to the risk involved. The higher the yield, the greater the chances that the borrower will not repay. Unlike Treasuries, which are backed by the "full faith and credit" of the federal government, corporate bonds are only as good as the company that issues them. Hence the importance of a good, reliable ratings system.

Non-Taxable Municipals. Lehman tracks a number of municipal bonds, or bonds issued by states or localities. The index tracks four separate long-term offerings.

Hybrid U.S. Convertibles. Created in 2003, this index covers convertible securities, which for the sake of simplicity are bonds that can be converted into stock.

Fixed-income funds can invest in stocks, but if they do, they tend to choose dividend-producing preferred stocks without much price movement. But bonds are the mainstay of these funds, particularly corporate bonds and government-backed mortgage securities. These have a fixed payoff rate that is called their return.

These funds, it is important to note, do carry a risk that is tied directly to the interest rate. The higher the rate, the lower the price for these types of funds and the lower their value. The lower the interest rate, the greater the value of bond funds and the more their capital grows.

When you are investing in a bond fund, stability is the next consideration. The riskier the investment, such as with lower-rated corporate bonds (a list if ratings can be found in the next section), the higher the yield. The safer the investment, the lower the yield. The stability of bond funds is better than that of stock funds, but the principal is not as safe as with money market–type funds.

Funds that invest in government-backed securities tend to be the best bet because of the full government backing that they carry. "Government-backed securities" refers to those issued by the United States Treasury. These are debt instruments that come with the slogan "backed by the full faith and credit of the federal government."

These bonds are usually bought based on maturity. The T-Bill matures in 90 days to 1 year. Treasury Notes are issued with maturity dates of 2 to 10 years. Treasury Bonds are sold to investors with maturities ranging from 10 to 30 years.

Municipal bond funds or tax-exempt bond funds are essentially just that. These funds invest in municipal bonds, which usually have longer maturity dates, lower ratings, and, of course, because of those risks, higher yields as well.

Municipal bonds are issued to fund a wide variety of civic projects. To entice investors, the interest received from these bonds is usually free of taxes on the state and federal level. These bonds can still have tax consequences, and when buying a fund that holds munis, this should be considered. In fact, the tax on the capital gain from a municipal bond can actually be taxed at the regular income rate.

These types of funds are not as sensitive to interest rates, although there will be some movement in the prices of these funds (remember, lower interest rates mean higher prices and vice versa).

If you include these types of funds in your portfolio, the income produced by them is free of federal taxes and in some cases of state taxes as well.

Using the Ratings

The following are summaries of the definitions of Moody's ratings for long-term bonds. There are other credit agencies of similar prominence, but for the sake of this discussion, we will use Moody's.

Aaa Best quality, with the smallest degree of investment risk.

Aa High quality by all standards; together with the Aaa group, they make up what are generally known as high-grade bonds.

A Bonds that possess many favorable investment attributes. They are considered upper-medium-grade obligations.

Baa Medium-grade obligations (neither highly protected nor poorly secured). Bonds rated Baa and above are considered investment grade.

Ba Bonds with speculative elements; their future is not as well assured. Bonds rated Ba and below are generally considered speculative.

B These bonds generally lack the characteristics of a desirable investment.

Caa Bonds of poor standing.

C The lowest-rated class of bonds, with extremely poor prospects of ever attaining any real investment standing.

We will, I promise, discuss bonds in more detail in later chapters.

Beyond Our Borders

Other types of funds that warrant a mention are international funds and emerging market funds. The growing attraction of exchange-traded funds (ETFs), real estate investment trusts (REITs), and funds that invest in a wide variety of sectors and disciplines may have a place in your portfolio.

Here's how we will approach these funds. We like them, and they are necessary in a good portfolio, but they carry additional risk, and they are not always right for everyone.

These funds act like a fuel enhancer, giving you a better opportunity to diversify and spread your investments across a broader horizon. Even if you were to invest in each type, they should never exceed 20 percent of your total portfolio.

We will discuss risk at length in a later chapter, but for now we will just say that the reward for exposure to some risks is not worth the exposure. International funds will become less distinct as more American companies become a little less domestic and a whole lot more international. Even now, it has become increasingly difficult to determine crossover holdings.

International refers to stocks offered by companies whose country of origin is not the United States. The foreign stock exchanges located in London, Germany, France, and Japan are the most widely recognized. Every country that has an economy has some sort of stock exchange, even Iraq.

In the Real World...

Here is a list of the major international exchanges.

AEX (Amsterdam)

All Ordinaries (Sydney)

ATTRACT40 (Stockholm)

CAC–40 (Paris)

DAX (Frankfurt)

FTSE (London)

Hang Seng (Hong Kong)

Ibex35 (Madrid)

Mib30 (Milan)

Nikkei 225 (Tokyo)

Straits Times Industrials (Singapore)

S&P/TSX Composite Index (Toronto)

If you dedicate 20 percent of your portfolio to international funds, you need to be aware that because of the ever-diminishing size of the global marketplace, you may be tracking funds similar to those offered in the United States. In the not-to-distant past, the global business borders were more clearly defined. Now, the world has gotten smaller and because of that, domestic and foreign investments are, in some instances, so interrelated that they have become similar in terms of risk and reward.

It's better to stay domestic for the most part despite the attractive returns that some of these funds have posted in recent years. Morgan Stanley Capital International (MSCI) offers some of the best international indexes.

Emerging market funds are filled with risk and possibility. Once again, these should be kept to only a small portion of a good portfolio. These are funds that look for opportunities in places where the economies are growing. While emerging markets are often financed by bigger countries, exposure to this group, unless it is done in very limited quantities, can be very risky. Once again, many U.S. companies already have a stake in or a partnership with many of the companies operating on foreign soil.

In the Real World...

The following is a list of emerging market indexes as tracked by Dow Jones:

Regional

Latin America Stock Index

Pacific Stock Index (excludes Japan)

Southeast Asia Stock Index

Dow Jones Country Indexes

Brazil Stock Index

Chile Stock Index

Indonesia Stock Index

Malaysia Stock Index

Mexico Stock Index

Philippines Stock Index

South Africa Stock Index

South Korea Stock Index

Taiwan Stock Index

Thailand Stock Index

Venezuela Stock Index

For some, exchange-traded funds have added a much-needed shot in the arm, allowing mutual fund investing in an open-market situation. Until now, I haven't said much about how mutual funds arrive at their price.

Mutual funds are priced at their net asset value, and, quite frankly, that price is not as important as it seems. Mutual fund investors can get caught up in that number, checking their portfolio online daily, looking for slight price shifts.

This can be hard on your psyche. Mutual fund prices do not move like stock prices. They do go up and down, but the price you see listed is based on the total of the stocks in the fund.

The net asset value of a fund is calculated by the fund at the close of business, giving the investor an average price for all of the investments in the fund. The NAV is set at the end of the closing day on Wall Street. The trouble with this approach is how often the prices for those securities change throughout the trading day.

Next time you call in sick from work, spend the day watching a station like CNBC. While it doesn't have the same excitement as a daytime soap, the changes in share prices throughout the day as news comes in, earnings are reported, or economic reports are issued can provide some entertainment. Stations like CNBC have their purpose, but for the utterly confused investor, they should be just watched for the spectacle of it. It is those ever-shifting prices and that four o'clock close that helped to bring about ETFs.

Investors wanted a price that reflected what was happening here and now, without waiting until the markets closed. The American Stock Exchange proved the perfect venue for just such an activity. ETFs offer a growing array of sector index funds that are actively watched, traded, and rebalanced throughout the day depending on the amount of money available to invest.

So what do you compare them to, if not to the index that they suggest they are trying to beat? How about to themselves? There are basically three types of ETFs. *Open-end index funds* have a number of special features that make them different from their mutual fund counterparts. These funds can use derivatives (basically contracts, either between two parties—over the counter—or on an exchange, based on some sort of future value) and loan securities. A *unit investment trust* pays dividends directly to the shareholder and has a little more leeway to drift beyond its core index. A *grantor trust* allows the shareholders to vote their interest (mutual funds do this by proxy); unlike the other two types of ETFs, this type of fund is not registered with the SEC under the Investment Company Act of 1940.

Which ETF is which?

Exchange-traded funds use a variety of abbreviations to describe the underlying index they are mimicking. For instance, SPDR is ETF shorthand for Standard & Poor's Depositary Receipts; these are a form of unit investment trust, as are Diamonds, nicknamed for the index they track, the Dow Jones Industrial Average, and Cubes, which were introduced during the height of the stock market craze in the late 1990s to track the top 100 Nasdaq stocks (this fund once had a ticker symbol of QQQ, hence the name Cubes; it has since been changed to QQQQ). Merrill Lynch's HOLDRS, or HOLding Company Depository ReceiptS, act as a grantor trust type of ETF. Select Sector SPDRs and iShares are forms of open-end index funds.

SPDRs, Diamonds, and Cubes were among the earliest traded indexes. SPDRs were first introduced in 1993 using the ticker symbol SPY. SPDRs track the S&P 500, and their price on any given day is based on one-tenth of the value of the index. The Dow Jones Industrial Average is tracked using the ticker symbol DIA. Introduced in 1998, this index is priced at one-hundredth of the value of the Dow. Cubes were introduced in 1999, with the ticker symbol QQQ and later QQQQ; they are priced at one-fortieth of the value of the top 100 Nasdaq stocks.

It should be noted that because ETFs are essentially traded like stocks but track an index, some of this discussion about their use in your portfolio will take place further on when we look at owning individual stocks.

Because these funds have some distinct characteristics, comparisons, while seemingly straightforward, are often difficult to understand.

When Porsche entered the SUV market several years back, aside from the price, the car was basically designed the same way a Ford Explorer was—to go off-road, carry more passengers and cargo, and be something that was not quite a truck and not quite a car. While both the Porsche SUV and the Ford Explorer did the same things, they were fundamentally different.

ETFs differ from mutual funds in the following ways:

1. ETFs tend to have a lower expense ratio than mutual funds, but mutual funds don't have trading costs (at least not on the surface). When you buy

or sell an ETF, you incur and pay a broker's fee. Mutual funds have the same cost, but it is spread among all of the shareholders in the fund and shows up as a fee—which is why a fund with a low turnover is preferable to one with a high turnover.

2. ETFs are traded throughout the day, whereas mutual funds are priced once a day at the four o'clock close of the markets. (Once again, this continual pricing leads investors to watch prices. Even with that feature, ETFs are still best held over the long term.)

3. ETFs disclose their holdings on a daily basis, whereas mutual funds do so on a quarterly, semiannual, or annual basis. (As the fund manager moves into and out of a stock, the value of the portfolio changes. Some mutual funds are so large that any changes in their holdings cannot only move markets but damage their share price when they eventually sell.)

4. ETFs have greater transparency, especially in pricing, because the share price is determined by the underlying value of the index based on supply and demand, whereas mutual funds are priced using net asset value. (This is a plus for some investors.)

5. ETFs are immune to redemption concerns, whereas mutual funds must make provision for shareholders who exit the fund. (When markets are in transition—in other words, on the way down—mutual funds must sell shares to accommodate those shareholders who want their money. ETFs do not have this problem.)

6. ETFs have lower portfolio turnover than mutual funds, and because of this, they actually receive a better tax treatment. (When a fund is forced to sell shares, there is always a tax consequence. In an ETF, the taxes are paid by the owner of the fund, whereas in a mutual fund, the remaining shareholders pay a portion of the tax.)

7. ETFs can generally be used only in self-directed retirement funds such as IRAs, whereas mutual funds are available in all types of retirement plans. (That could change in the future as ETFs, which are still a relatively new product for investors, gain wider acceptance and understanding.)

8. ETFs have no minimum investment requirements (although HOLDRS require you to buy what are called round lots, or multiples of 100 shares per transaction), unlike mutual funds, which generally require you to commit some specified amount of money to the fund to start your investment. [The exception to this is mutual funds held in 401(k) plans, which do not require any specific initial investment.] Many mutual fund companies

charge an initiation fee; Vanguard recently raised its fee for funds purchased outside of a retirement account. That fee is often discounted for funds used inside an IRA. This may seem prohibitive to first-time buyers, but there are reasons for it. Fund families want you to join and, more importantly, stay. Each transaction costs money, which in a mutual fund is shared by all shareholders. To keep those costs down, mutual funds put restrictions on frequent traders.)

9. ETFs can use a number of strategies, such as options (to be discussed at length further on), while mutual funds cannot unless they are specifically chartered to do so. (It is true that ETFs have far more latitude in achieving their goals than mutual funds. Keep in mind that with each new tool comes new risk. The straightforward nature of the mutual fund is still best for the utterly confused investor—and for those who are not so confused.)

10. ETFs can be used the same way stocks are, permitting some advanced and often riskier strategies such as shorting, while at the same time giving the investor a great deal more flexibility when it comes to shifting from one sector to another, which mutual funds, because of their trading restrictions, cannot. (Frequent trading increases volatility. Volatility can increase an investor's return, but at what cost? Over the long term, finding a mutual fund that shares your goals and investment ideals will provide you with better returns and, as a side benefit, a good night's sleep.)

And after all of that, ETFs may not be right for the utterly confused investor. I'll tell you why. We have already spent a lot of time discussing how you approach investing. In the next couple of chapters, we will spend a good deal of time wrapping ourselves around some sort of mind-set, one that allows us to be confident in not only how we will invest, but why.

The why is very important. Investing is about making money, growing your investments, and becoming better acquainted with your inner investor. It is, and I will not be the first one to say this nor will I be the last, the *you* in this equation that is the biggest obstacle in the path to becoming successful.

Some of the challenges for the utterly confused investor are overcoming those innate fears of loss, feeling confident during those moments when you might be tempted to second-guess your decisions, learning when to admit you may have been wrong, and appreciating your skills when you are right.

We are all about the long term. While ETFs are best suited to that approach, their ability to be traded throughout the day makes them quite the opposite.

The next step will be to discuss strategies for getting started and staying invested. There are numerous methods and theories on the best way to keep your money involved to net the best advantage; most of these are good in theory but fail when given the test of time. So the best way to use time is to make this enemy of so many strategies your ally.

We are going to take the time to work through many of the more difficult aspects of mutual funds. Many of the questions and answers that are included in the next chapter will give you some background, some additional language skills, and, with luck, the beginnings of your involvement with your investments on a personal level.

CHAPTER 12

On the Defensive

◆◆◆◆◆◆◆◆◆◆◆◆◆◆◆◆◆◆◆◆◆◆◆◆◆◆◆◆◆◆◆◆◆◆

One of the most important driving skills you can learn is the ability to move your eyes quickly from one feature to another. You must be able to check your mirrors with just a glance while rapidly assessing your situation. You must also be able to use the instruments on the dashboard without jeopardizing your view of the road.

Here are a number of questions that will help you navigate that instrument panel; with any luck, they will become part of the skill set you need if you are to drive your investments safely. Many of these questions will give you just the right dose of cynicism as well. Driving defensively is just as important a piece of advice for an investor as it is for a driver.

What Is Dollar Cost Averaging?

In the financial world, there are many and varied schools of thought and an almost innumerable variety of strategies. No single method has proved better over the long run for both the beginning and the seasoned investor than dollar cost averaging (DCA).

The idea is insanely simple. You invest equal amounts at regular intervals over a period of time and allow compounding to work its magic. This method, which is the one usually used when purchasing shares in retirement funds [IRAs and 401(k)s], spreads the cost of those shares across the inevitable higher and lower periods.

One school of thought suggests that dollar cost averaging, in essence, reduces risk. To investors, a lack of risk suggests a lack of reward as well. When you reduce your risk, you may reduce your returns.

I'll admit that I regularly suggest that folks put their tax refund directly into their retirement accounts. Many people who are on the paying end on April 15 try to offset some of their tax bill by making a large fiscal year-end contribution to their IRA in the hopes of lowering the bill that Uncle Sam is charging them.

While the idea behind this is sound, the method leaves something to be desired. Investing a lump sum works best if you have timed the market in such a way that you have hit the fund's NAV at its yearly low. Since there is little likelihood of that happening—it's possible, but not probable—investing a steady stream of money over a long period of time is by far the best method.

Where do I get the money to get started?

I have also been known to say, "Fix those tax returns so that you *don't* get that big tax refund. March into your personnel department," I continue, "fill out a new W–4, and stop paying the government more than you need to." This advice is aimed at those folks who get those huge tax windfalls every year. Taxes often involve complicated issues, and I am not a tax professional. But for those who file a simple return, have a relatively straightforward tax situation, and have not had many changes in their situation over the course of the year, they could have funded a good dollar cost averaging approach to successful investing by investing the amount they were overpaying in taxes each week or month. For instance, a $2,000 tax refund amounts to $166 a month that could have been invested, drawn interest, and created the beginning of a healthy portfolio. Or you can keep giving the money to the government, which will return it the following year with no interest or gain.

There are other approaches to DCA that add a little more risk to the equation. According to M. A. Milevsky of York University in Toronto, investing one-half of the amount you are planning to invest in a lump sum and investing the remainder over the last six months of the dollar cost averaging period permits greater returns without increased risk.

But remember that the market often makes quick and dramatic moves on both the upside and the downside. Investing evenly over the year allows you to buy at both highs and lows. This method favors beginning investors, but it is also the first tool of disciplined investing. This is what leads to wealth. The result of this can be quite extraordinary and convincing.

For example, suppose you are 25 years old, which would be an optimum time to begin your investment life. Suppose you contribute a small amount to your IRA, say $100 each month, until you reach age 65. (You can actually contribute $4,000 annually to these types of accounts, and $4,500 if you are over 50.) Suppose you receive a modest 8 percent return on your investment and you are in a 25 percent tax bracket.

Age	IRA Account	Taxable Investments (Tax-Deferred)
26	1,299.60	1,274.70
30	7,669.96	7,217.94
35	19,097.03	16,980.12
40	36,121.59	30,183.30
45	61,485.50	48,040.49
50	99,273.95	72,192.05
55	155,572.83	104,856.72
60	239,449.48	149,035.25
65	364,412.74	208,786.11

For 40 years, you have put $100 a month away. Some years have been better than others, but overall you have had a measly 8 percent return, slightly below the industry average. You have put $48,000 away for your future, and your balance is now $364,412.74.

Suppose, though, that like many of us, you got a late start and you want to play catch-up. Let's suppose you are 40 with a 25-year horizon until retirement. Suppose you maxed that IRA with the full $4,000 a year, had the same 8 percent rate of return, and were in the same tax bracket.

Age	IRA Account	Taxable Investments (Tax-Deferred)
41	5,415.00	5,311.25
45	31,958.18	30,074.77
50	79,570.94	70,750.49
55	150,506.61	125,763.86
60	256,189.80	200,168.69
65	413,641.46	300,800.22

Dollar cost averaging achieves what no other method could hope to achieve: steady and almost predictable returns. While there will always be disputes and debates on how best to judge those return on investment numbers (in the previous example, we used 8 percent), the markets tend to be more up than down historically.

With dollar cost averaging, it is the down markets that prove the most profitable in the long run. Because you are purchasing shares at a lower price, you can buy more. If the NAV of your mutual fund is $5 and you purchase $333 worth ($4,000 divided by 12 months equals $333.34), you will have purchased 66 shares.

If the NAV falls to $4, the same $333 will purchase 83 shares. If the share price reaches $6, the same $333 will buy only 56 shares. Using DCA will allow you to buy more shares in a down market (without this discipline, many folks will opt to buy less if they think the markets are underpriced) and help you resist the urge to buy more shares in an up market (people like to jump in when the markets seem the strongest, buying more at a higher price).

Dollar cost averaging takes the personality we bring to the marketplace out of your investment strategy.

Are There Certain Investments That Are Better, Taxwise, for Retirement Investing and for Investing Outside a Tax-Deferred Plan?

It is one thing to go on record suggesting that you take advantage of whatever retirement plan is offered to you. And I do this often quite often, even though I know that in many instances, the company you work for will have such a limited selection of mutual funds and stocks that using the plan almost seems to be not worth the trouble. (Companies that offer a limited selection of funds are more common than those with wider offerings. If your plan has limited offerings, opt for the S&P 500 index. You can diversify your holdings outside of the plan, if necessary.)

Tax efficiency is usually not on your mind as you sift through your plan's offerings. People tend to look at growth and performance, fees and management tenure, rankings and riskiness. We will consider, it seems, everything but taxes—which, if you think about it, should be our first concern.

There is a strategy you should use in these *tax-deferred* accounts before you look at all of those variables. In order to pick which investments will be best suited for you to use in this type of plan, one that is designed for long-term holdings, it might be better to think about your possible tax bill in the future.

While death and taxes are often referred to as the only two things you can count on in this life, knowing what your future tax rate will be is almost harder to predict than when you will actually expire. You can take steps to protect your health and well-being, and you can even rely on medical science to give you a longer life, but predicting your final hour is next to impossible. We hear about actuarial tables being extended to accommodate our chances of prolonged life.

The taxpayer—that's someone who works for the federal government but doesn't have to take the civil service examination.

Ronald Reagan

Your tax rate is much harder to predict. When 401(k) plans and IRAs first became popular, it was widely believed that people would have a much lower tax rate after they retired. They would be earning less, and because of that drop in real income, their tax bill would be substantially smaller. Now, with current deficits increasing each year and the simple fact that those bills will need to be paid, there might be something amiss with the lower future rate theory. (Someone has to pay the bills, and that someone is the taxpayer.)

Tax-deferred plans allow you to put money away for the future, when, if things turn out as planned, you will be taxed at a lower rate.

One of the mainstays of 401(k) plans is the index fund. These funds make it easy for the less-than-experienced investor to buy a broad basket of stocks, stocks and bonds, or just bonds. From a tax perspective, this is not a good idea. In the *current* tax environment, keeping index funds in a taxable account outside of a retirement account can be a better move.

For those of you who have a difficult time disciplining yourself to keep accounts outside of your tax-deferred plan funded, making the best of what is inside your employer's plan is still the best choice. The ability to take a pretax deduction and, more importantly, making this investment automatically can create something in a situation where there might be otherwise be nothing. But if you realize how much of your retirement is in your own hands, you might find that discipline easier to embrace.

So which types of investments would be best kept inside a tax-deferred account like a 401(k), a 403(b), or a traditional IRA? The answer is really all about the taxes each type of fund pays and whether deferring those taxes until a later time would be a wise move.

Open your retirement account with index funds. Once you become savvy enough to open a second (taxable) account outside your 401(k) or IRA, use index funds in that account. Inside your retirement account, roll the assets from your index fund into one or more actively managed funds.

Mutual funds that are actively managed should be kept inside your tax-deferred accounts. Because of their high turnover and the possibility that you will incur capital gains taxes because of the fund's frequent short-term selling, these types of funds tend to generate a higher tax bill than investments held longer than a year. Keeping these investments inside your retirement plan eliminates any capital gains tax in the short term. As of right now, investments held less than a year are taxed at your marginal income tax rate, while those held longer than a year receive a 15 percent bill.

Some folks have taken popular advice and cycled some of their gains into high-yield junk bonds. If those investments are not kept inside a retirement account, the tax bill on these types of funds can come as quite a shock. The same thing goes for corporate bond funds, whose yields tend to be higher as well.

Real estate investment trusts (REITs) and funds that hold them should be kept inside tax-deferred accounts. REITs get a corporate tax break because of rules that force them to distribute 90 percent of their profits to their shareholders. When mutual funds hold REITs and trade them frequently, the tax efficiency deteriorates rather quickly. Deferring this little tax issue until retirement will net you the best results taxwise.

The better retirement plans offer some brokerage services. If they do, and if they allow you to buy stocks other than your company's equity, use the account to buy stocks that you do not plan on holding for the full year. Once you have held a stock for 12 months, any gains on the stock can be considered long term and are eligible for the 15 percent tax treatment. When buying stock, tax-deferred accounts are better for short-term holdings.

Outside of these plans, it is a different story. Index funds, by far the prevalent offering inside tax-deferred accounts and the first choice for the conservative investor, are actually treated better outside these accounts. One reason is the lack of turnover. Turnover generates taxes.

These funds tend to be mimic a basket of stocks that is rebalanced only on rare occasions. Index funds are balanced to allow a predetermined exposure to certain stocks. An index fund based on the S&P 500 does not hold equal amounts of each of the 500 companies in that index. Instead, they are weighted to match the percentage of the index represented by each stock to allow for better overall performance and, to some degree, a smaller amount of risk.

(The reference to "weight" is usually used when we talk about size. In this case, the size of a company is its capitalization, or the value the market places on their shares multiplied by the shares outstanding.)

Sometimes these funds do need to be readjusted. Because this is done so infrequently, and because it is done in a tax-friendly manner when it does occur, index funds are better held in accounts where the taxes are paid as the growth occurs.

Inside many company-sponsored retirement plans, companies offer their own stock, with the caveat that it cannot be sold until the employee reaches a certain age or leaves the company. This kind of buy-and-hold strategy is better used outside of these plans. Using accounts outside your retirement plan to pick a basket of diversified, dividend-paying stocks that are not included in any index funds you may be holding is a far better move for long-term holdings.

If you do plan on buying stock in the company you work for, never allow it to become more than 5 percent of your total portfolio. That means 5 percent of all your investments, not just your retirement account. Buy your company's stock through an index fund.

Even though exchange-traded funds (ETFs) are bought, sold, and priced on the exchanges each day, they should be held for longer than a year to take full advantage of what they offer. For that reason, ETFs should be kept outside your retirement plan. ETFs usually hold a basket of equities and are not taxed until you sell them. Taking the 15 percent tax hit after 12 months allows you the best of what could be a highly taxed situation.

Municipal bonds, debt issued by states and local governments to fund civic projects, and funds that trade them are best suited for the long term and should be kept outside of your tax-deferred accounts. In many instances, these funds are free of state as well as federal taxes, which would make their tax treatment much more favorable in an account where the tax obligation is clear. Even in accounts such as a Roth IRA, the return on these tax-free bonds may be subject to taxes when the funds are distributed..

So given these tax consequences, you should take the following five steps when investing:

1. Index funds and funds with little turnover should be held *outside* of a tax-deferred account. Look at your fund's turnover ratio. If it is less than 50 percent over a 12-month period, the fund is probably tax-efficient and should be kept outside of your tax-deferred accounts. Some balanced funds may also qualify.

2. Consider the real yield on your bonds and bond funds. Corporate bond funds, high-yield junk bond funds, and other bonds with healthy yields should be kept *inside* tax-deferred accounts. Being taxed at current rates can have a serious impact on those yields. Municipal bonds and the funds that hold them are free of state and federal taxes and should be held outside a tax-deferred account.

3. REITs have special tax considerations. If they are owned inside a mutual fund and are traded frequently, capital gains can begin to mount in spite of the generous distributions. Keep them *inside* your retirement plans and defer the tax consequences.

4. Stocks that you plan on holding should be kept *outside* retirement plans; actively traded stocks will get better treatment *inside* these plans.

5. ETFs, despite how easy they are to trade, should be held for the long term. Keep them *outside* of your tax-deferred accounts. Many ETFs are indexed and have the same tax considerations as index funds. Some, however, have become increasingly focused on specialized sectors. The only time an ETF should be kept *inside* a retirement plan is when it is so narrowly focused that it may create some outsized gains, tempting you to relinquish your position and take profits.

Since there is a limited amount of space inside your retirement plan [$15,000 annually for your 401(k), $20,000 if you are over 50; and $4,000 annually for your IRAs, $4,500 if you are over 50 and by 2008, that contribution will increase to $5,000], don't use up valuable tax-deferred contributions on something that may not serve the original purpose.

However, if funding your 401(k) is all you have done so far, any contribution is better than none at all.

How Often Should You Review Your 401(k), Your IRA, or Other Retirement Savings Accounts That Hold Mutual Funds?

The short answer is, review any and all financial accounts each time you receive a statement. You should do this to confirm that any automatic contributions have been made as scheduled. If you purchased additional shares by any other means, check to see that the transaction was made in a timely manner.

Reviewing your funds to adjust your account to reflect your targeted goals should be done once a year.

It is no mean feat to get folks to invest in their future. Just ask any poor soul placed in charge of employee enrollment in a company's defined-contribution plan or, as these plans are commonly known, the 401(k). In the largest companies in the country, the ones with the highest likelihood of having a self-directed retirement plan, only 70 percent of the employees use the 401(k) plans. The numbers get even worse when you look at smaller companies. The reasons all seem to boil down to the same set of answers: "I haven't gotten around to it" or "I need to pay the bills first" or "I can't afford to" or "the company doesn't match." In other words, there is no good answer as to why they don't. But I have a good idea of what the real answer may be.

And so does Congress. The vast array of offerings is often staggering for even the seasoned investor. The average plan offers 15 funds.

The seasoned investor is prepared to shuffle through the paperwork and read the material provided with some sort of grasp of the information being offered. It doesn't, however, guarantee that the investor will make the right choice.

The seasoned investor will look at a prospectus to get certain information, but to many of the newly enrolled plan members, the prospectus will seem like so much gibberish. In general, 401(k) plans primarily direct their participants to mutual funds, an investment vehicle that allows the investor to participate in the markets with investors of similar disposition who need a professional money manager to manage their money wisely. To their credit, mutual fund companies are now doing a better job of explaining what they are doing and why. Even more important, they are explaining their fees much better.

But what about the employee who has failed to enroll in a plan at work? On August 4, 2006, Congress approved a heavily debated bill that will change the retirement landscape. Although the full effect of the bill, known as the Pension Protection Act, will not be felt until 2008, it will have an impact on workers who have pensions (allowing companies to change those plans from defined-benefit plans to defined-contribution plans) and 401(k) accounts.

The bill seeks to address not only those who are not invested in their retirement plans, but those who are underinvested. These investors will get help from the plan administrator using acceptable rates of return as a benchmark. If an you are underinvested, your plan will get a sort of intervention to adjust your contributions and your goals.

The bill will also allow step-up contributions made on your behalf. This simply means that the employer along with the plan administrator will view your account against a retirement horizon and can increase your pretax contribution to get you to those goals in a more timely fashion.

For automatic enrollees, the first year of participation will save 3 percent on your behalf. The second year, this contribution will increase to 4 percent, 5 percent in the third year, and 6 percent in the years after that. The PPA requires an employer to contribute 3.5 percent if the employee contributes 6 percent or more.

The PPA will also look at investors who have failed to achieve a good investment balance. In some cases, advice will be given to the employee as to the best investment for his age.

The root cause for this change, aside from the profits Wall Street can make with this significant shift in how retirement plans are used, is investor laziness. If folks use these plans, they fail to keep them in their sights. The best investor pays attention. The best investors are skeptical. As these changes take place, your due diligence will be even more important. The advice that will be offered will come at a cost and may be skewed toward profits to the plan administrator's bottom line.

Regardless of this bill, the plan administrator should be concerned with a number of things in order to achieve what the participants want. Investors might find only a few funds to choose from or, worse, so many that they are staggered by the choices. Inside a 401(k) plan, the selection is often limited to the funds that one family offers, and sometimes the offerings do not include all the funds that the mutual fund company manages.

 Some choices we live not only once but a thousand times over, remembering them for the rest of our lives.

Richard Bach

Whether there are too many choices or too few means little or nothing to investors if they are unable to put what they know into practice.

Faced with the decision on where to put their money once they enroll, new investors ought to keep just two things in mind for the first year: the amount they wish to invest each pay period and what allocation or lifestyle fund best matches their age.

Regular and even contributions are the key to the success of the investment. Dollar cost averaging has never been debunked the way so many other formulas designed to give investors a window on the world of investing that only they will be able to see through have. Growing your retirement nest egg by contributing the same amount of money each and every month not only will provide you with the best advantage in every market condition, but will also allow you to move seamlessly from the world of the uninvested, the unprepared for the future, to the world of the involved. A 401(k) plan allows you to do this before taxes are taken out, deferring the tax bill until retirement, when your tax bracket may be more favorable than your current one.

The key to dollar cost averaging is consistency. With regular investing, you hit the markets at all sorts of levels, removing the psychological and emotional strain from the act of investing. This strain is very real. It makes you want to buy in with the crowd as the markets rise and makes you want to sell as the markets descend. (This crowd emotion is very well documented; the most recent case that comes to mind occurred in January 2000.)

Removing this emotion allows the investor to buy more shares when they are less expensive and to buy fewer when they are more expensive; by doing so, it averages the investment money across a broad range of market highs and lows.

Is There a Fund That Does It All?

Most 401(k) and similar retirement funds offer a fund that seeks to target your retirement goal and invest your money accordingly.

An allocation or lifestyle fund basically makes the adjustments necessary to keep your investment at the right level of diversity. Diversity is the balance between stocks and bonds that provides the investor, new or seasoned, with protection when the crowd overreacts and sends the markets gyrating madly in one direction or another.

For the seasoned investor, someone who has an understanding of the 401(k), now celebrating its twenty-fifth birthday this year, this is the most important part of retirement planning. These investors may not feel that allocation funds are the best tool available. They believe that they can actively manage the diversity that allocation funds provide by spreading their investments across the world of large-cap, mid-cap, small-cap, and international funds. They probably understand their tolerance for risk and how their age plays a part in their ultimate goals.

The new investor, however, has little knowledge going in, but wants to be as equally well exposed with the least amount of effort. As the "path of least resistance" needed to encourage new investors, two-thirds of the companies that manage 401(k) plans now include lifestyle or asset allocation offerings.

These types of funds seek to blend conservative, moderate, and aggressive investment strategies and make them age appropriate. For the youngest investors, the fund would be tipped heavily toward risk. That risk might involve a heavier investment in stocks, and those stocks might be ones that are focused on growth rather than older companies whose growth has slowed.

These funds are easy to spot among your plan's offerings. They are often accompanied by some distant date. For instance, if you plan to retire in 35 years or so, the fund might be listed as a 2040 or 2050 fund.

In an attempt to explain risk, the scholar Philippe Mongin developed an concept called Expected Utility Theory (EUT), which states that "the decision maker" (in this instance, the investor) needs to chose "between risky or uncertain prospects by comparing their expected utility values." Mongin suggested that utility depends on our expectations multiplied by the probable outcome.

So simply, investors need only look at their age to determine which fund is right for them. Perhaps, and for the sake of space, we'll agree with that statement. The younger you are, the more aggressive your portfolio should be.

If new investors choose a fund with an approach that matches their age, they may actually find themselves doing better than investors who claim to be more knowledgeable.

Lifestyle or asset allocation funds are not only for the new investor. They are also worth a look for the investor who brings a little more knowledge to the table. The key to any plan's success remains simple: invest frequently and evenly, and diversify.

What Is Herd Mentality, and How Do I Avoid It?

Although we may not like the reference, as shareholders in a mutual fund we are essentially part of a group, members of a financial herd all seeking to be led in the most profitable direction by our mutual fund managers. When we act in unison, we refer to this as "herd mentality." Markets can move dramatically up or down when investors act as a group.

Few are able to point the finger at any one particular group as being to blame for the rise and fall of any particular market. However, a recent study by Harvard Business School professors Erik Stafford and Joshua D. Covel has found that mutual funds may be the culprit, and that the forces they exerted on the markets in the period leading up to the bursting of the bubble are still at play.

This study, called "Asset Fire Sales (and Purchases) in the Equity Markets," takes a detailed look at how mutual fund managers react to certain market events that affect their cash inflows and outflows. The belief that mutual fund managers were forced to sell to cover redemptions in the event of poor performance and to spend money on stocks when they did exceptionally well was often thought of as being fund-specific. It turns out that these actions had a wider effect on how the markets moved than was previously thought.

Mutual funds that are expecting poor performance for the quarter will often anticipate that the shareholders in the fund will flee to some other, better-performing fund or sector. This "voting with their feet" effect can be felt when the fund is forced to sell large quantities of stocks to cover the redemption of the fund's shares.

Investors in funds that are performing poorly see no reason to hold on for better days; they want their money, and they want it now. Most equity mutual funds, often as a requirement of their charters, keep very little cash on hand; instead, they favor full investment of the available funds. Therefore, the fund must sell some of its holdings to get the money it needs to pay the shareholders who are selling. Until this report, it was unclear just how much of an effect this was having on a specific sector or, in some cases, the overall market.

On the flip side, funds that have had stellar quarters have found themselves flooded with inflows of money as investors seek to hitch themselves to the rising star. This sudden spike in cash reserves must be spent—once again because of the relatively small percentage of cash that a fund's charter permits it to keep on hand—forcing the fund manager to buy additional stocks. While some funds that are overwhelmed with money and see relatively few good buying opportunities will close their doors, it often takes them up to a full quarter to do so, and by then, it may be too late.

The professors called these fund events *forced purchases*. The effect of this type of buying in the open market, often targeted at a specific sector, was to push prices higher until someone sounded the warning and the whole sector crashed. In some cases, the overpricing affects the whole market, and the professors point out that this may have been the reason for the crash in 2000.

While one large fund may not have the power to bring down a whole sector, its actions are seldom isolated, as the underlying stocks' sudden change in value alerts other holders of those equities—which, by coincidence, happen to be other large funds—to buy or sell as well. The possibility of missing a run-up in price or failing to recognize a potential fall forces other funds to react. These forces at work in the marketplace are often governed by program trades, computer-driven buy/sell programs that allow fund managers to put purchases or sales of some stocks in their portfolio on autopilot. These programs react to one fund's fire sale or forced purchase by jumping in automatically and buying or selling the same or similar stocks.

Individual investors seeking to profit from this movement do so at their own risk. The reports of a mutual fund's holdings are often several months old by the time they are made public. Buying the holdings of a top-performing fund in hopes that the stocks in the portfolio will rise as a result of the manager's forced purchases runs the risk that the stocks will become, in the market's mind, overpriced. Chasing the fire sale that happens at poor-performing funds, the individual investor will try to short the beaten-down shares held by the fund. The market might also work against this idea, as the shares of the stocks that the fund has sold may to reach a bottom and become a sudden value.

The best way to benefit from this kind of fluctuation is to pick top-performing actively managed funds whose managers have proven their expertise over a long period of time (five years or more). For those who prefer indexing, the diversity does provide a good deal of protection from these fluctuations. For instance, the Dow Jones Wilshire 5000 index, an index that tracks the total market, has returned an average of 12.4 percent over the last 25 years.

What Is Soft Money?

Soft dollars are basically the cost of a trade over and above the actual transaction cost. Brokerages that trade for fund managers bundle their services when they contract with a money manager. Currently you are paying for this service.

Soft money is not easily understood. So be patient as we take a look at something that might be both necessary to a successful return on your investment and, at the same time, something that you find loathsome.

We have spent a healthy chunk of time looking at the topic of fees. Who pays for what and why has been at the heart of many of the scandals that have racked the mutual fund industry. And as unpleasant as they may seem, these fees are, in their most simplified form, the cost of doing business.

Once an investor determines what type of risk tolerance he or she can stomach, the search for funds that match that criterion begins. The most conservative among us will choose an index fund, a passively managed mutual fund whose holdings usually mimic some index. The manager of this fund has little in the way of trading to do apart from rebalancing or adjusting to changes in the index that the fund is following.

Investors who can tolerate greater risk will want to have an actively managed fund. This type of fund requires the manager to make investment decisions in order to remain fully invested and increase the returns on the portfolio. Portfolios with higher returns are often compared to indexes, so performance that is better than that of your peers is important.

That performance costs money, not only in terms of timely trades, but for the research that supports those trades. Now the question has to be asked: should you pay for this, or should the fund company?

Whether this research is good is another matter that we will get to in a minute. Shareholders generally have no problem with the cost of executing a trade. We understand that stocks need to be bought and sold, and that doing so involves a certain handling fee. But the core of the soft money problem falls into an area governed by "safe harbor" rules. Safe harbor rules were first brought into focus with the amendment of the Securities Exchange Act of 1934. So-called bundled services have become safe harbors for passing such costs on to shareholders, making us pay for not only research but computers and software as well. Bloomberg terminals, the preferred desktop trading tool, do not come cheap, by the way.

But problems and more questions start arising when these safe harbors are abused. Should shareholders pay to send their managers back to school for such things as professional development? Or pay for the phones? No, we shouldn't.

More problems can be found with the bundled services themselves. Often brokerages use other small, independent firms to execute trades, with the brokerage acting as a middleman or reseller. This means that had the mutual fund family done a little shopping, he or she could have saved a little money by using the less expensive service directly.

This, of course, points to a need for more transparency, not only for us, but for the managers of our money. And this, of course, leads to a cry for regulation that isn't really needed.

If soft money is going for research, then everyone should know how much that research costs. Outlawing the use of third-party research would not be a good step. Much of the good-quality research comes from these small independent firms, and the cost of that research might well translate into excellent returns.

Is it worth the cost? It may come as a surprise to most of you, but fund companies are also publicly traded companies, with shareholders and profit and loss statements of their own. Soft money helps the fund companies recover some of the costs of doing business by passing them on to the wrong shareholders—namely you.

Estimates of the loss of profits for fund families' shareholders if soft money were halted are somewhere in the 6 to 8 percent range. Faced with the need to pay for these services with cash, many managers might find the services that enable them to provide the mutual fund shareholders with better research and more quickly executed trades not worth the cost. That might turn a good many active managers into passive "closet" indexers.

For now, a little belt-tightening and a little more transparency would be good for all parties concerned. The belief that you have to spend money to make money may be worth holding onto when it comes to active management.

What Is a Hard Close?

There are two definitions for this term. One refers to closing mutual funds; the other, to the closing of the trading day.

Mutual funds can grow so large that they actually become too cumbersome to operate. Keep in mind that each time an investor adds new money or a new investor jumps on board, the fund manager needs to invest that money. Sometimes stocks that fit the fund's charter become either too expensive or so scarce that they are not worthy of the fund manager's attention, and so the fund family is forced to say "enough!" and close the fund.

In many instances, funds are closed to new investors, but those who already own shares in the fund are allowed to continue to send money. At the end of April, four of Fidelity's largest funds closed their doors to new investors (Fidelity Growth Company, with $30 billion in managed assets; Fidelity Mid-Cap Stock, with $12 billion; Fidelity Advisor New Insights, with $6 billion, and flagship Fidelity Contrafund, with $65 billion).

Sometimes the fund becomes so large that the fund manager closes the fund to all investors. This is called a hard close.

The other definition—and it's a shame that we even need to discuss this—involves with a fund's failure to close the trading day in a timely fashion.

Mutual funds moved along nicely for decades. Behind the scenes, though, there were a few people who found a way to manipulate their returns at the expense of other shareholders. This caught the eye of the Securities and Exchange Commission, the investment industry's highway patrol.

Because of this country's time zones, the markets that close in the East at 4 p.m. close in the West at 1 p.m. Some mutual fund transfer agents continued to trade after the close, giving their clients the opportunity to trade late in the day. You might say, so what, and you might be justified in saying so. But after the trading day closes, news often continues to be released, some of which will have an impact on the following day's trading.

Because many mutual fund users are large pension plans, the cry of foul was heard—but it is as yet unheeded. Even if the SEC does decide how to rule on this subject, it warrants a mention for the utterly confused investor.

This issue, while seemingly small, can have a negative effect on your returns while allowing a select few to benefit. This, according to groups like the American Society of Pension Professionals & Actuaries (ASPPA), creates two classes of investors. Because much mutual fund trading takes place through intermediaries, those second-class investors may miss a whole day's trading.

Should the SEC rule on this issue, and it has been on the table for over three years, the costs to the mutual fund industry would be significant. And those costs would be passed on to the 95 million households nationwide that use mutual funds to finance their retirement and pension plans.

One last thing of note, and certainly not the least, is the diligence you need to maintain on subjects that seem of little consequence. Whenever there is money involved, there will be someone or some group that is trying to benefit from your inattention. You wouldn't drive down the highway putting on makeup while balancing a bowl of Cheerios on your knee, all the while talking on your cell phone (at least, I hope not).

Driving requires diligence on your part, and not just for your own safety. Mutual funds, or any investment, for that matter, also require you to pay attention, at least once in a while.

What Is a Hedge Fund?

In the short span of five years, hedge funds have made inroads into the market, and their participation is creating more volatility and, quite frankly, mayhem. Although this exclusive club for the rich(er) among us has rather high entry fees, these funds are beginning to make inroads into middle America. But before we go forward, let's take a step backwards.

Hedge funds are the autobahn of investing. Sleek, fast, and (more or less) without rules, they were created to enable the wealthy to take greater risks with their money. Mutual funds are heavily regulated, with charters that limit them to a certain investment style. Hedge funds are not. Hedge funds are allowed to do whatever is necessary to make money.

Recently, hedge funds have found themselves in the news for numerous reasons. Mutual fund managers are being lured by their handsome pay packages: investment stars can receive 20 percent of the profits *and* 2 percent of the assets under management. With this kind of compensation, hedge fund managers will do anything to keep investors and attract new ones.

Hedge funds have begun to have an increased effect on the investment community outside of their elite world. They have become more vocal about corporate governance (a subject that we will discuss at length in Chapter 15). Their trading flexibility (something that mutual fund managers eye with envy) has begun to have a ripple effect on the markets. In fact, it was just that type of freewheeling, try-anything-to-make-a-buck attitude that lured many fund managers to the sort of unstructured freedom and rich payday that working for exclusive clients provides.

Because of this small investor pool, sudden moves can wreck havoc in the markets. When mutual fund shareholders want to leave their fund, the fund manager sells shares and gives the departing investors their money. In a hedge fund, the ripple effect of a large investor—or, worse, several of them—demanding that they be allowed to redeem their shares can make headlines.

As a rule, hedge funds have strict redemption policies. In many instances, investors are not allowed to redeem shares whenever they want. Instead, hedge funds have "lock-up" periods that can last as little as three months or on the quarter to as long as a year.

Only recently has Wall Street begun to worry about this unregulated group. The potential for sudden selling has led the SEC to reconsider. There was a time when the mutual fund industry was used as a barometer for the market. Analysts charted the inflows (when purchases were made) and outflows (when investors removed money or redemptions) of investors' money as indicators of market sentiment. It was widely believed that changes in investment objectives, which could be easily tracked by following fund flows, would provide some insight into how the markets might move.

The problem that now undermines this indicator is the current unpredictability of hedge funds. According to AMG data, "the nature of the flow change or sentiment shift is as important to understand as the relative direction and size of the change." AMG has begun providing additional information about these trends in the hopes that specific inflows or outflows would provide a better look at the overall market while uncovering specific moves. This information was previously lumped into broad range reporting by the Investment Company Institute, the industry's trade association.

But this sentiment information does not reveal much about the participation of hedge funds. Information on these of funds and the strategies that govern them comes with a long disclaimer, much lengthier than the standard mutual fund mantra of "past performance is not an indication of future results."

Hedge funds are not for the faint of heart—or the short on cash.

Is the Prospectus Important?

It is, if you understand it. At the heart of the prospectus, a balance sheet of your fund's operation, are numerous tidbits of information about the fund's operations, holdings, and fees and the manager's goals for the future. But recent studies suggest that prospectuses may soon be a thing of the past.

The Investment Company Institute (ICI) has conducted studies on the use of prospectuses by investors. What these studies uncovered was the lack of importance that the average investor placed on these publications.

At a general meeting held in May 2006, the ICI suggested that almost two-thirds of the investors who buy mutual funds care only about fees and historical performance. Its survey goes on to say that financial professionals acting on behalf of fund investors purchase over 75 percent of the funds for their investors' portfolios.

This industry lobbying group may get its way if its survey, *Understanding Investor Preferences for Mutual Fund Information*, has any effect.

What the survey found was an increased preference for graphical depiction rather than the current format of written disclosure. The use of summaries instead of the current way the industry publishes its results was preferred by 90 percent of the 700 investors surveyed. This group was asked about mutual fund considerations when the fund was bought outside of typical retirement plans.

The information that these investors seek, in order of importance, is as follows: almost 75 percent considered fees important, and 69 percent thought that historical performance was of importance. While the riskiness of the investment came in a close third, only a little over half of the surveyed investors considered the comparisons to indexes important.

This book has given the role of the fund manager much greater importance than the ICI study suggests we should. Based on its survey, the role of the fund manager barely registers with investors, being mentioned by only 25 percent, and there is little concern among investors over their voting powers or proxy.

While the Internet has provided investors with a great tool—the graphical content and what many believe is up-to-date information and concise reporting aside—it is the combination of information provided from many sources that is important.

The prospectus has improved in recent years and is now much easier to comprehend. Unfortunately, you will need to take a few minutes to read through it. Snapshot glimpses at who is managing your money and how it is being managed do not make an investor successful. In many instances, a quarterly review is all the average investor needs.

The full ICI report can be downloaded from http://www.ici.org/pdf/rpt_o6_inv_prefs_summary.pdf.

What Is XBRL?

In a speech delivered to the American Enterprise Institute in Washington, D.C., on May 30, 2006, Christopher Cox, the chairman of the Securities and Exchange Commission, offered his view on something that should give all investors hope that data will be available in real time online. This would be a marriage of disclosure and technology that Mr. Cox has begun to refer to as *interactive data* rather than XBRL, the cumbersome term that is currently being used.

This comparative tool will be what active and, more importantly, passive investors need to help them determine how well their defined-contribution plan is doing. Even passive investors, the ones who may not have any real clue about how a company compares to other companies in the same industry, will be able to find this out.

Mr. Cox explained how interactive data would work. Each important part of a prospectus would be tagged. Those tags would allow interested investors to find the sections they are curious about and get all of the information immediately. No more settling back on the porch on a lazy summer afternoon to read through a company's financial statements and its 10-K (published once a year) and 10-Q (published three times) filings.

So far, the system has proved to be exactly what investors need, even if they may not know it yet. Getting good information to investors has always been most troublesome for companies that fly under most investment radars.

Investors will now be able to compare small- and mid-cap companies with larger ones in the same sector, allowing them to discover hidden gems among firms with low profiles but great numbers. This will, Mr. Cox feels, give small companies increased access to the money they need to grow their enterprises.

XBRL will also tag content of interest such as footnotes and analytical discussions, making it harder for companies to hide dirty secrets within pages of incredibly boring information. No longer will we need to wait for analysts to ferret out the information. It will be available via RSS (Really Simple Syndicator) on a news aggregator as well.

The full text of the speech can be found at http://www.sec.gov/news/speech/2006/spch053006cc.htm

Speaking of Fees, What Are 12b-1 Fees?

This term refers to a 1980 ruling by the SEC that allowed mutual funds to charge the shareholders a fee for the financial guidance the fund receives. Fees for the services of these investment professionals can vary in mutual funds with different classes.

The Investment Company Institute has reported that 63 percent of the fees charged by mutual funds goes to pay for these services. The rule allowing mutual funds to charge their shareholders for certain expenses is a throwback to a time when investors could buy mutual funds only from brokerage houses. The fee, which was once paid at the time of the transaction, has since evolved into a number of methods of payment, all with their problems.

When the 12b-1 was first allowed, it gave mutual funds the opportunity to spread the costs of those brokerage services over time. New classes of the same fund were created: class A funds usually had a front-end sales charge levied on new investors in the fund, class B shares were offered with an exit fee or a back-loaded sales charge, and class C shares are often no-load.

Each of these funds has an ascending 12b-1 charge, with the no-load fund paying the highest rate. The ICI also reports that this fee not only goes for services like brokers, but also helps pay for advertising and administrative services.

The biggest funds often have low 12b-1 fees. Sometimes referred to as a distribution fees, these come directly off the performance of the mutual fund. Because federal law requires funds to report on a net basis, whenever you see a performance percentage listed for a fund, the expenses have been factored in.

Be very cautious of this fee if your fund has closed (sometimes a mutual fund will close its doors to new investors, as discussed earlier in this chapter), but it continues to charge you a 12b-1 fee. Be very cautious if the fee doesn't go down as the fund increases in size. Be very cautious if the fund charges more than 1 percent.

The mutual fund industry is quick to point out that because of this fee and its full disclosure, competition for your investment dollars has driven the cost of investing down. Whether these fees are necessary in a fund with a large amount of money already invested or a fund from a large, established family will always be a source of debate. The fee is understandable in smaller-sized funds, but it should be decreased if the fund swells in size.

What Is the Difference between Growth and Value?

Growth funds invest in the stocks of companies whose business dynamic is still growing. The stocks of older, mature companies are not often considered-growth stocks because of the companies' established markets, predictable earnings, and solid reputation.

Growth stocks can be defined as stocks that have shown better-than-average growth in earnings and are expected to continue to do so through discoveries of additional resources, development of new products, or expanding markets.

Value stocks, on the other hand, are those of companies that have earnings and good price-earnings ratios (called P/Es), but whose prices are somewhat depressed, making them good value.

In a bull market, which is a market with upside numbers that look very good, picking beaten-down companies that have fundamentals and earnings and therefore "value" can often be a challenging and lonely endeavor. Most investors tend to look at growth stocks as the true place to grow your money. Value investors are looking for the same thing, but in the meantime, they would like to own something that gives them some assurances that if they look the other way, the company will still be there when they look back.

Suppose My Mutual Fund Invests in Companies That Have Products or Services That I Disagree with on a Moral or Ethical Basis

While socially responsible investing has yet to make the same inroads performance-wise as its less socially responsible counterpart, the idea behind such funds and the screening they employ is sound.

Socially responsible funds will screen companies for various infractions, such as tobacco revenue, ties to nuclear energy, or even the manufacture of handguns. Driven by moral beliefs, socially responsible funds use an ethical filter when considering companies for their portfolios.

Socially responsible funds may also favor companies that are environmentally friendly and have proactive work policies designed to embrace diversity, culture, and indigenous rights.

These funds often also screen for animal testing, military involvement, gambling, and alcohol. Catholic Equity Fund A screens out any company involved in abortions.

Here is a short list of the largest fund families in the socially responsible world.

Ariel Mutual Funds
200 E. Randolph Dr., Ste. 2900
Chicago, IL 60601–6436
Phone: (800) 292–7435
Fax: (312) 612–2702
thepatientinvestor@arielcapital.com
www.arielmutualfunds.com

Citizens Funds
One Harbour Place, Ste. 400
Portsmouth, NH 03801–3274
Phone: (800) 223–7010
Fax: (603) 433–4209
welcome@citizensfunds.com
www.citizensfunds.com

Calvert
4550 Montgomery Ave., Ste. 1000N
Bethesda, MD 20814–3329
Phone: (800) 368–2748
Fax: (301) 654–2960
www.calvert.com

Domini Social Investments LLC
P.O. Box 9785
Providence, RI 02940–9785
Phone: (800) 225–3863
info@domini.com
www.domini.com

The Catholic Funds, Inc.
1100 W. Wells St.
Milwaukee, WI 53233–2332
Phone: (877) 846–2372
Fax: (414) 278–6558
dhanrahan@catholicfunds.com
www.catholicfunds.com

The Dreyfus Corporation
200 Park Ave., 55th Fl.
New York, NY 10166–0001
Phone: (800) 896–8170
Fax: (212) 922–4861
info@dreyfus.com
www.dreyfus.com

LKCM Aquinas
301 Commerce St., Ste. 1600
Fort Worth, TX 76102
Phone: (800) 423–6369
Fax: (817) 332–4630
www.aquinasfunds.com

Mennonite Mutual Aid (MMA)—
MMA Praxis Mutual Funds
1110 N. Main St., P.O. Box 483
Goshen, IN 46527
Phone: (800) 348–7468
Fax: (574) 534–6631
mmapraxis@mma-online.org
www.mmapraxis.com

Parnassus Investments
One Market, Steuart Tower, Ste. 1600
San Francisco, CA 94105–1407
Phone: (800) 999–3505
Fax: (415) 778–0228
shareholder@parnassus.com
www.parnassus.com

Pax World Funds
222 State St.
Portsmouth, NH 03801–3853
Phone: (800) 767–1729
Fax: (603) 433–4697
info@paxworld.com
www.paxworld.com

Here are the top-performing socially responsible funds over a five-year period:

Ariel Fund	12.30%
Winslow Green Growth Fund	10.48%
Ariel Appreciation	9.34%
Citizens Small Cap Core Growth Fund	8.80%

What Is a REIT?

A REIT, or real estate investment trust, is a company that buys, develops, manages, and sells real estate assets. REITs allow participants to invest in a professionally managed portfolio of real estate properties. REITs are essentially pass-through entities, which basically means that they are designed to pass their profits from their investments in income-producing rental properties on to their shareholders.

Historically, REITs have had their share of ups and downs, both from a tax perspective and from an investment standpoint. There was actually a time in their history where you could have been taxed twice on your investment, once at the corporate level and then again at the investor level. But that changed with the post–World War II demand for these types of investments. When Eisenhower passed the real estate investment trust tax provision in 1960, REITs became pass-through entities. Their popularity increased in the 1980s with the Tax Reform Act of 1986, which allowed REITs to manage their properties directly. Several years later, pension funds were allowed to invest in them and receive the income and appreciation that they provide.

REITs come in three basic flavors: *equity REITs*, which invest in and own properties, collecting rents; *mortgage REITs*, which act as lenders and collect interest on those loans; and *hybrid REITs*, which are a little of both. These companies are often traded on exchanges and are a healthy source of income and appreciation for not only pensions, but also insurance companies, bank trusts, and mutual funds.

REITs pay dividends, which not only add to their attractiveness, but also allow them to shine in their indexes. REITs paid an average of 7.3 percent over the last five years of the 1990s, which was six times what the Russell 2000 index of small-cap stocks paid. And therein lies the rub. Many of these companies qualify as small-capitalization concerns, and this makes it difficult for mutual funds to purchase them. A company that is too tiny doesn't have the liquidity that a large mutual fund needs. But they do provide a steady stream of income, low volatility, and stability, along with good returns.

The National Association of Real Estate Trusts lists the top reasons to invest in REITs as performance (over the last 30 years, the Dow has returned 8.8 percent, the S&P 500 has posted a gain of 12.70 percent, and REITs have outperformed those benchmarks with a handsome 13.80 percent), dividends (in all but one year over the last 20 the dividend has outperformed when compared to the Consumer Price Index), and diversification (a small allocation to REITs can reduce some risk, especially when you consider the historical run that REITs have had).

Here is a short list of the largest publicly traded REITs:

ABN-AMRO Real Estate Fund
(800) 443–4725

American Century Real Estate Investments
(800) 345–3533

AIM Real Estate Fund
(800) 959–4246

CGM Realty Fund
(800) 345–4048

Fidelity Real Estate Investment
(800) 544–8888

Franklin Real Estate Fund
(800) 342–5236

ING Equity Trust Real Estate Fund
(800) 334–3444

INVESCO Advisor Real Estate
Opportunity Fund
(800) 525–8085

John Hancock Real Estate Funds
(800) 225–5291

Neuberger Berman Real Estate Fund
(800) 877–9700

Oppenheimer Real Estate Fund
(888) 470–0862

Scudder RREEF Real Estate
Securities
(888) 897–8480

T. Rowe Price Real Estate Fund
(800) 638–5660

Vanguard REIT Index Portfolio
(800) 662–7447

Van Kampen Real Estate Securities
Fund
(800) 421–5666

Where Are ETFs Traded?

ETFs have given the American Stock Exchange a much-needed boost. Because they are exchange traded, they give the investor a great deal of investment flexibility. While the credit risks are high and ETFs are more susceptible to market fluctuations, their low costs make them an attractive alternative for *some* investors.

Those who are attracted to low fees will find ETFs worth a look. An average ETF will charge its shareholders a smaller fee than a mutual fund. The average ETF levied a 0.42 percent fee, while mutual funds as a whole averaged fees of 1.13 percent. Bond funds posted lower fees of 0.90 percent. The real difference: mutual funds have no brokerage fees.

In the following sections, you will find a list of ETFs along with some pertinent information about each investment. The list is by no means complete. New exchange-traded funds seem to be appearing daily, chasing ever-narrower investment sectors in the hopes of allowing investors more focused opportunities.

Cubes

The Nasdaq 100 Index Tracking Stock, commonly referred to as Cubes from its ticker symbol QQQ, is an exchange-traded fund that tracks the Nasdaq 100 Index by investing in the constituent stocks. This index, which is reviewed quarterly and rebalanced annually, is a modified market-capitalization-weighted composite of 100 of the largest and most actively traded nonfinancial companies listed on the Nasdaq stock market.

The Nasdaq 100 Index includes companies in several major industry groups, including computers and office equipment, computer software and services, telecommunications, retail/wholesale trade, and biotechnology.

SPDRs

Standard & Poor's Depository Receipts, commonly referred to as SPDRs, are a group of exchange-traded funds that track various Standard & Poor's indexes. They are traded actively on the American Stock Exchange.

SPY	SPDR 500
XLY	SPDR Consumer Discretionary
XLP	SPDR Consumer Staples
XLE	SPDR Energy
XLF	SPDR Financial
XLV	SPDR Health Care
XLI	SPDR Industrial
XLB	SPDR Materials
MDY	SPDR Mid Cap 400
XLK	SPDR Technology
XLU	SPDR Utilities

iShares Funds

The iShares funds are a family of open-ended exchange-traded funds that seek to track the performance of an array of market indexes, such as the Russell 2000 Value Index or the Dow Jones US Consumer Cyclical Sector Index.

Fund	Style
iShares Russell 2000 Index Fund	IWM Small-cap index
iShares MSCI South Korea Index	EWY Pacific/Asia ex-Japan
iShares MSCI Belgium Index	EWK Europe stock
iShares MSCI Sweden Index	EWD Europe stock
iShares MSCI Hong Kong Index	EWH Pacific/Asia ex-Japan
iShares MSCI Taiwan Index	EWT Pacific/Asia ex-Japan
iShares MSCI France Index	EWQ Europe stock
iShares MSCI Japan Index	EWJ Japan stock
iShares MSCI South Africa Index	EZA Diversified emerging markets
iShares MSCI Brazil Index	EWZ Latin America stock
iShares MSCI Austria Index	EWO Europe stock
iShares MSCI Netherlands Index	EWN Europe stock
iShares MSCI Italy Index	EWI Europe stock
iShares MSCI Spain Index	EWP Europe stock
iShares MSCI Germany Index	EWG Europe stock
iShares MSCI Switzerland Index	EWL Europe stock
iShares MSCI Singapore Index	EWS Pacific/Asia ex-Japan
iShares MSCI Canada Index	EWC Foreign large value
iShares MSCI UK Index	EWU Europe stock
iShares MSCI Pacific ex-Japan	EPP Pacific/Asia ex-Japan
iShares MSCI Mexico Index	EWW Latin America
iShares Russell 3000 Value Index	IWW Large value
iShares S&P SmallCap 600 Growth	IJT Small growth
iShares Dow Jones US Consumer	IYC Large blend
iShares Dow Jones US Energy	IYE Specialty—natural resources
iShares MSCI EAFE Index	EFA Foreign large blend
iShares S&P Global Energy Sector	IXC Specialty—natural resources
iShares Russell Midcap Value Index	IWS Mid-cap value
iShares Morningstar Mid Value Index	JKI Mid-cap value

iShares Russell 3000 Index	IWV Large blend
iShares Morningstar Large Value Index	JKF Large value
iShares Russell 1000 Value Index	IWD Large value
iShares Dow Jones US Total Market Ind	IYY Large blend
iShares MSCI EAFE Growth Index	EFG Intl Multi-cap Growth
iShares Russell Midcap Index	IWR Mid-cap blend
iShares S&P 1500 Index	ISI Large blend

Diamond Funds

Diamonds is the common name for a specific index ETF that seeks to track the Dow Jones Industrial Average (DJIA) by investing in the constituent stocks of this index.

Diamonds Trust Series I Average index	DIA Dow Jones Industrial

streetTRACKS Funds

The streetTRACKS funds are a family of exchange-traded funds that are marketed by State Street Capital Markets and represent ownership in the streetTRACKS Series Trust, an index fund that consists of separate portfolios of common stocks. Each fund is designed to track a specific index, such as the Dow Jones Total Market Index Series (U.S. large-cap value, U.S. large-cap growth, U.S. small-cap value, U.S. small-cap growth), the Morgan Stanley Internet Index, the Fortune 500, or the Fortune e50 Index.

streetTracks DJ Wilshire Small-cap Growth	DSG small-cap growth
streetTracks DJ Wilshire Small-cap Value	DSV small-cap value
streetTracks Wilshire REIT	RWR REIT
streetTracks KBW Capital Markets	KCE Specialty—financial
streetTracks DJ Euro STOXX 50	FEZ Europe stock
streetTracks DJ Wilshire Small-cap	DSC Small blend
streetTracks KBW Bank	KBE Specialty—financial
streetTracks SPDR Homebuilders	XHB Large blend
streetTracks SPDR Biotech	XBI Specialty—health

streetTracks SPDR Dividend	SDY Large value
streetTracks DJ Wilshire Mid-cap	EMM Mid-cap blend
streetTracks KBW Insurance	KIE Specialty—financial
streetTracks DJ Wilshire Mid-cap Value	EMV Mid-cap value
streetTracks DJ STOXX 50	FEU Europe stock
streetTracks DJ Wilshire Large-cap	ELR Large blend
streetTracks DJ Wilshire Mid-cap Growth	EMG Mid-cap growth

Best of the Best—Five Years Running

Here is a brief list of the top mutual funds, broken down into their respective categories. All are U.S. stock funds. These performance numbers are as of August 31, 2006, and are to my best efforts accurate. They will, however, change over time. They are meant to be representative, not a suggestion that you invest in any of these funds.

Over the last six years, this marketplace has been an interesting one. Small-cap and mid-cap funds have done extremely well despite calls for their demise from the large-cap investors. So far, this has not happened—which is not to say that it won't. Large-cap funds will have their day in the sun adding to the argument for diversity.

If you have learned anything from Part II, it should be caution. Investing is fraught with perils, but they are not insurmountable. We will discuss your attitude as an investor further as we move into individual stocks and bonds.

Type/Fund	Ticker	Five-Year Performance
Bear Market		
Prudent Bear	BEARX	7.41%—no load
Conservative Allocation		
Permanent Portfolio	PRPFX	13.26%—no load
Franklin Income Adv	FRIAX	10.40%
Franklin Income A	FKINX	10.19%

Large Blend

MassMutual Select		
Focused Value S	MFVSX	11.75%—no load
MassMutual Select		
Focused Value Y	MMFYX	11.63%
Janus Contrarian	JSVAX	12.11%

Large Growth

Columbia Marsico		
21st Century Z	NMYAX	14.89%—no load
Marsico 21st Century	MXXIX	14.84%
Columbia Marsico		
21st Century A	NMTAX	14.58%

Large Value

Yacktman Focused	YAFFX	14.28%—no load
Yacktman	YACKX	13.45%
Hillman Focused Advantage	HCMAX	12.37%

Mid-Cap Blend

Fidelity Advisor		
Leveraged Co Stk I	FLVIX	26.38%—no load
Fidelity Leveraged		
Company Stock	FLVCX	26.03%
Fidelity Advisor		
Leveraged Co Stk T	FLSTX	26.65%

Mid-Cap Growth

Baron Partners	BPTRX	16.61%—no load
Delaware		
American Services I	DASIX	14.29%
Delaware		
American Services A	DASAX	14.04%

Mid-Cap Value

ICON Materials	ICBMX	15.45%—no load
Hotchkis and Wiley		
Mid-Cap Value I	HWMIX	15.94%
Hotchkis and Wiley		
Mid-Cap Value A	HWMAX	15.68%

Moderate Allocation

Bruce	BRUFX	28.96%—no load
FPA Crescent	FPACX	12.63%
Waddell & Reed		
Adv Asset Strategy Y	WYASX	12.37%

Small Blend

Bridgeway Ultra-Small Company Market	BRSIX	22.15%—no load
Perritt Micro Cap Opportunities	PRCGX	19.74%
RS Partners	RSPFX	21.07%

Small Growth

Bridgeway Ultra-Small Company	BRUSX	24.12%—no load
FBR Small Cap	FBRVX	19.30%
Dreyfus Premier Enterprise A	DPMGX	16.57%

Small Value

Schneider Small Cap Value	SCMVX	21.74%—no load
Hotchkis and Wiley Small Cap Value I	HWSIX	18.24%
N/I Numeric Investors Small Cap Value	NISVX	18.56%

Bond funds cover an incredibly broad spectrum. Here is a full list of the types of bond funds available for investors and a single fund that tops the five-year category. All funds listed are no-load. (The utterly confused investor should stick with a long-term government or a long-term bond fund.)

Bank Loan		
Morgan Stanley Prime Income Trust	XPITX	5.66%
High-Yield Muni		
Nuveen High Yield Municipal Bond R	NHMRX	8.63%
High-Yield Bond		
Loomis Sayles Instl High Income	LSHIX	13.77%
Intermediate-Term Bond		
Loomis Sayles Investment Grade Bond Y	LSIIX	9.35%
Intermediate Government		
Huntington Mortgage Securities Trust	HMTGX	5.56%

World Bond		
Templeton Global Bond Advisors	TGBAX	12.31%
Emerging Markets Bond		
GMO Emerging Country Debt Sh III	GECDX	21.25%
Long Government		
American Century Target Mat 2025 Inv	BTTRX	8.32%
Long-Term Bond		
Vanguard Long-Term Investment Grade	VWETX	6.62%
Multisector Bond		
Loomis Sayles Strategic Income Y	NEZYX	14.30%
Short Government		
Analytic Sort-term Government Inc	ANSTX	4.50%
Short-Term Bond		
DWS Advisor Short Duration Plus Inv	DBPIX	4.75%
Ultrashort Bond		
Managers Short Duration Government	MGSDX	3.29%
Convertibles		
Davis Appreciation & Income Y	DCSYX	9.73%

I should point out that some of the best bond funds have incredibly high minimum deposits. The best overall bond fund for the last five years would like $25,000,000 just to let you in the door.

Staying Focused

 I mentioned early in this chapter that even though mutual funds seem like investing on cruise control, there are some things that you should be aware of if you decide to just let the investment run itself. Further along, we will discuss executive compensation at companies and the effect it can have on your stocks.

One has to wonder why mutual fund managers do not take a stronger stance against excessive compensation. Fund managers who run index funds seem willing to turn their heads and ignore the problem. Are you willing to let them ignore the high pay that CEOs often receive despite their performance? Some fund managers, as I mentioned earlier, receive incentive fees for their performance, but many of those same fund managers are unwilling to cry foul when their corporate counterparts receive an extraordinary amount of pay for a job not so well done.

While judging fund managers on their performance and tenure, take into consideration not only their stance on executive pay—they have a fiduciary responsibility to the shareholders in their funds, and they often vote your shares by proxy—but their own compensation as well. While prospectuses may no longer be in vogue, the prospectus is the only place you can find information about these issues. Take the time to read it, and if you have any questions that this book has failed to cover, call the fund company and ask.

Chances are you will need to. So far, there is no real effort at disclosing managers' compensation. Ask.

There may come a time when your mutual fund closes its door to new investors. This is a signal to leave the fund. While the reasons for closing a fund are varied, it is most commonly done because of the fund's size (however, underperformance closed a wide variety of funds following the fall of the markets in 2000; some were absorbed into other funds in the family, and some were simply sold, with the investors having the option of reinvesting in another fund).

We discussed this earlier. When a fund becomes too big, it is time to take your assets and head for the door. If the closed fund is inside your retirement account, move the assets to another fund to avoid the penalties for early withdrawal.

Historically, once a fund closes its door to new investors (and sometimes to current ones), the fund fails to perform as well as it did when it was open.

The problem is more profound in the largest funds. For a large funds, selling the stock of a particular company without affecting the price of the stock can take weeks. In smaller funds, the opportunities to find other companies to invest in are much greater. Yet they still close.

One additional skill that you need if you are to move forward may actually sound counterintuitive. Think again about how you drive. You may be concentrating on the road ahead, but you do so with any number of distractions clamoring for your attention. Yet you still arrive home safely each day. As we continue on, it may be not what you know but how you apply that knowledge. In fact, not thinking about it may be the best thing you can do as an investor.

The Distracted Investor

Ap Dijksterhuis, a psychologist at the University of Amsterdam, did a study, and what he found may reveal a hidden talent that you already have. We all have it, but many of us just don't know how to apply it.

The good doctor did a study showing that conscious thinking was not as good as unconscious thought. Dr. Dijksterhuis conducted the experiment in an attempt to find out whether a distracted mind was capable of making better decisions than a focused one. He tried to determine whether the old adage of "sleeping on it" was more advantageous to the decision-making process than a focused and concentrated approach.

The basis of his experiments was simple. He believed that, on a normal day, the average person is presented with a wide array of information, much of which demands attention. Dr. Dijksterhuis found that if the test subjects simply deferred these decisions—in essence, allowing the unconscious mind, the one that hums silently in the background, to mull over the information—the subject would, more often than not, make the right choice.

In other words, snap decisions are not necessarily natural to our thought processes, and if the results of this test are true, they are just plain bad for us as investors, whether we are utterly confused or not.

On any given day, we are faced with tough financial decisions, some more important than others. Often we react impulsively. This has been written off as being human nature. But Dr. Dijksterhuis thinks that we are mentally wired to wait. That brief period of thinking about it unconsciously allows us to take all of the stored information in the brain and blend it with the new information that we may be just now receiving. That brief period of thoughtfulness, he found, allows the mind to make astute judgments about a wide variety of things.

Dr. Dijksterhuis sought some simple answers. Why he asked, do we often take only some of the information that we need to make the right decisions into account and leave other important considerations out of the process? Snap decisions are often fraught with emotion and impulse.

In his lectures on the subject, he often uses the example of the home buyer who purchases the house she desires without any consideration of the commute. Would that buyer have made the same decision if she had had an opportunity to think about the amount of time she would be spending in the car going to and from her house each day? He suspects not, fuel prices aside. Too much emotion is involved in the purchase of a house, the complexities of the financial negotiations are often stressful, and the demand of timeliness, especially in hot housing markets, makes the parsing of all of the information nearly impossible. Having the luxury of enough time to allow the information to not only sink in but also associate itself with the knowledge that we already possess can make all the difference in the world.

In his experiments, Dr. Dijksterhuis gave his students information on four cars, each with its own list of features. He did this rather quickly in rapid succession. He then asked the test group of 80 to split into two smaller groups of 40.

One group was instructed to try to remember all of the information by thinking about it. The other test group was given anagrams to solve in order to distract them from thinking about the information they had been presented.

What is an anagram?

Anagrams are delightful plays on words in which common words or phrases are rearranged to make new words or phrases. Author Anu Garg (*http://www.wordsmith.org*) suggests that such turns of phrase, such as Clint Eastwood being an anagram of Old West Action, are just plain fascinating. Someone once said, "All the life's wisdom can be found in anagrams. Anagrams never lie." Anagrams include such obvious examples of turns of words as Kyoto, which was the former name of Tokyo; also, the word *senator* can be changed to *treason.* Curiously, you cannot rearrange the word *anagram* to make another word or phrase.

Not surprisingly, at least to Dr. Dijksterhuis, the students whose minds had been happily working away at the word puzzles retained far more information, and as a result, they had clearer recollections of the information and were able to make more informed decisions about the cars.

So it goes with investing. Although the information within these pages will lead you to think, do so unconsciously. Investing takes time, effort, and, in some cases, a level of passivity that makes many of us uncomfortable.

Investing is three things at once. First, it is an achievable gain. Second, it is an avoidable loss. The third thing is much more difficult and personal. It involves mastering the mental maniac in all of us. That mental maniac wants to make rash decisions, wants to follow the markets with great intent, wants to be where the in-crowd is, wants to take huge risks in the face of reason, and wants to sell low and buy high instead of vice versa.

The mental maniac inside us makes us believe that our emotions are part of what we are. Perhaps they are, but not when we invest. Our desire to be part of the group, to belong and participate, especially when the markets are hot and rising, makes us more prone to mistakes. In fact, that mental maniac, if it is allowed to take hold, negates the first two things an investor needs to be.

PART III

◆◆◆

Long-Term Coming

CHAPTER 13

The Vast Open Spaces of Wall Street

◆◆◆◆◆◆◆◆◆◆◆◆◆◆◆◆◆◆◆◆◆◆◆◆◆◆◆◆◆◆◆◆◆◆◆◆◆◆

Robert Pirsig wrote:

> If the line wiggles, that's good. That means hills. If it appears to be the main route from a town to a city, that's bad. The best ones always connect nowhere with nowhere and have an alternate that gets you there quicker. If you are going northeast from a large town you never go straight out of town for any long distance. You go out and then start jogging north, then east, then north again, and soon you are on a secondary route that only the local people use.
>
> The main skill is to keep from getting lost.

He and his son Chris, he tells us, navigate roads using "dead reckoning, and deduction from what clues we can find."

Long-term investing harnesses the great American spirit of adventure. It offers thrills and sometimes chills. It offers riders on those open roads the opportunity to feel the wind in their face (and, hopefully, more often at their back).

It allows you to map out a destination and travel there on a road that heads over the hill just ahead and around a bend that holds who knows what beyond your line of sight.

And that is why we have been taking investing one step at a time. You need to give yourself time to learn how to navigate. You are not alone, and once you get behind the wheel, you will quickly learn how other drivers drive and how you should react to them. You will come to learn how traffic moves, and you should adjust your driving to these changes.

On the open road, even though other travelers have journeyed there before you, you are beginning to blaze a trail that will be yours alone. No one else on the road has your temperament. No one else on the road has chosen the same destination. No one but you.

 What the Experts Say   Successful investing is anticipating the anticipations of others.

John Maynard Keynes

No matter how you choose to navigate the road ahead, there are numerous considerations to plan for. You need to be prepared for unforeseen tweaking and tuning, and have the ability to change course if need be and take a road less traveled.

Long-term investors take into account numerous things that are wholly foreign to short-term investors—even though the two types of investors have the same fundamental goals. Long-term investors take a more conservative approach by taking into account a wide variety of considerations, from taxes and inflation to the choice between growth and value. They are concerned with what happens while they are holding the stock. Corporate governance and economic factors, trade and deficits, good buys and timely sells, and the responsibilities of ownership all play major roles in the success of long-term investing.

Long-term investors take their age into consideration. They realize that this plays an important role in how they should allocate their money. They are able to grasp the simple notion that they need to achieve balance in their portfolio. And most importantly, they understand that a steady approach to investing using the only time-proven method to achieve long-term wealth, dollar cost averaging, will help quell the emotion that runs through all of us.

By considering age, balance, and continuity, the financial ABCs, investors will find themselves using both common sense and intuition to their fullest.

How do I approach a long-term plan?

When the subject of age comes up in a conversation about investing, it is usually broken into three distinct categories: young, middle-aged, and near or at retirement. This is an oversimplified way at looking at investing. It should be thought of instead in terms of the types of investing: retirement, asset protection, and speculation. *Retirement* should be the foremost goal of any financial plan. This basically allows the investor the peace of mind that comes from knowing that the future is secure. *Asset protection* involves investing in mutual funds outside of a retirement plan, preferably funds that are indexed to the total market, whether through a total market fund or divided among several different indexes. *Speculation* can take place even when the investor has a long-term plan. It is not solely the domain of short-term investors—they just use speculation in a different manner. Long-term investors use a calculated and measured form of speculation.

Beneath the broad brushstroke of age lie far too many factors that are individual to each of us. Some of the most important ones, however, should be taken into consideration.

Age does not prevent you from getting behind the wheel of your car and heading off into the sunset for parts unknown. It will, however, make you more likely to think twice about this the older you get. Acting on impulse diminishes in most cases because age has taken some of the rogue intuition that you may once have had and replaced it with a more thoughtful emotion: common sense.

Investing does not discriminate when it comes to age. You should, however, be discriminating at every age.

When you have a long-term horizon, the make-up of your conservative portfolio should not enter into your decision to buy individual stocks. Once you have fully funded your retirement account and your additional investable assets are diversified and balanced in mutual funds held outside that retirement account, you can set aside some money for your portfolio of individual stocks; this should be kept separate from those other accounts and accounted for differently.

The same principles that you used in your other investments will come into play when you begin to look at individual stocks. The same discipline that helped you successfully invest in your future and your mutual funds will be employed again in the purchase of equities. You will need to be vigilant and diverse. You will need to have a good understanding of who you are and what your goals are.

If you are of an appropriate age, you will be able to embrace many of the nuances that can make long-term investing in equities so important.

Considering Taxes

Before we continue with this little investing journey, I feel the need to clarify one small detail. The references I will make to long-term versus short-term investing are based mostly on tax considerations—nothing more and nothing less. Once you venture out of the relatively safe haven of mutual funds—more specifically, indexed ones—and move into the world of individual equities, long-term and short-term become one and the same. Taxes are the only difference.

Currently, the tax rate on long-term capital gains (gains on anything held longer than a year) and dividends is 15 percent through 2010. If this rate expires, it will revert to the previous rate, which averaged 20 percent. Short-term gains (gains on anything held less than a year) are taxed at your ordinary income tax rate. Low-income investors pay considerably less.

 Two roads diverged in a wood, and I . . . I took the one less traveled by, and that has made all the difference.

Robert Frost

Regardless of the length of time you hold the stocks, the same amount of involvement is required. Holding stocks for the long term requires less strenuous effort. Short-term investing, on the other hand, demands your attention much more frequently. As we enter into the discussion of long-term investing in Part III and short-term investing in Part IV, you should remember that any successes you may have with either form of investment depend wholly on your temperament.

Few people can bring sufficient market savvy to their investments to win consistently. Many try to do so because they don't know whether they have that kind of savvy until they try it for themselves. Consider the eight thousand or so mutual funds and ETFs that are available. We discussed quite a few of them in Chapter 12. A good many of these mutual funds are run by people—not machines or algorithms or theories on market footprint or whatever mechanism designed to beat the markets modern science can dream up.

Many of these same money managers have risen to the top of their field as a result of their financial skills, and yet not all of them beat the markets. Not even close to half of them do so. In fact, the number of mutual funds that manage to beat the markets is more like one in six.

You could be the one who manages to do so. Five others may try, but you may be the one who is able to understand and apply the straightforward discussion that awaits you in the rest of the book.

To reiterate, once you begin investing in individual equities, the length of time you hold a stock, whether it is considered long-term or short-term, affects only the taxes. The tax implications are relatively easy to understand. Stocks that are held for less than a year do not get favorable treatment under the tax code (they are taxed at your regular income tax rate); stocks that are held for more than a year pay a capital gains tax of 15 percent—at least for the near future.

Taxes are always a consideration when owning equities. Buying long-term simplifies the equation somewhat and lowers the bar on the amount of returns you need to net in order to pay the tax collector. But other things besides taxes also come into play—inflation, for one.

This little-understood mechanism is not as easy to grasp. As a consumer, you probably believe that you understand the way inflation works. However, inflation is about erosion, not prices. And because of that, it affects your investments.

What is this mysterious effect that inflation has on money and consequently on your investments? Inflation is a naturally occurring phenomenon of commerce. Even before there was money, when barter was the way business was conducted, inflation crept into the equation. If one man sold goats to another, the cost of those goats, paid for by whatever was agreed upon, would depend on market conditions. Was it a good year with lots of rain that watered lush plains to graze on, or was it hot, forcing the goat herder to expend a lot of additional energy to find good grazing land? Once the conditions for producing a product or raising a goat affect the worth of the item or animal, inflation comes into play.

You might wonder if inflation ever reverses itself. If a good year followed a bad year, would the price for the product or goat decline? From a consumer's standpoint, the answer would probably be no. Once a price level has been reached, discounts never seem to be as deep.

But perhaps we need look no further than your gas tank.

Recently, the cost of gasoline in the United States rose to new levels. We have a natural tendency to look for reasons for price increases on basic necessities such as food and fuel. (Curiously, those two commodities are excluded when inflation calculations are done in the core Consumer Price Index, the one that the nation's top bankers at the Federal Reserve study for signs of increasing or decreasing prices. What is left is a core number, without the volatility.)

Yet, when prices reached and exceeded three dollars a gallon for gas, we failed to recognize that even those prices may not be as high as prices once were in today's dollars.

The following table appears on the California Energy Department's Web site. The effects of inflation are clearly charted, showing the peak prices and adjusted prices that include the effects of inflation. The far right column illustrates the true cost of a gallon of gas on different dates in today's dollars. But be warned, inflation is more about the availability of money to borrow than about the actual high price of the actual commodity. File this under "This I believe although I cannot prove it," but had there been enough consumer confidence at the time that gas prices hit their all-time high and enough money to borrow to buy it, then the reality would not have seemed as harsh.

Historical Yearly Average California Gasoline Prices per Gallon 1970 to 2005 Based on 2005 Dollars, Adjusted for Inflation (Gross Domestic Product Implicit Price Deflator)

Year	Yearly Average Price	Price Peak (2005 = 100)	Price Deflator Adjusted for Inflation	Yearly Average Inflation (Dollars)	Peak Price Adjusted for Nominal (Dollars)
1970	$0.3415		25.10	$1.3606	
1980	$1.2280		49.26	$2.4929	
1981*	$1.3460	$1.660	53.89	$2.4977	$3.0803
1990	$1.0900		74.37	$1.4656	
2000	$1.6634	$1.847	91.15	$1.8249	$2.0263
2001	$1.6366	$1.954	93.33	$1.7536	$2.0936
2002	$1.5138	$1.622	94.88	$1.5955	$1.7095
2003	$1.8308	$2.145	96.61	$1.8950	$2.2203
2004	$2.1200	$2.402	98.51	$2.1521	$2.4383
2005	$2.4730	$3.056	100.00	$2.4730	$3.0560

*Refers to the all-time historic high for fuel prices in today's dollars.

The long-term investor needs to understand inflation for what it is. Back in 1981, when gas prices peaked, that was equivalent to over $3.08 a gallon in today's dollars, adjusted for the inflation that has occurred between 1981 and today. But this is looking in the rearview mirror. What happens to the worth of your money (or the value of your investments) when inflation is applied to the equation?

The average inflation rate for the period covered in the table is 4.7 percent. This number includes a very difficult inflationary period in American economic history. The central bank closely monitors the economy to prevent this type of inflation from recurring. Yet, inflation in some form will always exist, and because of this, it needs to be taken into account when developing a long-term plan.

When doing inflation calculations, it is popular to use averages that exclude those periods of high inflation, but the effect of inflation remains. On forward numbers spread out over a huge period of time, inflation can average 3 percent. So if your investments returned you a modest 7 percent during the period covered by the table (35 years), your real rate of return after inflation would be around 3.88 percent—before taxes.

The best illustration actually uses forward-looking numbers. It is also the easiest to comprehend. Suppose, for the sake of the calculation, you wanted to reach a goal of $100,000. You would need to save around $240 a month for 35 years to reach that investment goal using the simplest of calculations ($100,000 divided by 420 months = $238.09).

You want your money to grow, so you invest it and hope for a moderate growth of 7 percent. The goal is reached much earlier than the time horizon we have set, but you keep investing. You continue to make 35 years worth of contributions month after month, growing that nest egg until, almost miraculously, it is worth $435,000.

But then, to make the calculation work, we need to factor in inflation. Since 1920 the historical average for inflation has been 3 percent. Once that is factored in, our investment is whittled down to a worth of just under $155,000. While this is still considered a gain to the naked eye, the effect of 3 percent inflation on a 7 percent gain over that period of time results in a real return of 3.88 percent.

Consider the effects of inflation on your investment dollar. Suppose you invested $1,000 in 1970 (the same year gas was 34 cents per gallon or, in today's dollars, $1.36) and received a modest rate of return, somewhere in the 7 percent range. At the end of that same 35-year period (the same one used to track the inflation of gas prices), you would have amassed a small nest egg of $11,569 (time and compounding are truly magical events). Factor in an inflation number of 3 percent, and that $11,569 is now worth $4,112 in today's money. Use the real inflation rate that encompasses some of the worst inflation years of our recent history, and that $4,112 is now worth only $2,318.

But that may not be a good way to calculate inflation. Carlos Lozada, in a paper titled *Are Equity Investors Fooled by Inflation?* (National Bureau of Economic Research, May 21, 2006; http://www.nber.org/digest/oct04/w10263.html) thinks that simple calculations such as this do not reveal exactly how inflation affects equities. He also thinks that the way most financial professionals calculate it is the right way to determine whether inflation has a real effect on the price of a stock.

Most financial pros like to use a Fed model for determining the yield of the stock. While the price of a stock can be easily seen, the dividends and earnings of a stock are not accounted for when only the price of the stock is used in the calculation. In the Fed model, the change in the price of a stock is added to the dividend and the stock's earnings to arrive at a yield. Because earnings can change year after year for any number of reasons (for example, new debt, successful product introductions, or improved productivity), the yield on a stock, using the Fed model, will fluctuate as well. Dividends are usually declared, and while taken directly out of earnings, they are considered a constant number.

Bonds, as we learned in Chapter 11, have yields as well (they move in the opposite direction from the bond's price). The Fed model assumes that in any given portfolio, there is only so much in the way of available dollars to invest. If the yield on bonds rises (while their price goes down), investors might be swayed to move away from stocks and buy bonds instead.

But what causes bond yields to increase? While there many factors feeding bond traders' legendary worrying, nothing grabs their attention like inflation or fears of inflation. Their fear stems from the market's reaction to inflation.

Inflation creates a vicious circle, with price increases being passed on to a workforce that is demanding more money in wages to compensate for the higher costs of getting by. When this happens, the Federal Reserve Board will be forced to raise interest rates in an attempt to slow the economy down. This has a decidedly negative effect on businesses. When the Fed begins to move against inflationary pressures, the profitability of a business is affected.

When that happens, the risk premium rises. Risk is a factor because investors need to be compensated for taking it, and that often shows up in the yield of a fixed-income offering. Using the Fed model, you would simply add the bond yield to the risk premium to end up with what is called the normal stock yield.

In other words, inflation and risk determine the stock yield. What this means is, when inflation is high, it is normal to feel that your money isn't buying as much as it should. And technically, it isn't. This effect trickles over into the equity markets. When inflation is high, investors become risk-averse, choosing to ignore investments like equities or bonds. The increased cost of living has a dampening effect on investors' enthusiasm, the profitability of the companies they invest in, and the reward received for the investment. Investing becomes simply not worth the risk.

Bond offerings get increasingly higher yields and lower prices to entice investors. The late Franco Modigliani and his writing partner Richard Cohn discovered that stock yields actually increased during periods of higher inflation, making equities more of a bargain than when inflation was low.

The long-term investor should know two things about inflation and equities. First, dividend growth is likely to outpace inflation. Companies that are able to raise their prices and keep their profitability high will entice investors with higher dividend payments. Second, inflation actually misprices stocks. This has been called the inflation illusion, and if you watch the markets on a regular basis, you will marvel at the knee-jerk reaction that takes place when inflation worries persist.

How does inflation affect the markets?

One week in May 2006, the Dow lost 2.6 percent and the Morgan Stanley index that tracks emerging markets (relatively new players on the global financial scene) fell 15 percent on inflation fears. The Federal Reserve in the United States, along with foreign central banks—but acting independently of one another—continued to make remarks about slowing down an overheated global economy. Rising interest rates do not necessarily make companies less profitable (except when comparing them to a time when rates were lower), but investors sell nonetheless. Once the fear of inflation takes hold, herd mentality can grip the markets. The selling is usually done in anticipation of a move by the Federal Reserve Board to raise short-term interest rates (the fed funds rate, or the rate that banks charge one another for overnight loans). Raising interest rates slows economic growth, makes borrowing more expensive, and, if done in a timely manner, curbs inflation.

If Modigliani and Cohn are correct in their assumptions, when inflation increases, the real value of a stock relative to its price actually declines, making equities a better investment. During periods of low inflation, the two suggest that stocks will be overvalued.

I'm going to mention, oh so briefly, defensive investments against inflation. There are two types of investments that, because of how they operate, can provide you with some inflation protection—sort of.

Both *TIPS,* or *Treasury Inflation-Protected Securities,* and *REITs,* or *real estate investment trusts,* provide a long-term investor with some hedge against the possibility of rising inflation. The problem with both types of investments has nothing to do with inflation, however. It has to do with taxes—an inflationary pressure that is a direct result of your lawmakers, not an aftereffect of any economic condition.

TIPS are a relatively new type of investment. They made their debut in 1997 as a way to hedge your portfolio against the possibility of inflation. You can buy these securities without a fee through the Treasury Direct program. They are issued twice a year in January and June, and because they offer that inflation protection feature, they generally pay a lower rate than a standard 10-year Treasury.

The purpose of TIPS is to protect your principal (the money you put into the bond). If inflation rises, you still get paid your interest every six months just as you would if you held a regular security, but your principal is readjusted for inflation based on the Consumer Price Index (CPI). Should the opposite economic reaction, deflation, occur, then your principal is protected.

What is the difference between inflation, deflation, and stagflation?

Deflation is often referred to as the opposite of inflation. Both are tightly tied to money and credit. We feel inflation most often in the increased cost of the goods we buy. But in truth, *inflation* occurs when money is readily available to borrow but costs more to borrow, in which case the prices of goods need to rise as well. Think of the economy as a balloon. If you fill it with products (productivity) and available credit (borrowers who are willing to pay their loans back with interest because they feel confident—that's the key—that they will be able to pay it back), the balloon expands (this is often referred to as a growing economy) and you have inflation (which is why central bankers like Federal Reserve Chief Ben Bernanke worry so much about too much inflation). *Deflation* happens when confidence disappears, credit gets tight, and productivity slows. Lower prices only follow. *Stagflation* is the worst of those two evils. It occurs when the economy is not growing. but prices are rising. U.K. Chancellor of the Exchequer Iain Macleod is credited with coining the word. Stagflation is the result of a sudden price shock, such as an unexpected spike in the price of oil.

Not to be ignored are *deflation* (a point during a recession when the rate of price increases falls because retailers can no longer pass on increases) and *reflation* (a government intervention using fiscal policy or monetary stimulus to give the economy a boost). *Hyperinflation* refers to a time when prices increase at such a rate as to be considered out of control.

The problem with TIPS is the taxes. Because you are taxed on the cash payments and the inflation adjustments made to the principal at your current income tax rate, these securities should be held either inside of a tax-deferred account like an IRA or a 401(k) or in a bond fund. They are a long-haul investment, and that is why they need to be mentioned. One other thing about TIPS: they are designed to protect your principal, not to make buckets of money. In most cases, the real yield on a TIPS might not exceed 2 percent.

REITs, like TIPS, should be kept tucked away inside a tax-deferred retirement account—if possible—and owned through a mutual fund (see Chapter 12 for a fuller discussion of REITs). The temptation to buy REITs like stocks can be hard to avoid, but do it anyway.

Inflation may be a worrisome event, but it is far from the most problematic. The job of the Federal Reserve Board is to keep just enough money in circulation and available to borrow to keep you feeling confident that things are okay. Providing just the right amount of grease to the wheels to keep things moving along smoothly is not an easy task.

The short-term interest rates that the Fed is responsible for setting, the ones that receive so much attention that they warrant a mention on the evening news, actually mean little to the average person.

Those who do care about those rates and how they might affect the economy have spent weeks forecasting the increase/decrease, have remade their portfolios to accommodate the change, and get the news the minute it is released. In other words, by the time a rate change is news, it is old news.

The rate that the Fed most commonly changes is the Fed funds rate, or the rate at which banks lend to one another on an overnight basis. What happens after that is just good business. The banks lend the money to new borrowers at higher rates and on and on. The better the borrower's credit, the lower the rate. Despite what you might think, the Fed funds rate has little to do with housing prices. It really has little to do with the concept of long-term investing.

When it comes to buying a company—which, in simplest terms, is exactly what you do when you buy a share of stock—short-term interest rates mean little in terms of the performance, the governance, and, ultimately, the survival of your investment.

What role does the Federal Reserve Bank play in fighting inflation?

The Fed bankers begin to raise rates at the first sign of inflation and keep doing so until the economy slows to the point where it is continuing to grow, but is not growing so fast as to overheat. If the Fed stops raising rates, inflation tops out within the year and begins to fall. This has happened repeatedly over the last 25 years or so. There is a direct correlation between the time when inflation peaks and the time when the Fed stops raising rates. It should be noted that the Fed has access to a large amount of economic data and uses this information to tweak interest rates. When inflation or the threat of it seems imminent, traders monitor the Fed's actions closely.

There is a pecking order when it comes to investors. Bondholders are placed before stockowners in all matters financial. I preface this brief discussion of bonds and other fixed-income investments—because it's important—with that disclaimer because if you are a stockholder, bondholders are essentially lending to you as well as to the company. You share a responsibility for the company's payback priorities. As a shareholder/owner of the company, you always pay the people whom you owe (the bondholders) first, not yourself. (We'll talk about corporate governance and CEO pay packages in Chapter 15.)

But bonds also involve risk. Even though they are the slow horse to equity's fast car, bonds, and particularly bond funds, have a place in a diversified portfolio. The question, however, is how much of your portfolio to devote to bonds and the risk you run if you don't get it quite right.

You may find yourself in a position where you must diversify a portfolio outside of your retirement plan. If that is the case, using a bond fund is preferable to owning individual bonds. Bond fund managers generally get the best price when buying bonds for their funds—they get a buy-in-quantity break that the average investor doesn't receive. They can also juggle the huge amount of credit information involved in corporate securities and sift through the economic news and interest-rate nuances that affect government offerings, all the while allowing us along for the ride at a fraction of the cost of owning these same securities individually. It is easier for bond fund managers to ladder, a method of bond portfolio building that staggers maturity dates, keeping as much money as possible invested and earning interest.

When it comes to bonds, risk is a hard thing to pinpoint, even for the seasoned investor. It is particularly difficult for the utterly confused investor. We firmly believe that we can achieve great wealth with our retirement investments, and while that is a comforting thought, it is not always a realistic one. So we invest. We invest for the future through our retirement plans. And then we invest outside those plans using mutual funds. All the while, in the back of our minds, we realize that we need to grow our money while at the same time protecting it.

You should have the lion's share of your portfolio in equities if you are just beginning this long investment road. The portion you keep in equities should, however, begin to taper off as you age. In a portfolio held outside your retirement accounts, the issue becomes more about protecting gains than simply diversifying.

Diversification, if you will recall, requires you to invest across a wide range of sectors to keep your money safe from market swings. Rather than taking money off the table, so to speak, finding someplace to keep that money involved, if only in a passive way, becomes very important. This is when you consider the protection that bond funds provide.

 Of course. I favor passive investing for most investors, because markets are amazingly successful devices for incorporating information into stock prices.

Merton H. Miller

Granted, everyone's circumstances are different. But incorporating bonds, or, more specifically, bond funds, as some percentage of your portfolio is important. Even if they are hidden inside of a balanced fund, a fund that invests in both equities and bonds, you need to protect what you have gained.

Bond funds invest in bonds, which essentially are a form of debt. The price of the debt that these funds buy is directly related to the *yield*. You will hear those two terms, *price* and *yield*, used when bonds are discussed because they tell a great deal about a bond or a bond fund.

The type of debt issued and who issued it will determine the credit risk. The lower the credit risk, with the government being the best borrower, the higher the letter rating the bond is given (see the discussion of bond ratings in Chapter 11). Try to avoid funds that invest in bonds with a B rating or less.

Companies issue bonds because they need money and cannot get it on the open market in any other way that they consider sufficiently favorable. So they make a deal with the bondholder: I will pay you X amount in interest if you buy this bond. This essentially makes you the lender.

These investments have three types of risk, which makes individual investments in bonds a particularly treacherous road for the inexperienced investor. Each of these three factors can undo a perfectly good plan and undermine a good investor's intentions.

There will come a time in every broker/client relationship when the phone call will be made. The call will most likely begin with, "Boy, have I got a stock/bond for you." Brokers do their best business with their largest clients. If you have a broker, but your account is relatively small, your contact with that broker will be minimal at best. Online brokerages list the cost of client contacts right up front, discouraging most direct contact from ever occurring. So when your broker calls you on the phone, just say thanks for thinking of me, but no thanks. If the millionaire clients passed on this incredible opportunity, so should you.

The creditworthiness of the borrower should always be the first consideration. The last thing bondholders want is a default on the bonds they hold. When a company cannot pay back the loan you have given it and defaults on the bond, you lose not only the regular interest payment, but also a large portion of your principal. As a bondholder, you are first in line for repayment, ahead of the shareholders. Still, the amount of money you get back when a bond defaults, something that usually happens only when a company goes bankrupt, can be pennies on the dollar, depending on the judge's decision.

On the flip side, when the company pays back the bond and the interest due, you win. The higher the likelihood a company that might default and not pay back the money due, the lower the letter rating, the higher the yield, and, of course, as with anything risky, the higher the profit potential.

A second form of risk is the chance that the debt will be paid off early and the bondholder will be denied the potential for any additional income from the bond. Bonds that permit this are referred to as *callable bonds,* and this can add to your losses in the form of unrealized returns when the borrower refinances the loan.

Third, interest rates add risk to the investment, and that affects bonds. In a bond fund, this risk is lessened, as the investments in the fund carry different maturity dates (when they are due to be repaid), and interest rates, which are set by the Fed, will have a greater impact on bonds with longer maturities.

In essence, a higher yield on the longest bond (30 years) suggests that the economy will be stable and not too inflationary. When yields on those bonds are low, the belief that inflation could be a factor in the near-term economy is making investors shy away from committing money to fixed-income securities for too long.

This is where the fund manager has a decided advantage over the individual. Interest-rate risk can be avoided by laddering, a process that involves investing in a wide variety of bonds with different maturity dates. Individual bondholders have a difficult time laddering. The ability to avoid sudden drops in price or yield or having to reinvest when the markets are not favorable is improved by laddering.

It should be noted that risk is further lessened with insured or government bonds. Bonds issued with high yields can be a telling sign of risk. The yields are highest when the risk is greatest. The risk is greater because of the kind of the debt the bond represents and who issued it. Investors should pay close attention to this because the higher risk indicates the potential for greater returns or losses.

Including bond funds in your portfolio will diminish your risk in the equity markets, but these funds should be only a small part of a young investor's portfolio. If, however, you have started late, including a good balanced fund should provide you with enough diversity to weather any sudden downturns in the market.

Fixed-income funds do have real risk and, depending on the investment strategy of the fund, some reward. From the contact that I have had with many of you, your investment plans are focused on making your money do the most for you while you are still working. Bond funds can protect a portion of. this investment adequately for the long term.

What is a yield curve?

The yield curve refers to the differences between the yields on fixed-income securities with different maturities, from the shortest-term bill to the longest-term bond. When the yield on a short-term bill is higher than that on a long-term bond, the yield curve is said to be *inverted*, an indication that investors are not confident in the economy and are purchasing short-term securities. When the yield curve is *flat*, there is growing worry that the economy is not doing well, but the reasons are hard to grasp. Mixed signals of economic strength result in flattening yield curves. A *normal yield curve* suggests that the economy is good for the long term. Investors are willing to buy Treasury offerings with longer maturities because they believe that the economy will continue to be good.

Bonds Can Be Divided into Four Distinct Categories

There are four distinct types of bonds: government bonds, municipal bonds, corporate bonds, and zero-coupon bonds.

Government bonds are broken down into three basic categories based on the length of time that the bond issuer, in this case Uncle Sam, has before he must pay you back. Treasury bills have maturities of less than a year; if you want to get technical, they aren't bonds at all because of their abbreviated maturities. Notes can have maturities of 1 to 10 years, while bonds have maturities in excess of 10 years.

Don't be fooled into thinking that the government bonds of all countries are safe. Depending on the stability of the country (and the United States is considered among the world's most stable), defaults can happen. A default is basically a failure to repay the lender—which is you—what is owed.

If you are looking for a slightly better return, which in the world of bonds means a slightly higher yield, *municipal bonds,* or *munis,* can be a nice fit. Once again, you are looking for economic stability in the municipality to which you are lending your money. The riskier the borrower is (cities do go bankrupt and become unable to pay their creditors), the higher the yield that is offered to investors who are willing to take the chance.

Munis, however, are generally free from federal taxes, and if you live in the state in which the muni was issued, the entire return on your investment can be free of taxes. Because of that tax-free feature, munis generally offer lower yields than their taxable counterparts. Once your money has been taxed, munis are a good place to park it.

The next level of fixed-income investing involves *corporate bonds*. Corporations default more frequently than municipalities and governments, and because of that, investors rely heavily on the credit rating of the issuer. Once again, the higher the offered yield, the greater the chances that the company might default on the loan. When the risk is extremely high, the bonds are referred to as junk.

There are numerous types of corporate bonds, some of which would best be avoided by the individual investor. Let the bond fund manager determine the advantages and disadvantages when it comes to convertible bonds (bonds can be converted into shares of stock) or callable bonds (bonds that the company can pay back before they mature).

Why, you may ask, are these not considered good? Changing your status from bondholder to shareholder makes the company less liable to you. You may end up with shares, but remember, when or if the company gets into trouble, you as a shareholder are last in line. Bondholders prefer to be creditors of the company, not owners.

Convertible bonds do have a certain attraction for investors. Under the right circumstances, such as during periods of surging stock market prices, the investor that holds convertible bonds will see a steady stream of payments (at a lower yield than traditional bonds), and if the value of the stock exceeds the face value of the bond, a profit as well.

Convertible bonds work best for companies that are at a turning point in their growth cycle. These companies may not want to commit to the higher interest normally paid by corporate bonds, but instead feel that the stock market will price in the profit when the yield does not.

Here is a simple example of how convertible bonds work: A company issues a $1,000 convertible bond with the promise that the investor may buy the stock for $100. The bond is worth 10 shares when converted.

If the stock is currently trading at $50 a share, investors can collect the interest while they wait for the markets to increase the share price. Investors can lock in their profits if the stock exceeds the $100 a share price. If the price of the stock never reaches that point, investors will receive less than bondholders would receive in terms of yield had they held a regular type of corporate bond. And last, the buyer may have missed gains in the stock if the price increased as the bond was being issued.

Convertible bonds are considered a worthy risk if the company is likely to have good growth potential. This usually applies to smaller companies, although blue-chip companies will also issue these types of investments. If the stock appreciation does not occur, the investor has essentially lent the money to the company at a very good rate with little to show for it.

A callable bond may on the surface seem like a good idea. You get your money back before its due date. However, no lender likes to have this happen, and neither should you. It is possible that when you get your money back, there will be no good place to reinvest that cash. Worse, your interest payments cease, stopping the flow of income that you expected or perhaps even relied on.

Callable bonds allow the company to find a cheaper loan elsewhere. This could be possible because of several factors. The economy may have changed, making money cheaper to borrow, or perhaps the company's credit ratings have improved, enabling the company to repay its higher-rate bonds and issue lower-rate ones. The company may actually be borrowing from one bondholder to pay another. The investor is usually paid for this early redemption in the form of a call premium, a dollar amount over the par value.

Corporate bonds can be issued with payback periods of as long as 12 years. Short-term is considered less than 5 years, while intermediate-term offerings are usually in the middle, at 5 to 12 years.

Zero-coupon bonds offer the investor something slightly different. They initially discount the bond and sell it to you for less than its par or face value with the promise that, while you will not receive cash interest, you will get the full face value of the bond when it matures. Savings bonds work this way. When you buy a savings bond at $50, you are actually buying a promise that the government will pay you $100 (full par value) in 17 years—with interest. That

What is par value?

Par value differs in meaning depending on which type of securities is being discussed. With equities, par value is simply an accounting number; it has no real relationship to the price of the common stock. The par value of a preferred stock is determined by the dividend paid to the shareholder. In the case of bonds or other fixed-income investments, par value refers to the face value. In other words, when a bond is offered, a face value is assigned. Corporate bonds usually have a face value of $1,000, municipal bonds of $5,000, and Treasuries often come in denominations of $10,000. You will not necessarily receive par value when the bond is sold. Suppose you want to get out of a corporate bond. The price you will get for a bond if you resell it depends on what the market is willing to pay (the interest rate on the bond stays the same—only the holder changes). Suppose the company is offering new bonds at a higher rate of interest. To sell your bond, you must "discount" it by lowering the price. If the company is offering bonds at a lower interest rate than the bond you are selling, the price you will get increases because the higher interest rate makes the bond more attractive.

interest is calculated every six months and is 90 percent of the interest paid on five-year Treasuries. The value of series EE bond increases each month, while the interest paid to the bondholder (at redemption) is compounded semiannually. That interest, by the way, is exempt from state and local taxes. The federal tax is not due until the bond is redeemed. Series EE bonds are a favorite for education purposes because they receive additional tax benefits.

Like series EE bonds, I-bonds, or inflation bonds, come in denominations of $50, $75, $100, $200, $500, $1,000, $5,000, and $10,000. Unlike series EE bonds, they are bought at par value, and there is no guaranteed level of earnings. During inflationary times, your principal can increase; during deflationary times, your principal will not fall below par.

Before we move along, other long-term investments can include commodities, such as gold, or property, such as your home. Leave the commodities and currencies to the experts or invest in funds or ETFs that track them. There is a good deal of volatility in these areas, so be careful. In periods of inflation worries, the prices of commodities can soar. In periods where the inflation risk is low, they can often reach new lows.

While it deserves more of an explanation, the exact opposite happens with housing. When inflation is high, housing prices usually soften. When it is low, consumers feel confident, and they borrow as much money as they can. Homes should not, in my humble opinion, be considered an investment based on our current discussion.

 There is a great deal that goes into the purchase of a stock that investors often overlook. Companies are affected by any number of outside influences, from government regulations to investor involvement, all of which play a role in the profits of *your* business. The next chapter will encourage you to wrap yourself around your role as an owner of the company.

Not only will we discuss the important role of dividends to the long-term investor, but we will take a look at the best way to capitalize on stock ownership for the least amount of out-of-pocket fees.

CHAPTER 14

With a Goal in Mind

N o one really goes on a journey without a destination. Sure, there are travelers who meander for days, weeks, or months on end (lucky them!). But when the trip is over, they either return to where they started or stop at some other place. Either way, the traveler had an ultimate destination. Investing in stocks requires some consideration of this as well.

Where are we going? How do we want to get there? And by which route should we travel? All of these questions have merit. But the most important consideration is what to bring. What will we need for the journey ahead?

I mentioned this earlier, but for those who might have skipped a section or two, it bears repeating: investing is three things at once. First, it is an achievable gain. Second, it is an avoidable loss. The third, which is much more difficult and personal, is the control of the market manic inside of each of us—the one that wants to buy when the market is headed up and sell when it tumbles. That market maniac wants to make rash decisions, wants to follow the in-crowd, wants to take huge risks in the face of reason, and wants to sell low and buy high instead of vice versa.

But first, we need to determine exactly what the long term is.

 What the Experts Say The early bird may get the worm, but the second mouse gets the cheese.

Anonymous

An awful lot goes into determining what is the long term. Many researchers have found that most people consider the long term to be five years. Short-term investors (which we will discuss in Part IV) believe that each quarter holds a new investment worth considering.

The companies we invest in often make long-term plans and develop products with far-off completion dates and only probable profitable outcomes. Why, then, do investors look only at the here and now? Shouldn't we consider the distant future, the chances that the demographics of a company's markets will change (baby boomers have become a major consideration for many companies), that the economy will improve (or not), that governments will accommodate the business, or even that the company will still be there in 10 years?

Working in reverse, if you have been paying even passing attention to the news, you will realize that the chances of a company's remaining in business for 10 years seem slim. Companies with poor guidance or shady dealings disappear almost as fast as they become corporate leaders. Mergers and acquisitions (M&A) have become the new twenty-first-century way of growing a business. A company that wants to increase its market share, or perhaps buy a new technology rather than develop that technology on its own, will look for another company to buy.

M&A activity is often referred to as being a benefit to the shareholders. Unfortunately, the opposite is often true.

Let me explain briefly how that can be. A company that makes money can use that profit in several ways. From best to worst, the possibilities are: pay the shareholders a regular and increasing dividend, reinvest in the company by developing new products or services that can increase profits, use the profits as incentives to employees, purchase other companies, or repurchase shares of the company's stock.

Profits are the property of the shareholders. In a young and growing company, the shareholders agree that any profits should be used to "grow" the company. In the example above, I put shareholders at the top of the list. Once a dividend is declared, the shareholders should always be first in line because usually, but not always, the company is more focused on growing market share. (That's Wall Street speak for finding new customers.) Once they establish a product line, growth comes by enhancing those products, and to some degree, by developing new ones to replace the old.

When a company uses its profits to buy another company, it is essentially saying that the purchase will increase profits in the long run..

Governments can influence the outcome of a long-term investment. Governments generate regulations and laws that have an effect on how businesses are run. Many of these regulations and laws affect profits, and long-term investors need to pay attention to whether or not that impact is positive.

The Securities and Exchange Commission is the primary cop of the investment industry. It enforces numerous regulations, investigates corporate misconduct and wrongdoing, and generally acts as an investor advocate for proper conduct. The current head of the SEC is Christopher Cox. The head of the agency is appointed by the president and can change when the administration changes. The best agency heads are bipartisan and do their job with an eye on business vitality and shareholder protection. That's no easy task.

The members of the SEC are elected to staggered five-year terms. Five commissioners in all are split with no more than three members coming to the job with the same political affiliation. Christopher Cox, who was appointed by President George W. Bush in 2005, is the chairman. The rest of the commissioners are Paul S. Atkins, who is serving until 2008, Roel C. Campos, recently nominated to serve a second term, Annette L. Nazareth, who worked with former SEC Chairman Authur Levitt and has been a commissioner since 2005, and Kathleen L. Casey, the newest member of the commission, appointed in 2006.

Here is a list of the laws that the SEC enforces:

Securities Act of 1933

Securities Exchange Act of 1934

Public Utility Holding Company Act of 1935 (repealed May 8, 2005)

Trust Indenture Act of 1939

Investment Company Act of 1940

Investment Advisers Act of 1940

Sarbanes-Oxley Act of 2002

Securities Act of 1933

This act is also called the "truth in securities" law. It was enacted on the heels of the stock market crash of 1929 and the Great Depression that followed. It requires companies issuing securities to represent themselves honestly, using every available means to provide full disclosure of financial information and what the SEC refers to as "significant" information (http://www.sec.gov/about/laws/sa33.pdf).

Securities Exchange Act of 1934

This is the act that brought the SEC into existence and gave it its muscle. This act allowed the SEC to look at almost every aspect of the securities industry: "brokerage firms, transfer agents, and clearing agencies as well as the nation's securities self regulatory organizations (SROs). The various stock exchanges, such as the New York Stock Exchange and American Stock Exchange, are SROs. The National Association of Securities Dealers, which operates the NASDAQ system, is also an SRO. This ability to not only oversee but also regulate and register securities firms was accompanied by the disciplinary powers to enforce its regulations.

The act also identifies what Congress felt was improper conduct, forced the periodic reporting of company activities, and required companies whose assets exceed $10 million and that have more than 500 shareholders to file financial reports. (These reports are available to the public through the SEC's EDGAR database.)

The full text of this act can be read at http://www.sec.gov/about/laws/sea34.pdf.

Trust Indenture Act of 1939

This act outlines the agreement required between bond issuers and bondholders. This formal agreement is called a trust indenture, and it must be in place before a bond can be offered publicly.

The full text of this act is available at http://www.sec.gov/about/laws/tia39.pdf.

If at first you don't succeed, destroy all the evidence that you tried.

Steven Wright

Investment Company Act of 1940

This act organized the mutual fund industry. The act, which has come under scrutiny of late, basically requires a mutual fund to report financial and other information in the same way a company does. While the SEC provides oversight and regulation of mutual funds, it does not supervise their investment activities. (Hedge funds fall outside this act even though they appear to deliver the same basic service.)

The full text of this act is available at http://www.sec.gov/about/laws/ica40.pdf.

Investment Advisers Act of 1940

This requires firms or individuals who receive compensation for their advice to be registered with the commission. The act goes a long way toward protecting investors, but it was amended in 1996 to allow advisors who have less than $25 million under management to be free from registration. (A list of online brokers appears in Chapter 19.)

The full text of this act is available at http://www.sec.gov/about/laws/iaa40.pdf.

Why is Sarbanes-Oxley important?

The Sarbanes-Oxley Act (SOX) was more than a knee-jerk reaction to several corporate scandals. It was an important piece of legislation that created a Public Company Accounting Oversight Board, subjected companies to strict regulation and control of their relationships with their auditors, forced CEOs to sign off their companies' financial statements, mandated stricter disclosure within company financial statements, and required companies to give their shareholders an outline of the company's ethical standards. From an investor's point of view, analysts, the ones who delve into a company's inner workings and make recommendations about investments, must be free of conflicts of interest.

Sarbanes-Oxley Act of 2002

This act, sponsored by Senator Paul Sarbanes (D.-Maryland) and Representative Michael G. Oxley (R.-Ohio) changed the way corporations make disclosures to investors. This law has come under fire because of the high costs of internal audits and disclosures. However, while it is true that the initial costs are high, we have begun to see lower costs each reporting year. Whenever you see an analyst on television, anything that he or she says about an individual stock will come with a list of disclosures ranging from ownership (including family) to whether the firm the analyst works for has any relationship to the company.

The full text of the act is available at http://www.sec.gov/about/laws/soa2002.pdf.

The Role of Government

There is also no denying that the office of the president has an impact on how companies operate. While its effects are often debated among economists, the White House can do a great deal that is good or bad for business depending on what it does about taxes.

Is the president cutting taxes in the hopes of generating growth, or is he or she raising them to increase the government's solvency and to strengthen public entitlement programs? Is the White House spending money to generate economic expansion or reining in the size of the government?

Many economists like to think that monetary policy is what really affects the economy, but the influence of the White House, referred to as fiscal policy, can be felt. Here is a short list of presidential actions that had this type of influence: the Kennedy-Johnson tax cuts of 1964 (they resulted in an unprecedented economic expansion), Nixon's efforts to use wage and price controls to lower unemployment and inflation (this was coordinated with monetary policy from the Fed), calls by Presidents Ford and Carter for stimulation by the Fed (remember, it is the president who appoints—with congressional approval—the members and the head of the Federal Reserve Board, although they each have a fixed term), Reagan's huge tax cuts (the Fed raised interest rates to stave off inflation), and finally Bush Sr. and Clinton's focus on the huge federal deficits (giving rookie Fed chief Alan Greenspan the ability to get interest rates back down to normal, business-stimulating levels).

Presidents also have an effect on the nation's confidence that can often translate directly into business investments. Higher confidence includes hope that the economy will improve, and with it, the profitability of the companies we invest in. More and more, long-term investors need to look globally for trends that might affect business here in the United States. Increasingly, companies that many investors previously thought were operating only in the United States are exposed to foreign economies as well through mergers and acquisitions. (M&A activity can be spurred on by other reasons as well: Competition, the service the acquired company might provide, and often just to get a "foot-in-the-door" of a marketplace.)

Buy Me, Hold Me

Companies that want investors to hold their stock for the long term need to explain how their new products or services will affect their profits in the far future. This gives investors the confidence to continue to buy additional shares of the company. One of the surest ways to do this is with earnings and dividends.

Earnings and dividends are the fuel we need to travel the open road. Each earnings statement is a road map. Unfortunately, most of us think of earnings in terms of the simplest equation: buy something for a dollar, sell it for two, and the profit from the transaction is one dollar.

 What to Ask?

What is EBITDA and what does it tell investors?

Earnings are net income after taxes. A much less telling measure of a company's strength and economic viability is its *EBITDA* number. EBITDA is an acronym for Earnings Before Interest, Taxes, Depreciation, and Amortization. This method of looking at earnings removes the effects of financing and accounting decisions, requiring potential investors to estimate whether the company can handle more debt or pay for the debt it already has on the books. Don't be fooled by a company stating its EBITDA number. EBITDA is intended to evaluate profitability, not cash flow. For that reason alone, investors have had to ask themselves, why does EBITDA matter? It doesn't. A company using EBITDA may be hiding something that it doesn't want you to know.

The real fuel comes from a souped-up equation. The P/E ratio, or price-to-earnings ratio, is even more important than stand-alone earnings. It refers to the valuation of the company using the company's stock price and earnings:

$$P/E = \frac{\text{market value per share}}{\text{earnings per share (EPS)}}$$

For example, if a company's share price was $20 and the earnings the company posted over the last 12 months (called trailing earnings; when a company looks at earnings for the next 12 months, this is referred to as forward earnings) was $2, the P/E ratio would be 10.

Investors look at the P/E ratio in much the way we would examine gas prices on our road trip. For stocks, when a company has a high P/E ratio, it is generally assumed that the market is incorporating favorable future prospects into its calculations. Perhaps the company has expectations for higher growth in the future that would push earnings higher. When that happens, the P/E rises.

If the stock price of the same company rises to $65, the P/E ratio using the same 12-month earnings per share, or EPS, of $2 changes to 32.5.

A lower P/E, especially when there has been no change in the a company's earnings, can be a signal that the market suspects that the company may have to struggle during the next fiscal year. The market sets the price, while the company posts the earnings.

 The P/E number is only as good as the actual earnings of the company.

Here are some other terms that you might bump into during your search for the perfect long-term portfolio:

Earnings multiplier takes into consideration the prevailing interest rate.

Price multiple is another way to express P/E.

Relative P/E refers to the comparison between a company's P/E and the P/E for a comparable index (for instance, at the end of May 2006, Microsoft had a price of $23.77 a share and a P/E of 18.13; if you compare that P/E with the P/E of 25.20 for the industry that Microsoft is included in, Application Software, you will find that Mr. Softy is doing quite well— its P/E is neither too high nor too low).

Price-to-book ratio is the stock price divided by the book value of a company. Basically, book value is the company's assets less its liabilities and is calculated each quarter. Even more basic, book value relates to the worth of the company should it go bankrupt. (And I do mean basic. There have been several opportunities to delve into the different accounting methods used to calculate such things as book value. Generally Accepted Accounting Principles, or GAAP, are applied in situations like this. For the sake of our discussion, we will try to keep it as simple as possible.)

P/E-to-growth or PEG ratio combines growth potential with the P/E. The accuracy of such a ratio depends on the quality of the projection and the potential for growth. As with P/E ratios, be sure you are comparing not only apples to apples but time frames to time frames.

$$PEG = \frac{\text{price-to-earnings ratio}}{\text{annual EPS growth}}$$

It is important to compare apples to apples, though. The P/E of one company might be vastly different from that of another company in a different sector. The utterly confused investor should compare the P/E of one company to the P/E of a similar company in a similar industry or to the P/E of a similar index of stocks.

How do I use P/E ratios?

For comparison purposes, here is a list of industries, their market capitalization or worth (in billions of dollars, based on outstanding shares multiplied by the price of a share of stock), their price-to-earnings ratio, and their dividend yield (the amount of profits that the company distributes to shareholders, expressed as a percentage of the share price).

Sector	Market Cap	P/E	Dividend Yield
Basic Materials	$4,726.2B	14.48	2.28
Financial	$5,288.9B	15.64	2.69
Utilities	$829.5B	17.94	4.32
Conglomerates	$694.6B	20.40	2.25
Consumer Goods	$2,398.9B	21.59	2.32
Technology	$4,701.1B	25.47	1.86
Services	$3,020.1B	27.63	1.35
Industrial Goods	$944.6B	35.32	1.40
Health Care	$2,443.7B	57.03	1.75

When entire industries are used as a comparison tool, an individual stock and its P/E are compared to a broad median number, one that is related to the company's specific niche. Often these broad groupings can be further dissected to give an even narrower look at the P/E performance of similar companies.

Updated sector P/E and yield numbers can be found at http://biz.yahoo.com/p/s_peeu.html.

The best comparison is one between a company's recent results and its own past performance. Since this financial tell-all figure holds so much sway, the recent surge in stock buybacks is troubling. Although many reasons for these buybacks are given, the investor should see them for what they are.

When a company removes stock from the public domain by buying it back at the currently traded price, two things happen: the liquidity of the stock is decreased (the number of shares outstanding on the exchange is reduced), and the EPS increases even if the profits have not, since the EPS is calculated by dividing profits by the number of outstanding shares on the market.

Using a wide variety of indicators and historical information, predictions are often made about how the future might look. The following table gives some of the predictions made by Standard & Poor's for the 500 largest companies.

Date	The S&P 500 Projected P/E
12/31/2007	25.53
09/30/2007	23.92
06/30/2007	23.34
03/31/2007	22.37
12/31/2006	22.46
09/30/2006	21.33

Another reason that most investors should balk at such corporate actions—and we will get to your role in this in the next chapter—is that the company is squandering its profits on making a number look better and therefore making the company more attractive to investors. The earnings number used is only as good as the company, and this sort of sleight-of-hand maneuvering can make the P/E suspect.

The Importance of Dividends

I've mentioned dividends several times now, but I have failed to mention just how important they are to long-term investors. They are the octane in your fuel tank, the number that assures you that the leaders of your corporation are doing the right thing by their shareholders. When industries suffer from declines in overall share price for whatever reason, dividends keep investors around.

The role of dividends is extremely important, especially after the market declines in 2000. Consider the dividend yield provided by the S&P 500. With a dividend yield of about 1.74 percent over the 12 months ending in May 2006 and the estimated dividend payout over the next 12 months of 1.84 percent, almost one-fifth of the value of the index is being paid to investors in the form of dividends. If the index's value (profitability) increases by an average of 10 percent over that time period, and the dividend yield reflects the payment to shareholders, almost one-fifth or 1.84 percent of the S&P's profits are returned to the shareholder. The performance of the index or of a company is determined by using a combination of returns and dividends.

Paying dividends is now very much in vogue. Encouraged by a favorable tax environment, more companies are starting to pay dividends for the first time. This is a sudden change of heart for many sectors, including technology. Profits that were previously used for expansion have been distributed to investors who stuck with the companies.

What are dividends?

Dividends are a portion of the profits of the company that is distributed to stockholders after its managers have determined that those profits will not be needed to grow the business. Dividends are often paid by mature businesses.

The following table shows the top dividend-paying companies with the actual dividend and the yield. The yield is calculated by dividing the amount of the dividend by the share price.

	The S&P 500 Projected P/E	Dividend	% Yield
1	Citizens Communications	1	7.97
2	Peoples Energy	2.18	6.01
3	Nucor	2.9	5.96
4	Progress Energy	2.44	5.76
5	Apartment Invest & Mgmt	2.4	5.53
6	Pinnacle West Capital	2.075	5.29
7	Consolidated Edison	2.31	5.27
8	UST Inc.	2.32	5.26
9	TECO Energy	0.76	5.16
10	DTE Energy	2.06	5.12
11	Ameren	2.54	5.05
12	Verizon Communications	1.62	5.04
13	CenterPoint Energy	0.6	4.9
14	Embarq	2	4.9
15	Altria	3.48	4.88

(Data as of March 2006.)

And while the percentage of profits distributed to shareholders is still low, time might improve that situation. Once companies stop buying back stock and overcompensating CEOs, and begin to develop profits organically (a term that means developing them within the company, as opposed to buying competitors or companies that can help in manufacturing), dividends should increase.

 In May 2006, Congress voted to extend the capital gains tax rate of 15 percent through 2010. The number of households owning equities has climbed steadily, with the median household holding $65,000 worth as of 2005, with almost 90 percent of those investors using equity mutual funds to do the investing for them. The stocks of companies that pay dividends are outperforming those of companies that do not pay dividends.

The real importance of dividends to you as an investor lies in your ability to reinvest them. Just as you would reinvest all of your gains, including dividends, from your retirement savings at work or your individual IRA, and just as you would buy more shares of your mutual funds held outside a retirement account instead of taking income distributions, figuring out whether stocks are a good buy requires you to do much the same thing. An investor would have seen phenomenal gains (over 600 percent) in any 20-year period from 1871 to 2002 had he or she invested in the S&P 500 and reinvested the dividends.

Dividend payments are dependent on a number of factors. Industry growth and consistent performance are key. The performance of a dividend-paying company is determined by its annual income and its dividend yield.

The abilities of the CEO and the management team to lead the company in the right direction, weather downtrends, and seize opportunities are all factors indicating the quality of the dividend. Mature companies with established markets tend to pay dividends at a much higher rate than younger businesses.

Cash dividends are the most common form of dividend and are the type that is most coveted by investors who are looking for income from their investment. With the current tax rate (until 2010) of 15 percent on dividend income, real cash is considered very favorable.

How do you determine whether a company can pay a dividend?

Wall Street uses a financial statistic called *dividend cover.* The math works like this:

Dividend cover = earnings per share ÷ dividend

A company with a dividend cover of 2 is considered very reliable. A dividend cover that falls between 1 and 2 is a relatively accurate indicator of increased risk. In this case, the dividend has become a burden on the profits of the company, but not to such an extent that it is a danger sign for investors. When the dividend cover falls below 1, the company is paying more in dividends than it can afford and will probably need to reduce the amount it distributes if it cannot increase its profits. Substantial increases in profits are difficult for companies that have reached a level of maturity that does not allow for rapid growth. A dividend cover of 1 might also suggest that earnings from previous years are being used to cover the distribution.

The board of directors determines when the dividend will be distributed. On the *declaration date*, the board declares its intention to pay a dividend, creating a liability on the company's books. Each time a dividend is declared, the board of directors must approve it, and then a date of payment to shareholders of record must be set.

What is the date of record?

Shareholders who have properly registered their ownership, which is done automatically when you purchase the stock from a broker or, as we will learn soon, from the company directly, on or before this date will receive the declared dividend.

The real importance of dividends to you as an investor lies in your ability to reinvest them, usually without cost, in the mutual fund or the stock. Had an investor done just that, he or she would have seen phenomenal gains of 600 percent or more in any 20-year period between 1871 and 2002. Without a doubt, the easiest way to reinvest your dividends is to agree to do so when you sign up for an IRA or a company-sponsored plan like a 401(k), or simply when you buy a mutual fund outside of your tax-deferred accounts. But the easiest way to do it with stocks is by using DRIPs or DPPs.

Surprisingly, considering the ease of the transaction, the use of this type of investment program is limited. But before I get into the nuts and bolts of this investment tool, you need to remember what it is that you are trying to achieve. You are looking for a long-term investment that you plan on spending a little more than a few minutes researching. (That is a sly reference to the influence of the media and the vast array of financial information they reveal daily, hourly, and, in many instances, crawling below the screen.) You have decided to take your money, often hard earned, and invest it for a profit.

What are widows and orphans stocks?

This is a sort of antiquated terminology for a stock that pays a healthy dividend, issued by a company that has a relatively stable or dominate market share and that can be counted on for consistency. These three things were very important to people who were in need of regular and steady income, the kind that, in the days before the social safety net, widows and orphans might need. The best examples were utilities, which, because of a government mandate (monopoly), met the criteria easily. Now the term usually resurfaces when the stock market has hit a low and investors are seeking safety rather than growth.

Direct public purchase (DPP) offers the investor a way to buy stock directly from a company. The vast majority of the companies offering this require you to access the program through a brokerage portal like FirstShare or MoneyPaper. Each requires you to join the program before you buy your first share of stock; then, once you have become registered with the company of your choice, the business will contact you and allow you to set up further investments.

Acting like the perfect dollar cost averaging broker, Sharebuilders allows you access for as little as $4 a trade. We will discuss online and traditional brokers and their cost structures in Part IV, but Sharebuilders seems to have carved out a nice niche for itself.

As with all brokerages, you get what you pay for. For $4 a trade, you get the basic program, which allows you to buy stocks on a recurring basis. The company invests every Tuesday, apparently seeking to avoid spikes, bounces, or carryover news from the weekend. Getting access to the markets in this way allows you to build your portfolio one share at a time.

This is by no means a recommendation to use Sharebuilders. However, once an investor becomes committed to the goal that he or she has in mind, using a broker such as Sharebuilders makes it easier to follow through consistently.

		Advantage	Standard	Basic
In the Real World...	Sharebuilders' Fee Schedule			
	Subscription fee	$20 per month	$12 per month	None
	Automatic investments	20 included/month, $1/additional 6 included/month, $2/additional	$4 per investment	
	Real-time trade market orders	$11.95	$14.95	$15.95
	Real-time trade limit orders	$15.95	$18.95	$19.95
	Free IRA	X	X	$25 per year
	Free ESA	X	X	$15 per year
	Gain & Loss Tracker	X	X	
	PortfolioBuilder	X	X	
	Portfolio Tax Tool	X		
	IPO Priority Notification	X		

DRIPs (an acronym, of which there are far too many) simply means Dividend ReInvestment Programs. These programs are often the least expensive way of buying a stock; they are sometimes even free of charge.

DRIPS are a wholly different vehicle because they are limited to dividends. Currently, there are only about 600 companies (a full list can be found in Appendix B, along with their ticker symbols; go to their Web sites and follow links for investors) that actually provide a program that allows individual investors to use their dividends to buy stock on a recurring basis.

Most of the programs are straightforward and easy to use. For instance, Dow Jones Industrial Average member 3M explains the program in an easy-to-understand format that requires only a small amount of clarification.

Once you are on the 3M site (www.mmm.com), click on the link at the bottom of the page titled Investor Relations. Follow that to stock information. If you do decide to buy a company like 3M, you will want to look at the financial information available here as well as any other news that might affect your decision. I'm sure I don't need to remind you that the responsibility to do this comes with ownership.

Most sites that I visited, and I worked my way through all of the ones on the list, redirect you to a service such as a bank to hold your new shares. These services act as custodians and track your account. Each time a dividend is issued, the money goes directly into your reinvestment account and additional shares are purchased, either full shares or fractions thereof. In 3M's case, the minimum purchase is $10 (many have a minimum of $25) and the maximum purchase is $10,000.

This is a dividend summary for 3M dating back to 2000. The closing price for 3M in 2000 was around $43. As of this writing in mid–2006, the company's share price was over $70. Each time a dividend is paid, the amount is deposited directly into the reinvestment plan and used to purchase more stock.

Declared	Record	Payable	Amount	Type
5/9/06	5/19/06	6/12/06	$0.46	Regular Cash
2/13/06	2/24/06	3/12/06	$0.46	Regular Cash
11/14/05	11/25/05	12/12/05	$0.42	Regular Cash
8/8/05	8/19/05	9/12/05	$0.42	Regular Cash
5/11/05	5/20/05	6/12/05	$0.42	Regular Cash
2/14/05	2/25/05	3/12/05	$0.42	Regular Cash
11/8/04	11/19/04	12/12/04	$0.36	Regular Cash
8/9/04	8/20/04	9/12/04	$0.36	Regular Cash
5/11/04	5/21/04	6/12/04	$0.36	Regular Cash
2/9/04	2/20/04	3/12/04	$0.36	Regular Cash
11/10/03	11/21/03	12/12/03	$0.33	Regular Cash
8/11/03	8/22/03	9/12/03	$0.33	Regular Cash
5/13/03	5/23/03	6/12/03	$0.33	Regular Cash
2/10/03	2/21/03	3/12/03	$0.33	Regular Cash
11/11/02	11/22/02	12/12/02	$0.31	Regular Cash
8/12/02	8/23/02	9/12/02	$0.31	Regular Cash
5/14/02	5/24/02	6/12/02	$0.31	Regular Cash
2/11/02	2/22/02	3/12/02	$0.31	Regular Cash
11/12/01	11/23/01	12/12/01	$0.30	Regular Cash
8/13/01	8/24/01	9/12/01	$0.30	Regular Cash
5/8/01	5/18/01	6/12/01	$0.30	Regular Cash
2/12/01	2/23/01	3/12/01	$0.30	Regular Cash
11/13/00	11/24/00	12/12/00	$0.29	Regular Cash
8/15/00	8/25/00	9/12/00	$0.29	Regular Cash
5/9/00	5/19/00	6/12/00	$0.29	Regular Cash
2/14/00	2/25/00	3/12/00	$0.29	Regular Cash

A booked share is an actual issued share without the certificate. You can request a certificate, and the custodian can take actual certificates and deposit them in the account, but the paperless exchange, at no cost to you, is simply the best alternative.

It's hard to believe, but there is still more. You, the owner, also need to find a way to curb your enthusiasm, and for that we will need to discuss the bulls and bears, the finer points of investing, the necessity for your involvement in corporate governance, the role that CEOs play in the running of your company (much like mutual fund managers do for funds), and what questions you should ask when you attend a shareholders' meeting. That's right, they have meetings where they bring out the top executives to tell you the what-fors and the how-comes of the previous year while explaining the future of the company.

The most important goal of the next chapter is to make you understand that a fat portfolio does not make you smart.

CHAPTER 15

And the Wind at Your Back

The majority of us are optimists. We embark on a road trip with full expectations of blue skies and wide-open roads meeting endless horizons. But life isn't always like that, and neither is the stock market.

Bear markets happen as well as bull markets. These references to animals are apt. Consider the way the bull charges, plunging forward with strength and abandon. The term is naturally associated with markets that are on the rise.

A bear market conforms to our notions of pessimism, a desire to curl up and sleep off any news we don't want to deal with. These necessary "corrections" are the driving rain, the relentless headwind, and the pitch black of night all rolled into one. How you react involves much more than having good wiper blades or steely nerves. There is a purpose for bear markets, and that purpose serves the long-term investor well.

 In the Real World... People with optimistic dispositions are not to be deterred in their belief that they can confront trouble head-on. A study found that women with such optimism could cope with and ultimately deal with a diagnosis of breast cancer better than their pessimistic counterparts. Dr. Charles Carver of the University of Miami, who conducted the study with Michael Scheier of Carnegie Mellon University and others, said, "Pessimism was associated with denial and a giving-up response. Optimism was associated with positively reframing the situation, with women believing, 'This is not going to go away, so let me make the best of it I can.'"

Bull markets are caused by more than just enthusiasm and optimism. There are a variety of mechanisms in place that allow investors to feel confident about the future. When investors are pleased with a company's current earnings and dividends, they expect that its earnings and dividends will continue to be strong. Sometimes bull markets are encouraged by monetary policy (favorable interest rates set by the Fed) or fiscal policy (favorable tax environments for both investors and businesses). Sometimes the belief that something new has appeared that will change the world and people investing in that new discovery with unbridled optimism can push markets higher.

Recently the Dow Jones Industrial Average pushed through the 12,000 mark. This happened just as the latest bull market hit the beginning of its fifth year. Historically, bull markets do not run for very long periods and rarely do they top the previous bull market highs.

Investors should also be aware that there are two different types of bull markets and two different types of bear markets. Both can be cyclical and secular. This means that during a prolonged, or secular, bear market, stocks can make a good run known as a cyclical bull market. If a bear market signifies a period of either downward movement or, just as bad, no movement at all, a cyclical bull market can develop, giving stocks a small boost. In a secular bull market, a cyclical bear market can develop, halting the steady long-term gains that had been occurring over a long period. These are often called "traps." A secular bear might trap a cyclical bull and vice versa.

But things change, and investors forget. Once the comfortable warmth of optimism sets in, the idea that markets can go down often simply slips from our memories. Markets that are pushed higher by good news can fall simply because the reasons for the optimism need to be controlled.

One force is interest rates. The Federal Reserve has the job of making sure that markets don't overheat. The data it gathers to make its decisions cover more than inflation. If companies grow too fast, they overheat. Why do markets get so hot that the Fed feels that it needs to step in and change the dynamics of monetary policy?

Investors forget. They see each new high achieved by the markets as they rise as merely a stepping-stone. They buy into the hype that markets can go up without fail, day in and day out, up into the stratosphere. It is tempting to buy stocks that are setting new highs each day. Each time a stock reaches a milestone—52-week high, two-year high, all-time high—you must be very careful to see that the price and the earnings are still in alignment (i.e., the price-to-earnings ratio is still reasonable), the P/E-to-growth ratio has not become outsized, and the company's long-term prospects remain solid.

Unlike short-term investors, which we will learn about in the next section, long-term investors buy companies on the basis of a firm set of rules and criteria. Foremost among them is a calculation of the tax consequences, the broker's fees, and the possibility that you might unleash that market maniac inside you.

Once you fall prey to the notion that stock prices can be forecasted, you are opening yourself to equity blindness. The underlying factors that make a company worthwhile are discarded in favor of a price. That price may or may not reflect how well the company is doing. In fact, a rapidly rising stock price seldom does.

The day following the Dow Jones Industrial Average's new high, one of its leading components, Caterpillar, warned Wall Street that it would not be making its estimated profits. Analysts for investment companies meet with companies and make determinations or recommendations of where a stock price might move. By factoring in numerous tidbits of information, these estimates can drive investor interest.

Caterpillar was responsible for the lion's share of this latest bull market, gaining over 150 percent over the course of the last four years. The stock sold off quickly as a result.

What the Experts Say

You get recessions, you have stock market declines. If you don't understand that's going to happen, then you're not ready; you won't do well in the markets.

Peter Lynch

I mentioned earlier in the book that dollar cost averaging was the single best formula for dealing with these rough spots in the road. That's right. A bull market is a rough spot akin to accelerating into a driving rainstorm.

The talking heads come out of the woodwork to tell investors that the next new Dow high is a good thing. Despite every logical explanation, the markets continue to rise. Investors who jump in on the way up are actually worse off than investors who bail out on the way down. Investors' overoptimism allows them to become less risk-averse as a feeling of invincibility sweeps over them.

Before we move on, I should mention how the Dow Jones Industrial Average is priced. The Dow's price is a weighted average divided by a divisor that takes into account stock splits. The short explanation suggests an actual dollar price. Each time the Dow advances, the gain can be considered a dollar increase in the total index.

The Dow divisor can change periodically, but the method for determining the index's value stays the same. The current Dow divisor is 0.14418073. Suppose all the stocks in the DJIA opened and closed at the same price with the exception of one company. That one stock increased by one point. To calculate the Dow's increase for that trading day, you would divide one by the divisor(1/0.14418073). The index would have posted a modest gain of seven points or, more precisely, 6.9357.

DJIA = Sum of 30 Dow stock share prices / Dow divisor

Current Dow Divisor = 0.14418073

With Ownership Comes Responsibility

Once you have decided to build an equity portfolio, you have made a commitment to not only research the stocks before you buy them but become an active participant in the company. You will be alert to news about things that affect *your* company. You will take your responsibility as a shareholder seriously, acting as if you owned millions of shares. You will vote your proxies and actually consider attending a shareholders' meeting.

But when you decide to react only to prices, all of your good intentions are for naught. In order to control this, you need to set aside a certain amount of money to build the portfolio. You must replenish the cash in the portfolio on a regular basis as well. Remember that this account is separate from your retirement account and your taxable mutual fund account.

For dollar cost averaging to achieve what it was designed to achieve, you need to purchase the companies you decide to invest in regularly. This allows you to buy their stock at a variety of prices (be sure to keep good records of these transactions for tax purposes). If the company is doing a good job—paying a decent dividend or showing a willingness to reinvest the money in the business and not buying back its own stock—prices shouldn't fluctuate all that much. If they do, dollar cost averaging will adjust your exposure.

What is the best strategy for buying stocks?

Dollar cost averaging is still *the* best method for becoming a disciplined investor. You invest a fixed amount of money on a regular basis, usually monthly or quarterly. The idea is to buy the stock at a wide variety of prices. When the stock price is low, you will be able to afford more shares with the amount of cash available. When the price rises, the limited amount of available cash will keep you from committing too much. This method requires you to buy fewer shares when the price is inflated. It is important that the company is on solid ground with a successful history. Although this methods works well as a way of dealing with volatility, too much movement in the stock might be cause for a reevaluation.

There are certain things that are within your control, and it is important that you always ask yourself the following questions before buying any stock that seems hot:

Do you understand the cost of each trade? Long-term investors consider this cost tobe part of the share price, but because these investors trade infrequently, the costsare generally low. Allowing yourself to succumb to hype will lead to increasedbrokerage costs.

Do you understand the risks? The long-term investor puts only a certain amount into each portfolio. Once you are invested in your company's retirement plan or an IRA, your portfolio should be structured first with mutual funds (be diligent in looking at the costs of these funds) and then with stocks. One of the biggest risks in stocks is replenishing the funds allotted to the riskiest part of your portfolio—the one with individual equities.

Do you understand the tax consequences? There are few among us who trade in the short term with an eye to the tax consequences. The financial pressure that comes from taxes should make short-term investors wince. The long-term investor can defer her or his taxes until a time when her or his tax bracket is favorable (although there's no telling how capital gains will be handled after 2010).

Do you understand what long-term means? It means a commitment on your part to join other investors who also believe that a company can be run profitably and that the owners of the company can share in that wealth. To that end, you buy stock and stick around. I have seen all kinds of ways to try to control the urge to follow total strangers up the hill. Doing so makes no sense. You may once have considered yourself an utterly confused investor, but you should now understand the concept of common sense and intuition, should be able to take a deep breath and sleep on it, and above all, should take pride in ownership.

Learning about You, the Investor

In the course of your investing, you will find scandals and poor corporate governance. You will find CEOs getting paid seven or eight hundred times what the average employee receives. You will stumble across techniques and theories, formulas and charts by the hundreds. You will be tempted to go beyond simple research. Reading annual reports cover to cover may be beyond the average investor, but a few basic facts can be uncovered.

Understand the direction of your company. What did the CEO discuss in his or her letter to you? Is the CEO the kind of leader to whom you would commit your money to do with as he or she sees fit? You get the idea. You own the company, and you have a right to ask questions. Annual reports have gotten easier to read, with most of the important numbers conveniently located where investors can find them.

You will also enjoy the road more if you do these things. You can have the top down and still be a long-term investor. Long-term investing should be more than just a short trip from point A to point B. It should be a period of self-discovery for you as an investor. You can be passionate and passive. You can be cautious and creative. You can set achievable goals, avoid losses, and harness the market maniac inside you.

Power Corrupts

More as a reminder than anything else, the shareholders' involvement in the companies whose stock they own has become more important with each passing day. Or at least so it seems.

It took two years to prosecute the people who were responsible for the Enron meltdown. High-profile trials make the business sections of the newspaper read like so many tabloids. But the crimes of people like Bernard J. Ebbers of WorldCom (convicted of $11 billion in fraud that led to the demise of his company and sentenced to 25 years, which he has not yet begun to serve), L. Dennis Kozlowski of Tyco (convicted of raiding the company coffers to the tune of $150 million and sentenced to 8 1/2 to 25 years), and Martha Stewart of Martha Stewart Living Omnimedia (convicted of lying to federal investigators; served five months but remains under investigation by the SEC) are testimony to the arrogance that can creep into people who hold the top job.

Every shareholder is invited to attend annual shareholders' meetings to cast his or her vote to elect the directors of the corporation. There may be other shareholder matters discussed as well. Notices of these meetings are mailed within 10 to 60 days of the event, depending on the laws of the state in which the corporation is chartered. Special meetings can be called as well. These are important gatherings that you as an owner should attend if possible. Here is where your involvement in the company becomes one of you as a shareholder speaking directly to your CEO. You may ask about mergers or reorganizations, any amendments to the Articles of Incorporation, why the corporation's assets are handled in a certain way, and whether the company should issue certain securities or stock option plans.

The feeling of invincibility that surrounds company chiefs makes equity investing akin to driving without headlights. The CEOs at companies like Enron were ignoring the risks that their companies were taking, the debt that they were racking up and, worse, the due date for that debt, and whether the company had enough available cash to weather a storm.

Investors kept pumping up the stock of these companies, and these head honchos took it as a vote of confidence. As P/E ratios soared—at one time

Enron was valued at a P/E of 100—investors plowed even more money into the stocks. The alarming part of this arrogance was the pay that many of these executives was receiving

As a long-term investor, should you be concerned that the company head is making 350 times the average worker's pay?

How much is too much?

According to the compensation practice of Clark Consulting, CEO pay increased from 2004 to 2005 by 27 percent, making the average pay $11.3 million. While *pay* usually means the dollar amount the CEO was paid to do the job, the biggest rise for the chief executives came from compensation packages. These additional monetary awards, which can include restricted stock, options, and incentive payouts and bonuses, increased 15 percent in 2005. The SEC wants to enact 370 pages of new rules that will help investors by providing better disclosure of executive compensation.

If the CEO is truly a superstar, someone who exhibits the qualities necessary to propel the company further, parting with a portion of your profits as a shareholder to pay that person may be easier. The way those qualities can be measured include how well the stock has performed and the position of the company relative to its peers. If the company seems to be well led, chances are that the CEO is doing the leading.

Confidence, a not-so-tangible measure of success, can go a long way in keeping a company on track. We have spoken at great length about what you need to bring to the stock market, the knowledge you need to keep in your hip pocket, but what we have not discussed is the right price at which to buy a stock.

We wanted Nike to be the world's best sports and fitness company. Once you say that, you have a focus. You don't end up making wing tips or sponsoring the next Rolling Stones world tour.

Philip Knight

Look at the CEO. The markets price a stock based on the perceived value of the company. This is a backward-looking, forward-predicting measure of how well the company has done and how well it will do. The market often gives a company with solid leadership a higher price. Having a good product or the possibility of a new service is not enough to make a company's stock price rise. Having a CEO who can get the product to market or launch the new service flawlessly means everything to Wall Street.

So the stock price is almost irrelevant if the leadership of the company is on solid ground. Are there other ways to price a company? Of course, but you will still need to look at the top management for the answer.

Long shots do come in and hard work, dedication, and perseverance will overcome almost any prejudice and open almost any door.

John H. Johnson

Things sometimes happen to companies that are beyond the CEO's control. But Wall Street will forgive a misstep for only so long. It is up to the CEO to exert his or her influence over the situation, whatever it may be, and literally will the company back. But things that break sometimes take a long time to fix.

A value stock, as we discussed in Part II, is the stock of a company that has a good market footprint, a respectable amount of steady profit, and the good fortune of having fallen off Wall Street's main radar screen. (Look at the company's P/E ratio both currently and historically. A P/E that is too low for too long represents a risk.) If the CEO insists that a dividend be paid and offers the promise of better days, the stock may be a bargain for the long-term investor.

In the end, treat CEOs much the way you would treat the managers of mutual funds. Judge them by their tenure. If they are new to the job, give them a couple of years. Wall Street will show its faith through a steadily rising stock price. If they have been at the job for a while, the share price should have risen steadily over the last half of the time they were at the company. This measure is easy when markets are on the rise. Determining a good CEO during a bear market is not as easy, but certainly not impossible. An investor needs to look at the sector in which the company is grouped. Even in a down market, good companies will lead the way with good corporate governance and vision.

It may be a CEO's moment to shine, navigating the rough waters of difficult markets in order to convince investors that the company is worth investing in and, because the stock price might be depressed, could be an excellent, under-valued bargain.

How do you determine which CEO is best, which company is worth investigating, and which stock is priced right?

There are several excellent publications that warrant the long-term investor's attention. One is *Barron's*. This stately publication offers a wide-angle look at the markets once a week, gathering investment professionals for semiannual roundtables and examining and ranking a variety of financial happenings, from CEO pay to best new stocks. The reading tends to be heady at times, and the research is considered to be among the best. In fact, *Barron's* has been responsible for a good deal of investor enlightenment that has turned over-the-weekend readers into stock buyers come Monday morning. This is referred to as the "*Barron's* bounce."

The pullout sections can provide the new long-term investor with some great exposure to the language of Wall Street. You already have a solid base; now its time to expand your horizons.

The *Wall Street Journal* provides the best performance for the money. No monthly investment magazine comes close to the daily reporting provided by this paper. You will find that your "native talent" for investing can feed on the information tucked inside. The *WSJ* is an excellent place to keep abreast of what is happening to the stocks you own.

How you should use that news is another matter. If you are looking for an opportunity, the *Wall Street Journal* and *Barron's* can give you the seeds for your research. There may be reports of a new product, an emerging service, or a change at the top spot. These could all indicate that this is a company you may want to own.

Other excellent sources for print coverage of the markets and the business that surrounds them are the *New York Times*, which has revamped its business section to make it easier to use, and *Investor's Business Daily. IBD* offers certain tools that some traders employ to make decisions in the short term, namely, charts and analysis, that go well beyond what a novice might need. Nonetheless, the paper does round out the coverage offered by the three previously mentioned publications. All have good Web sites that add special online services. The *WSJ* and *Barron's* charge subscribers an additional fee; the *New York Times* so far does not.

But suppose these papers uncover something unsavory about your CEO, a potential disaster looming for an established product, or perhaps an accounting irregularity. Should you run for the door? Not necessarily. A CEO scandal is not the end of the world. Companies with viable products and good markets or market potential will survive and someday post another profit. It will be largely up to the board to decide whether replacing the company chief is best for the business.

The Board of Directors at many companies have begun to assert themselves in ways that can only benefit investors. In many instances, the board was considered a "rubber stamp," approving whatever management suggested. This is changing.

Directors are now seeking information beyond the filtered facts that company management so often gives. Directors are taking an active interest in investor complaints, employee sentiment, and their primary purpose, oversight. Board members must be careful to avoid setting policy, providing a check and balance to what management is trying to achieve.

Board members, much to their credit, are doing a good job of representing shareholders. This is easy to see as the average time a CEO has spent at the top job decreased with the board's involvement.

Each time you buy shares in a company, you must set yourself selling parameters. These mental boundaries will allow you to consider your options from a cool-headed perspective. On the sell side, you will need to determine what percentage a stock can fall before you call it quits.

Most people fail to realize that a 50 percent fall in a stock price means that the stock will have to appreciate 100 percent to get to even. Look at it this way: if the shares of Widgets, Inc., fall from $20 a share to $10, the stock will have to double in price, or increase by 100 percent, to get back to $20.

Keep this in mind when you hear someone talk about how much a stock has gained in a year. That percentage may not be telling the whole story.

I would be remiss if I didn't offer you some direction about selling a stock. The notion of dollar cost averaging almost forbids such activity. The idea that you can buy additional shares for less when the stock is down is what makes

DCA work so well for the long-term investor. But change happens, as the saying goes.

You should do more than just set a sell price and allow a sudden change in market sentiment force you to sell. On any given day, it seems, a company might offer guidance to Wall Street about upcoming products or performance that might trigger a sudden selling frenzy. Do you react in kind? Do you know enough about the company to understand what happened and why?

If there is any doubt in your mind about a stock in your possession, set a sell price. Doubt will drive your fear of loss. So set your selling price at no more than a 10 percent drop. That is a sizable fall even if the number seems small. If you are using an online broker, you can do this using a stop order. But why should you do this?

Stop orders are intended for stocks that are so volatile that they may fall 10 percent while you aren't looking. Long-term investors do not usually buy companies that will have such catastrophic falls before the investors have a chance to react. And if a company they own falls on some news or rumor, and they are confident of both the management and the direction of the company, they would probably see a drop in the stock price as an opportunity to purchase additional shares at a lower price. Stop sell orders work against that goal. (Some investors might even place a buy order at a lower price in the hopes of capturing a mid-market move during volatile times.) A stop sell order acts without considering the facts. Research the stock as soon as possible and make a decision. Don't let your computer do it for you.

I mentioned Caterpillar earlier and their contribution to the Dow's recent gains over the last four years. Their earnings warning saw the stock price plummet at the opening of the trading day following that record Dow close. Had you set your computer to sell that stock on a 10 percent loss, it would have sold your shares almost immediately. Is one earnings miss or one prediction that Wall Street's guidance might be too high worth selling such a strong stock with such an excellent performance?

If you had purchased the company at the last Dow all-time high back on January 14, 2000, you would have posted a substantial gain. In fact, $1,000 of Caterpillar stock purchased on that day would have been worth almost $3,000 by the beginning of October 2006. These kinds of decisions should not be left to a machine.

When you are buying a stock that is rising, you should be using dollar cost averaging. This will keep you from buying too much at too high a price. For tax purposes, keep track of which stock was bought when. If you do decide to sell, the profit or loss will be determined by whichever stock price you paid.

And never, ever, ever buy on margin. The costs of covering not only the brokerage fees and inflation but also the interest charged on your margin account can make the profit margin very thin.

Of all the skills you take away with you from this section of the book, the most important one is this: a fat portfolio does not make you smart. Keep your eyes on the road at all times. Overconfidence can make you unaware that your surroundings, the road you are on, are not yours alone.

 The only thing that can prepare you for what is next is what has already passed. You should have by now developed some idea of the discipline involved in investing. It requires due diligence, for lack of a better term, the kind of commitment that is all up front. The research and the questions asked ahead of time all give the investor who has stocked her or his portfolio with conservative funds and dividend-paying stocks a restful night's sleep.

But even the most seasoned and conservative investor lets that mental maniac loose on occasion. Short-term investing fills the basic human desire for risk and thrills. Part IV will give you the information and warnings that will allow you to invest wisely, even if you are assuming additional risk for no other reason than to assume additional risk.

What Every Investor Needs

CHAPTER 16
Just a Spoonful of Sugar

◆━━━━━━━━━━━━━━━━━━━━━━━━━━━━━◆

I wrote in the introduction: "A. J. Foyt, for example, has won the Indianapolis 500 four times in 35 attempts. The late Dale Earnhardt, despite having won over $27 million in his career as a NASCAR driver, started 676 races while winning only 76 times." Think about it for a minute. Mr. Foyt, even with his great skill, came in first only 11 percent of the time. His NASCAR counterpart had about the same winning percentage despite the larger number of races run.

Fans of racing, of which I admit I am not one, will be quick to point out that these drivers gained their reputation by finishing in the money, even if it was second or third, so often that they attained legendary status, even if they had only a 1 in 10 chance of actually winning.

Investors do not have a second or third place. Either they finish in the money or they do not. They either win or lose, and this is because the only race you are actually running when you invest on a short-term basis is one against yourself. If you desire speed, there are only two possibilities.

Short-term investors are faced with a number of challenges. Because they approach investing with such a narrow focus, they must consider any number of things that could affect their investments. Among them is liquidity.

Edward A. Dyl and Anne M. Anderson wrote a research paper for the New York Stock Exchange (NYSE) titled "Market Structure and Trading Volume" (Paper 2004–01). These two professors, Dyl from the University of Arizona and Anderson from Leigh University, focused their research on liquidity.

What is liquidity?

Liquidity is basically availability. To someone who is buying a company's shares on the open market, liquidity means that there are a good many shares available for purchase, which means that the buyer will get a competitive price based on supply and demand. If there are only a few shares available for trade, prices are usually higher than they would have been had there been a larger amount available.

When the professors wrote their paper, there was a good deal of concern about how the two major exchanges, the New York Stock Exchange and the NASDAQ, conducted business.

The NYSE is an auction market. When someone wants to sell stock, the shares that person makes available are sold to the highest bidder. Stocks are listed on the NYSE with a bid and an ask price as well as the last price paid.

When the NASDAQ conducts transactions, a dealer acts as the intermediary, taking the stock from the seller, finding a buyer for the shares, and completing the deal. This method can create some unusual accounting. For instance, and this example is used in Dyl and Anderson's paper (http://www.nyse.com/marketinfo/researchpaper/1081850295276.html), when an investor sells 100 shares, the transaction is booked as a trade by the dealer. When the dealer sells those shares to a buyer, another 100-share trade is booked, even though the same shares were involved. There were never, the two authors contend, 200 shares traded, despite the way the trade was booked.

How is that important to you? To the short-term investor, it creates the illusion of volume where there is none. Volume on the upside gives the appearance of enthusiasm, and volume on the downside might give the impression that something is wrong. That is often all that is needed to drive a short-term investor to look into a particular stock, mutual fund, or ETF (exchange-traded fund). Lack of liquidity drives a stock's price higher, and vice versa. Later we will talk about how liquidity affects a share's price in more depth. (Much more involved charts can be found here: http://www.smallinvestors.com/SP500/ NYAcharts.htm.)

According to the paper's authors, not only is short-term investors' interest piqued by lack of liquidity, but institutional investors, such as mutual funds, pension managers, and hedge fund investors, are affected as well. This group usually has large amounts of cash to bring to the marketplace. In many instances, these managers must use any cash they receive to purchase additional shares. Many funds require the manager to invest all or a large percentage of available cash in the market.

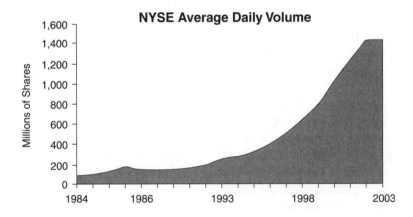

And the race is on. The normal rules of the road no longer exist. We have one goal, and all of the emotional discipline you may have developed thus far in the book will be for naught. If the information you get is not only accurate but timely, you can see how the short-term investor can get caught up in the spirit of the moment.

This effort to get money invested in presumably hot stocks becomes doubly difficult if the fund manager cannot find any appropriate investments. If the liquidity of a stock is too small, a large purchase might drive the stock price unnaturally higher. Remember supply and demand? This economic principle comes into play when demand outstrips supply: the price is pushed higher. Too high a price might not reflect the real value of the stock, and as a result, the buyer will pay too high a price relative to value.

So where can short-term investors find common sense and intuition at levels that will satisfy their urge to jump in at the next great notion or, as Netscape founder Marc Andreessen once called it, the next best thing?

Marc Andreessen rode the Internet bubble to its peak and came out unscathed. In a 2001 interview with FastCompany.com, he suggested that finding what people want is very difficult. He keeps a list of the top 10 ways in which his project might fail, appropriately dubbed, "Top 10 reasons we're going out of business." While the guys in legal hate the idea, he believes that a good level of paranoia is healthy. (http://www.fastcompany.com/online/43/andreessen.html.)

Even after the market came tumbling down, short-term investors have continued to embrace people like Andreessen. It is the pioneers, the people with the vision and innovation to chase their dreams, who are the focus of a short-term investor's intuition. And, if these investors use a certain amount of common sense, by taking the risk of supporting these innovators, they can help to uncover some of the great ideas that often are the foundation for great and long-lasting companies.

Short-term investors would have been able to spot business greats such as Intel. Back in 1968, Bob Noyce and Gordon Moore founded NM Electronics. Later that year, they purchased the rights to the name they currently use from a company called Intelco for $15,000. The year they went public, 1971, they booked their first million-dollar sales month and raised $6.8 million at $23.50 a share as a publicly traded company (ftp://download.intel.com/intel/ anniversary/35th.pdf). Intel has split its shares 13 times since its initial public offering, a move that creates greater liquidity by making more shares available for investors.

Issuing stock has come to be one of the best ways for companies to raise capital for expansion. In 1877, when Gardiner Hubbard and Thomas Sanders agreed to help finance the idea of a talking telegraph with Alexander Graham Bell, the Bell Company was born. The following year, it issued stock to seven shareholders.

Would the innovations brought about by Intel and Bell have had the same impact without the speculative impulse of the original investors? The real question is: When does a short-term investor, using his or her intuition, turn to the more conservative, common-sense side and become a long-term investor?

What's Next ▶ The next chapter is concerned with some of the basic differences between long-term investors and their short-term counterparts. Data and the accuracy of those data are what drive the short-term investor. Any number of reports, surveys, publications, or news events can force the short-term trader to shift strategies. In the following pages, we will look at some of the most important reports and explain what they are and what they mean.

As stated previously, another concern for the short-term trader is liquidity. In many cases, when a volatile stock is driven higher, chances are that few shares are being traded and they are changing hands rapidly. We will look at some of the pitfalls of buying companies with low liquidity, and offer an example of how some businesses can create great wealth with the help of short-term speculation and a little sleight of hand.

CHAPTER 17

How Fun Can Get Complicated

◆◆◆◆◆◆◆◆◆◆◆◆◆◆◆◆◆◆◆◆◆◆◆◆◆◆◆◆◆◆◆◆◆◆◆◆◆

T here are other telltale signs that define short-term investing that make it even more speculative. The first, and certainly not the least, is the risk. Short-term investors tend to be much more comfortable than other investors with the possibility that their intuition may one day desert them. It is the drive to be better than average, to get the higher returns that go with that assumed risk that keeps these investors looking for the next opportunity.

This is what makes it fun, at least for a small portion of your portfolio. The money that you put in your short-term account should be money that you do not need. Many of you have heard the expression, "Don't invest in the stock market with money you will need." While there is a germ of truth in the statement, it requires a little bit better explanation of its intent.

Investing in the stock market with money that you will need in the near term is sort of foolish. To really prosper from the benefits that investing provides, you need to commit money to the task for a long time. Only then will you receive the effects of compounding, tax deferral, and reinvested growth, to mention just a few, that time can provide.

Short-term investing requires a different type of commitment. I suggest that if you have reached this stage in your investing life, you place a fixed amount of money in an account and use only that for short-term investing. You may, of course, add to this account, but never do so to replenish losses. In other words, if the amount in the account is less than the original amount, do not add any more money to what is a loss.

Your short-term account should be built with money left over after you have paid your bills, fully invested in your retirement accounts, and acquired what Benjamin Graham first called "mad money." If this account does poorly, perhaps you do not have the native talent to invest where there is real danger of losing your money. If the account does well, celebrate, but by no means allow your newfound skill to trickle over into your safe zone: your retirement fund and your long-term savings. Keep these accounts separate.

Reports in the News

Short-term investors tend to be more data driven. They look at current information, using such things as quarterly earnings reports, economic indicators issued on a monthly basis, or just newsworthy events to try to channel their stock purchases in the most favorable direction.

Much of the data discussed in this chapter will be of little interest to the long-term investor (although, mind you, the long-term investor would do well to pay attention to the road at all times, and many of these surveys can hold a key to the future of the economy). However, because of the short-term nature of these reports, the short-term investor will see market-moving news within their decimal points of change.

Survey	Objective	When	Approximate Release Date	Sponsor
ISM Mfg Report on Business	Near-term indicator	Previous month	First of the month	Institute for Supply Mgmt., http://www.ism.ws/

This report looks at new orders and how much product is in the supply chain, and uses the information to draw a conclusion about the health of manufacturing based on prices and inventory levels. It now includes a salary report as well.

Employment Report	Job creation	Previous month	First Friday of the month	Commerce Department, http://www.commerce.gov/

On the first Friday of each month, the Bureau of Labor Statistics releases its jobs report based on two different surveys. The results of these surveys are often vastly different, and depending on whom you speak with, the data in each are superior to those in the other. The household survey, often the most politically favorable yardstick for those responsible for job creation policy, is based on a smaller number of people surveyed with a wider set of criteria for answers. The payroll survey, the questionnaire answered by over 400,000 businesses, is often considered incomplete and less revealing by policymakers.

The household survey covers 60,000 or so Americans, who are asked, many by proxy, such generalities as "who in the house is working?" The person charged with answering the survey may cite his own lawn-mowing job as employment, his unemployed father's freelance computer repair job as employment, and his mother's occasional catering business as work. That is why this survey is often touted as the whole truth, capturing all of the employed, even if their jobs are second rate or merely second or third jobs to make ends meet.

The payroll survey counts jobs. The information used in the survey comes from the businesses that create wage and salary work. Admittedly, it misses those entrepreneurs whose businesses may be growing from a sideline to mainstream work, but the chances are that those jobs will eventually show up as employee numbers in the future. While Uncle Harry's garage-based elixir production might be considered work in the household survey, the payroll survey will not show his work until he actually can call what he does work. But some economists point out that this flaw is not in need of correction. Self-employment is not always entrepreneurial in nature. Often it is the result of necessity and is more common in poor job markets; this is, as the economists are likely to say, countercyclical. That means transitory.

| Job Cuts | Job growth indicator | Previous month | First week of the month | Challenger, Gray, Christmas Inc., http://www.challengergray.com/ |

The company that conducts this survey specializes in outplacement programs for executives, middle managers, and long-term or highly valued employees. The survey seeks to measure the health of hiring, mostly from the top.

| Producer Price Index | Pricing indicator | Previous month | Mid-month | Bureau of Labor Statistics, http://stats.bls.gov/ppi/ |

The Bureau of Labor Statistics says that this survey "measures the average change over time in the selling prices received by domestic producers for their output." The prices included in the PPI are from the first commercial transaction for many products and some services.

| Michigan Consumer Sentiment | Current and future consumer concerns indicator | Current month | Mid-month | University of Michigan, http://www.sca.isr.umich.edu/ |

The University of Michigan conducts numerous surveys that try to determine the sentiment of consumers, investors, and wealthy consumers, and to offer regional data about consumers.

| Manpower Employment Outlook | Predictive indicator of hiring | Upcoming quarter | Every quarter | Manpower, http://www.manpower.com/mpcom/ |

The Manpower Employment Outlook predicts hiring practices not only here in the United States, but globally as well. The report is published quarterly, and although traders look at this report for guidance, it does not tend to move markets on negative news, but rather adds to the possibility that the future might be shifting based on how businesses staff their companies for growth or, on the flip side, a downturn.

| Consumer Price Index | Prices of sample products | Previous month | Mid-month | Bureau of Labor Statistics, http://stats.bls.gov/cpi/ |

This BLS survey measures the prices that consumers pay for a basket of goods. The Consumer Price Index (CPI) provides an indication of inflationary pressures. When the prices of fuel and food are removed (because of their volatility—fuel can be affected by speculation and geopolitical unrest, while food can be affected by weather—the prices of these two items can shift rapidly, skewing the index and clouding the actual price increases or decreases), the result is a core CPI number.

But the CPI is much more. Besides its effect on everything from social security to school lunch costs, the CPI gives economists the best look at how the economy is doing. The CPI's data collectors contact thousands of retail stores, service establishments, rental units, and doctors' offices looking for prices on more than 80,000 items. Included in the survey are eight major categories of goods and services.

| Wages/ Compensation Survey | Occupational compensation report | Previous month | Mid-month | Bureau of Labor Statistics, http://stats.bls.gov/ncs/ocs/home.htm |

This report can also offer a look at inflation. From the point of view of most economists, when wages and compensation begin to rise, this is a result of employee pressure. Employees will seek higher wages as a result of higher prices or a shrinking labor pool. The Federal Reserve Board is always looking for the right balance between prices and what it considers to be full employment.

Housing Market Index	Reports from home builders	Current month	Mid-month	NAHB, http://www.nahb.org/

The National Association of Home Builders, a trade association, publishes its report primarily for its members, but the report is also used to determine how much the consumer is willing to spend for housing. When builders are beginning large numbers of projects, this indicates a certain consumer confidence that the economy is doing well enough for buyers to be willing to buy homes. A slowdown in new housing starts might indicate that consumers are unwilling to commit to big purchases because of economic uncertainty. Consumers are responsible for about two-thirds of the overall spending in the economy, with housing being the largest consumer item.

Leading Indicators	Report on sector strength	Previous month	Mid-month	Conference Board, http://www.conference-board.org/

This is a backward-looking indicator of market strength. The Conference Board itself is a not-for-profit organization whose goal is to "conduct research, convene conferences, make forecasts, assess trends, publish information and analysis, and bring executives together to learn from one another."

Consumer Confidence	Consumer confidence in the economy	Current month	End of month	Conference Board, http://www.conference-board.org/

This is one of the many surveys that the Conference Board conducts, and one of the most telling in terms of confidence. The survey seeks to understand how consumers react to higher prices, shifts in the marketplace, natural disasters, and other such events, in order to help businesses align themselves with possible demand increases (if consumers are feeling optimistic) or slowdowns (if they are feeling pessimistic about where the economy is headed and the state of their personal finances).

Durable Goods	Details changes in sales of large items	Current month	End of month	U.S. Census Bureau, http://www.census.gov/indicator/www/m3/

This consumer survey allows the market to gauge how consumers feel based on their purchases of large durable goods such as refrigerators. If consumers are buying durable goods, chances are they are doing a number of other types of spending, such as remodeling, buying, or refurnishing new or existing homes. The bottom line is, when consumers spend, even if they are spending money that they do not have, economists feel good about the overall strength of the economy, and the markets react in kind.

Personal Income and Outlays	Reports on wage increases and spending	Previous month	End of month	Bureau of Economic Analysis, http://www.bea.gov/bea/dn/home/personalincome.htm

The Commerce Department publishes this report, as well as one on gross domestic product (GDP), to help businesses determine consumers' willingness to spend (or save) based on increases in their personal income and the chances that they will spend those increased wages.

So Much Data

Data have become much easier to obtain, easier to hype, and easier to understand. Then again, easy access has made those "easier to obtain" data more confusing. The investor is being pulled in numerous directions by Federal Reserve Bank observations about the economy and its control of monetary policy; earnings reports that may or may not be complete and may or may not be revised; surveys from government agencies attempting to pinpoint the future so that risk can be managed; and reports from any number of financial institutions that issue analysis, offer buy-sell-hold recommendations, tout the need to be fully involved in the markets or to stay out of the markets, and otherwise make their opinions known at every turn.

Which data are important? For the short-term trader, it depends on what the trader's focus is. Too often, short-term traders ignore any diversification advice. They need to be nimble and sure-footed, and tying up money for safety is not necessarily one of their key concerns—if they are concerned about safety at all.

What is fair value?

Essentially, fair value is a predictive number based on the purchases of futures contracts on indexes such as the DJIA or the S&P 500 that is used to determine whether the market will open higher or lower on any given day.

Reports on inflation and interest rates, energy prices and mortgage rates, insider trades and breaking news about new discoveries, whether good or bad, can all play a role in the short-termers' decision-making process. What news is important becomes, for want of a better definition, a personal decision. The information that appeals to you might not appeal to other traders. Left without anything but your intuition to temper your activity, the data that you choose to use can be considered less than standardized.

Markets invariably move to undervalued and overvalued extremes because human nature falls victim to greed and/or fear.

William Gross

Short-term investors tend to care little for a company's long-term prospects, its soundness, or whether the underlying business is properly run. They pay little attention to protecting themselves against losses, hoping that they will be nimble enough to get out of their investment at just the right time. In other words, short-term investors like speed.

You don't have to go too far back in history to see how these investors, the ones who approach the market from a purely speculative point of view, get in, get out, reap huge profits, and move on to the next rising star. Their actions can bring whole markets down. For proof, you need only look at the later part of the 1990s.

Looking for Proof

Those were frenzied days indeed. Each day, it seemed, some new company appeared with little more than an idea and offered its shares to the public through an initial public offering (IPO). Every company begins its publicly traded life with an IPO. During those heady days leading up to January 2000, you needed only the support of an analyst, the hype of a market strategist, and word of mouth to push an IPO into the stratosphere. Stock in these companies changed hands repeatedly, creating turnover rates that were absurd.

 Faced with the choice between changing one's mind and proving that there is no need to do so, almost everyone gets busy on the proof.

John Kenneth Galbraith

A turnover rate can help determine volatility. The more rapidly a stock is traded, or turned over, the higher the price can rise. If there are not a lot of shares available in the open market, the price can rise dramatically. The best evidence of that is Google, the search engine giant that went public with a relatively small number of shares available and high demand for those shares.

Even though many people did not understand the company, the company was not exactly forthcoming concerning how it did business, and the company even refused to reveal how well it was doing, investors flocked to the stock, pushing it from its initial offering of $108 price on August 13, 2004, to over $470 at one point. (On November 19, 2006, Google (GOOG) reached a high of $499.66, closing at $498.79.)

This lack of liquidity is evident in the number of available shares. Currently, insiders own 35 percent of the outstanding shares. The shares owned by insiders are usually locked up, a situation that prevents the sale of stock without certain securities filings made prior to the transaction. Institutions own about the same amount of shares and while they are not considered locked up, they are infrequently traded, making them essentially unavailable. On any given day, there are only about 100 million shares held by individuals and thus available for trading. Compare that to a company like General Electric, which has 10.32 billion shares available to trade (50 million are preferred stock). (56 percent of the total number of outstanding shares, or 5.88 billion shares, are held by institutions such as mutual funds and pension plans. The top five institutional investors are Barclays Global Investors Intl., 397 million shares; Capital Research & Management Co., 310 million shares; Fidelity Management & Research, 299 million shares; State Street Global Advisors, 294 million shares; and Vanguard Group, 263 million shares.).

The clearest evidence that these lessons about volatility have yet to be learned lies in the turnover rates. The NYSE publishes a list of turnover rates on its Web site. This monthly indicator shows how short term this normally long-term exchange has become. In the last four decades alone, the turnover rate at the NYSE has jumped from 20 percent (or five years for the average investor's holding of an equity) to 106 percent, or a little over 11 months.

Month		YTD
Feb–05	103%	105%
Mar–05	110%	107%
Apr–05	109%	107%
May–05	97%	105%
Jun–05	97%	104%
Jul–05	94%	102%
Aug–05	91%	101%
Sep–05	107%	102%
Oct–05	116%	103%
Nov–05	103%	104%
Dec–05	99%	103%
Jan–06	117%	117%
Feb–06	108%	113%

Data from http://www.nyse.com/marketinfo/datalib/1091545087955.html.

Some of this could be the result of the current favorable tax climate for capital gains. We will discuss the effect of taxes on equity trades a bit further on. Short-term investors need to receive a much higher overall return on their investments when they sell their stock than their long-term counterparts because taxes do not favor short-term holdings.

I mentioned liquidity earlier. Consider the following statement delivered by a CEO to his investors and employees:

"Our liquidity is fine. As a matter of fact, it's better than fine. It's strong."

That message was delivered by the late Ken Lay, the man who took a run-of-the-mill natural gas company and turned it—albeit illegally—into the seventh largest company in the United States. A comment like this, especially in hindsight, makes most investors shudder. Did Lay actually believe those words, or was he merely enticing investors to keep putting their money in his company?

For those of you who may be unfamiliar with what Enron was, cared little about the ensuing meltdown that caused thousands of investors to lose billions of dollars in individual portfolios and retirement accounts, or are unaware of the regulations that followed that event, here's a little story about how Enron did business.

This slightly paraphrased example of how Enron operated was sent to Alan Abelson anonymously by e-mail and was published by *Barron's* on January 28, 2001.

In a land where feudalism is the way of life, you have two cows. Your Lord is entitled to and takes only some of the milk.

Where fascism reigns, you might have two cows as well. Under a fascist regime, the government will seize both of your animals and hire you to take care of them. Then it has the audacity of selling you your own milk.

Those same two cows, owned by a farmer who lives in a communist state, the animals are yours to tend. The government in this case simply owns all of the milk.

Under capitalism, the law of the land here in the United States, if you have two cows, you could sell one and buy a bull. You would breed the animals and then watch as your herd grew in size. You could then sell out of the business you created, take the profits and invest them, and eventually retire on the income.

With Enron, you have two cows.

You borrow 80% of the forward value of the two cows from your bank, then buy another cow with 5% down and the rest financed by the seller on a note. This note would bear interest of twice prime. This note would also be callable, which means that the lender could call the note due, in this case, if the value of your publicly listed company falls below $20 billion. You have put up your stock as collateral so this calculation is very important.

You sell the three cows to your publicly listed company, using letters of credit opened by your brother-in-law at a different bank. You then execute a debt/equity swap with an associated unit so that you get four cows back, plus, as an added bonus, you get a tax exemption for a fifth cow.

There's more.

The milk rights of six cows are transferred via intermediary to a Cayman Island firm secretly owned by a majority shareholder, who sells the rights to seven cows back to your listed company. The annual report now tells the shareholders and analysts that you have eight cows with an option on one more. Your auditors say it's okay because they were in on the transactions and acted as consultants . . . after the fact.

Now you are all set to disclose, via press release and conference call with analysts, that Enron, a major owner of cows, will begin trading cows over the Web. Analysts call you the new economy, talk up your shares into the stratosphere and you sell huge amountsof stock.

This you use to buy the most expensive shredding machine available.

Plenty of investors bought into Enron for the long term, even when it was trading at 100 times earnings. They believed the founders and the folks running the company. There were no immediate signs that what those people were saying was wrong. Until someone blew the whistle.

Although the vice president of corporate development, Sherron Watkins, was labeled a whistle-blower, she wasn't quite timely enough to be considered one. What she did was write a lengthy, seven-page letter to her boss and her friend, the founder of the accounting firm Arthur Anderson, LLP. In the letter, which surfaced a full five months after the scandal that brought Enron down came to light, she wrote: "I am incredibly nervous that we will implode in a wave of accounting scandals. My eight years of Enron work history will be worth nothing on my résumé, the business world will consider the past successes as nothing but an elaborate accounting hoax."

Short-term investors often pay little attention to what happens inside a company. Many of them rely on current data as reported by any number of publications and by some business-specific media networks like CNBC to make trading decisions. Not all of them do this, but the influence of these highlighted news events makes frequent traders nervous, and nervous traders, well, they trade. Sometimes they trade on the rumor, and sometimes they trade on the news. Either way, short-term traders often do not take the time to fully assess all of the facts before committing themselves to a trade and executing the transaction.

It's time to identify short-term traders for what they are. We will continue to warn you as we go along about the speculative nature of this kind of trading; you should do it only after you have allocated all of the funds necessary to keep your portfolio balanced. Make sure no money heads into your short-term account from your tax-deferred retirement plans. The money invested in mutual funds held outside of your retirement accounts should get a similar "lockbox" treatment. Stocks that are held for their dividends and bought for the long term should also be kept separate from a short-term account. This will be the hardest thing to do, as the temptation to sell some of your profitable long-term holdings to make room for more speculative positions will be almost overwhelming. You will have to deal with this demon if you do not take precautions before opening a short-term account.

The next chapter discusses some of the emotions that drive short-term trading and the very real need to unleash them on occasion. With the proper understanding of the rules of this very different road, the short-term trader can achieve some successes—in the short term.

CHAPTER 18
Defining Short-Term

O ne or all of the following attributes can identify short-term investors.

They have a margin account. How much margin their broker could offer was key to their signing an agreement with that brokerage house. A margin account is a line of credit that can be used to buy stocks and is paid back at a specified rate. Many brokers will lower their margin rates for exceptionally large customers or frequent traders. One online company refers to these investors as Power Traders. Keep in mind that this fee for borrowing money must be included in the stock price, but we will get into that a little more further on.

Another telling sign is ticker fixation. Take a day off from work sometime and watch CNBC from dawn until dusk. While the stories of the day are repeated over and over again, from Squawk Box to the Closing Bell, the ticker remains the focus of the short-term investor. These investors look for price fluctuations, however minute.

In those heady days leading up to the stock market meltdown of 2000, this was the ribbon of success. Crawling across the bottom of the screen, the ticker showed not only how much a particular share was selling for, but also its increase (or decrease) in price and the amount of volume represented by each trade (this has since been eliminated). If a stock caught fire for some reason or another—and there were plenty of stories floating around in those days—its symbol would dominate the crawler all day.

The race was on, and the short-term trader, driving alone, would be jockeying for position against other traders looking for a near-term gain.

The mathematical expectation of the speculator is zero.

Louis Bachelier in *The Theory of Speculation* (1900)

For the short-term trader, each new story stock could mean an opportunity, a chance at a significant gain that could be received only hours later. Needless to say, the crawler was very infectious. The background chatter provided by the hosts and the constant parade of analysts promoting one company after another with inflated price targets caught more than one person's attention. Looking back, there were very few places you could go and not catch the broadcast. If a business had a television available for public viewing, everyone—or so it seemed—was watching CNBC.

No longer. Just try to find a television in the public domain that's tuned to that business station. Gone is the enthusiasm. There was a time when each trade showed the number of shares traded at that price. (The number of shares traded at a specific price are still there, crawling across the bottom of the screen.) Gone is the irrational exuberance. (In those days, even contrarian hosts seemed to act as straight men for guests with bullish sentiment.)

Bears don't live on Park Avenue.

Bernard Baruch

Now CNBC gets only an average 50,000 viewers per day, and the hosts often sound more bearish than bullish, more cynical than supportive, more cautious than speculative, and much less likely to have guests who take only the upside view.

In a Nutshell

Short-term traders are in it for the profit. They care little about dividends. They care little about corporate governance. They revile the Sarbanes-Oxley Act of 2002. This law came about as a result of what happened at companies like Enron, WorldCom, and Tyco. The bill was sponsored by Senator Paul Sarbanes (D.-Maryland) and Congressman Michael Oxley (R.-Ohio) and was designed to protect investors from corporate scandals. The bill, in a nutshell, forced CEOs (people who held prominent positions within their companies like Ken Lay) to sign off on all accounting reports. (The full report on the law can be found at www.law.uc.edu/CCL/SOact/toc.html.)

Short-term traders are also open to new and riskier trading techniques. While we will look at more of these techniques in Chapter 20, short-term traders will be the ones who are most apt to use short selling.

What is short selling?

Short selling, often referred to as shorting a stock, is a bet, pure and simple, that the price of a stock will go down. The wager that the investor places works like this: the investor borrows shares of stock, usually from a brokerage house. (Brokerage houses have various securities available for customers to purchase.) The short seller then sells those borrowed shares. Later, the investor replaces the shares with newly purchased ones. What the investor is trying to do is to purchase the replacement stock at a lower price. The difference between what the investor sold the borrowed shares for and what he or she paid for their replacements is his or her profit or loss.

A short seller can make money if the stock that he or she replaces the borrowed shares with was purchased for less than the sale price of the borrowed shares. Of course, the short seller also needs to include any dividends (the short seller must pay the owner of the borrowed shares any dividends distributed while the shares are borrowed), any interest charges for borrowing the shares, and, of course, the trading costs levied by the brokerage house. However, if that stock goes up instead of down, disaster awaits. When a stock is rising, the upside can be unlimited. Short selling is a very risky undertaking and is not recommended for a novice investor. It requires careful thought even by experienced investors.

Short-term traders believe that all money is mad money. Benjamin Graham first coined this term. He suggested that an investor could engage in short-term speculation with about 10 percent of a portfolio. It was, he went on to add, to be kept separate from the investor's regular holdings. This sage investor went on to say that an investor should never add money to this account. If the short-term investments do well, wonderful. If that portion of the portfolio loses money, however, the investor should take the lesson to heart and stop speculating.

Graham was adamant about this, believing that the best that could come from such an account would be a loss.

So why did he suggest it at all? He recognized that there is something inside every investor that needs to be harnessed. The desire to run with the pack, follow the leader whether the market heads up or down, and do whatever is popular is overwhelming.

I agree. Once a portfolio has been built around the long-term prospect, the short-term trader can emerge from inside an investor, but only for a small percentage of the investor's money. History has shown us that short-term trading is wasteful and not very profitable for the majority of investors who engage in it. The markets have many hidden dark corners that are out of sight and out of reach for the average investor. The chances that you will find something that no one else notices are exceedingly small. There are numerous market forces at play behind the scenes that you have little control over, and you have little time to react when something happens.

A short-term trader can always see the finish line. That single focus can often blind him or her to what is happening on the periphery.

The short-term trader is also faced with a mathematical question as well. If such a trader buys a share of stock, what is a good time to sell that stock? The trader should consider the cost of the buy order, the cost of the sell order, the interest rate charged by the margin account, the tax implications of the sale, and the target profit before he or she feels as though he or she has made money.

 The next chapter begins with another discussion of risk and ends with a list of online brokerages. In between, we will cover how to hire a broker, how to define what kind of trader you are, and how to calculate risk.

While short-term trading did not invent the Internet, it has profited from the Internet's existence. In the next chapter, we will break down the world of online brokerages, where fees seem to keep getting lower (for the largest accounts) and the service is getting better (again, for the largest accounts). Along the way, we will talk about secure transactions, internalized orders, and what to ask your broker should you ever have the need to speak.

CHAPTER 19

Investing Is a Team Sport

Investors are the great adventurers of our time. They understand little about what is in front of them, yet they seem to understand the basic pitfalls. Jill Fredston, the codirector of the Alaska Mountain Safety Center and author of *Snowstruck: In the Grip of Avalanches,* wrote in a recent op-ed piece in the *New York Times*, "We tend to see what we expect to see, what we want to see or what we've seen before. The more we want to do something, the more likely we are to make unchecked assumptions and pay attention only to the data that tells us what we want to hear."

Although she was talking about the dangers of avalanches, something that many backcountry enthusiasts are well aware of but whose warning signs are regularly ignored, her observation of human nature tends to characterize us as investors as well. Do we see only what we want to see? Do we look only for a future that is part of our vision? Do we ignore what we know and plow forward, even though we know better and are aware of the consequences?

What the Experts Say

Speculation is an effort, probably unsuccessful, to turn a little money into a lot. Investment is an effort, which should be successful, to prevent a lot of money from becoming a little.

Fred Schwed, Jr.

She goes on to say, "If we didn't take risks, we might forget we are alive." But how much risk is too much? How much living can we expect to do when we are faced with the downside of bad decisions? And are our good decisions, the ones that proved profitable for us in the past, something that we should expect to be able to repeat in the future without fail? Do we "make unchecked assumptions and pay attention only to the data that tells us what we want to hear"?

So far, we have discussed the need for time, the "sleep on it" factor that can help us with our decisions. We have assessed the balance between common-sense and intuition to understand how short-term investors think differently from their long-term counterparts. And we have looked at the need to have a grasp of what drives the markets and the investor, even if it required repeating some basic principles in the process.

We have also looked at what makes short-term investors tick. Their specula-tive energy is necessary to find and support new and interesting industries, as they act like equity pioneers and chase new ideas into uncharted territories; on the flip side, they add volatility to the markets, create a sense of panic among all investors, and have created two new industries to cater to their needs. The first is data, and the second is online brokerages.

This chapter will discuss both of these significant influences on the short-term trader and how they affect the market for all of us. We opened with a discussion of risk, and we should continue this discussion.

Risk is always there, but you need to recognize it. Without it, investing would be far less profitable, and there would be little need for books such as this one. From my point of view, risk is a much-needed ingredient in investors' experi-ence. But how do we tell the good risk from the bad, the right risk from the wrong, some risk from more risk than we are comfortable with?

Assessing personal financial risk has always been the hardest task an investor can undertake. Short-term investors embrace risk much the way the skiers and snowshoers that Ms. Fredston speaks about do. They plow forward, cocooned in their own assessment of their skills and literally hoping for the best. They begin to assume that the next loss will be something they will overcome.

They often do not give damaged portfolios enough time to repair them-selves. They also often fail to give themselves enough time to absorb the lessons learned and, by doing so, recover their commonsense, brush off their intuition, and reassess their plan.

In a short-term investor's portfolio, reinvestment is something of an anomaly. Too often, short-term investors fail to diversify their holdings. They own more stocks in a specific sector than is prudent, and they hold mutual funds that resemble one another in terms of holdings. For these investors, reinvestment simply means that they are prepared to get back into an industry that has done poorly because of the perceived value of something they see as cheap. Inexpensive stocks aren't always a good value. Nor has the risk been removed because the price has dropped.

Risk involves determining a future net worth. For the individual, that determination is incredibly difficult. For the marketplace, the determination of future net worth involves what the authors of the paper "Coherent Measures of Risk" (Philippe Artzner, Freddy DelBaen, Jean-Marc Eber, and David Heath; http://business.tepper.cmu.edu/display_paper.aspx?id= 4459) call supervision.

In the Real World... David Heath wrote the paper "Coherent Measures of Risk" in 1998 along with Philippe Artzner, Freddy DelBaen, and Jean-Marc Eber. Specializing in applied probability, Dr. Heath has held a position at the University of Illinois since 1969. What made this paper most intriguing was its attempts to measure risk. While much of the paper is filled with complicated financial equations, it has been helpful for the financial industry in determining how much to charge for margin accounts, whether a brokerage's position needs to be adjusted, and whether the Securities and Exchange Commission (SEC) is using the proper tools to assess risk.

Short-term traders are doing without several key safeguards when they strike out on their own and try to determine risk. According to the paper, investors need some sort of regulation in place. While the SEC and associations such as the NASD (National Association of Securities Dealers) provide some protection, acting as an insurance policy of sorts or, as the paper calls them, a guarantor of last resort for acceptable risks. These market regulators can, by default, help the short-term investor decide on the worthiness of the trade. Based on the ability of the companies traded on the major exchanges to meet certain requirements such as timely filings and regulations, traders can make better decisions. If short-term traders believe that their mistakes can be fixed through regulation, they might find this to be more true after the fact than helpful in the determination of risk in the present.

Even if they don't realize it, short-term traders rely on the security of the transaction rather than the execution of the trade. The promises made by an exchange's clearing firm, while generally assumed by the short-term trader, are not always included in the measurement of risk.

And lastly, the paper calls the "trade-off between severity of the risk measurement and levels of activities in the supervised domain" a key factor in determining an exit option, setting a selling price, and otherwise performing the job of an investment manager. Can a short-term trader be all of these things and still be able to figure out how much risk he or she can take?

For the sake of this discussion, short-term traders have been unjustifiably lumped together. They come in a wide variety of flavors, although I'm sure they would consider what they do to be a discipline rather than an activity. It is tempting to blame market volatility on day traders, swing traders, and position traders, but I won't. Far too many people believe in what they are doing and are fully aware of the troubles they face and the risks they are taking. While the results are not as disastrous as an avalanche, many of these traders have come to rely on their reactions rather than on what they know.

What's in a name?

Day traders buy and sell stocks throughout the day. They look for price fluctuations and attempt to profit from them. Normally, a day trader begins and ends the day without any holdings.

Swing traders usually have a longer time horizon, but not by much. They will establish a position in certain stocks and prepare to act when these stocks move in one direction or the other. These traders are driven by data and charts. The risk they assume involves unknown events that could potentially harm them overnight.

Position traders use more technical analysis and look at trends. Often these traders look at moving averages and historical numbers, and they are frequently influenced by talk radio, television, and investment newsletters. They are always in search of confirmation that they have made the right choice.

Unlike Ms. Fredston's backcountry adventurers, who have a good knowledge of the dangers that await them but choose to ignore some of the basics, short-term traders often are unaware of the amount of risk involved in their activity. Can online brokers be to blame?

Because short-term traders understand that there are costs associated with each trade, they are always on the lookout for the cheapest trade possible. You will not find this with a traditional broker. The advent of online brokers revolutionized the way stocks are traded.

Online brokers can be broken down into two distinct categories: browser-based and software-driven. Although there are hybrid online brokers that allow their clients to trade stocks using software and check their accounts using the Internet, we'll limit our discussion to browser and software trading.

Online brokerages have come a long way over the last decade. Many of the names that you associate with online trading have a history that dates back to the deregulation of the securities industry. Ameritrade opened its doors in 1976 as First Omaha Securities. Charles Schwab had a similar beginning. Mr. Schwab began as the author of a newsletter in 1974, selling his investment opinions for $84 a year. Deregulation gave him the opportunity to open a discount brokerage with a focus on investor education.

Since then, the industry has matured and consolidated, and it now offers investors an often bewildering array of services and fees. It is important to make several serious decisions when you are shopping for an online broker. Beyond all the hype that accompanies their publicity campaigns, the differences among brokers are very real and can have a deep impact on how you profit from their services.

How do I pick a broker?

Begin with brokerage fees, as the fees charged for trades, asset management, and other such functions vary from broker to broker. Because you are fully aware of what you are doing by this point, the cost of the trade is the primary consideration. While you may take advantage of some of the numerous other features offered, such as charts and research or actual assistance by a live broker on occasion, a short-term trader's day-to-day needs are based almost entirely on costs. One thing is for sure: all brokers discriminate based on portfolio size. One of the best of the bunch is Siebert (www.siebertnet.com/, 800–872–0711). Although the base fees are $14.95 for a trade of up to 1,000 shares, people with large accounts and active traders can negotiate commissions and fees. Charles Schwab (www.schwab.com/, 800–308–1486) will knock a cool $10 per trade off its commissions if your account is larger than a million dollars. Accounts under $50,000 pay the full $12.95. Fidelity (www.fidelity.com/, 800–343–3548) bases its commission costs on number of trades, offering $10.95 for accounts with 36 or more trades and more than $25,000 and $8 for traders making 120 trades a quarter. Otherwise, you should expect to pay $19.95. All these firms provide additional services. A list of online brokers, both browser-based and software-based, appears at the end of this chapter.

The criteria you use in making your decision will depend largely on how flexible you are. No brokerage is the be-all and end-all for investors. Each brokerage has some attractive features, and each has drawbacks. If you prefer to look only at the costs of the trade, you might not be enticed by the research or customer service that a brokerage offers. Short-term traders usually have a defined set of likes and dislikes when they look for a broker.

Here are few things to look for in an online broker.

Although we will get into the pricing of a stock later on, this is extremely important to the online trader. Time is money for many active traders, and price improvements are necessary if a brokerage is to stay competitive. What brokers have done is close the gap between the actual sale price of the stock and what the bid was. A higher price relative to the bid can mean that the brokerage was unable to get the trade done in a timely fashion.

Software-based brokers usually do better in this area, but not always. If your broker internalizes orders, chances are that you will be paying slightly more for a share than with a quicker routing of the order.

What is an internalized order?

Internalized orders are a very touchy subject among brokerages. There is little likelihood that your broker will even discuss the issue with you. This is odd considering there is no hard-and-fast rule concerning the best execution of a trade. An internalized order basically is an order that is filled by the broker from stock that it already owns. On the surface, this doesn't seem so bad. But brokers often treat such orders as if they had gone to the exchange with your money and bought the stock at the ask price. There are conflict of interest issues, but so far there is no solid proof that brokers are working against their clients' interest when they internalize orders.

People who use the Internet on a regular basis are comfortable with much of the new technology that has been introduced to make the online experience more pleasurable. Online brokers are constantly trying to improve the way their sites function, increasing their usability by beginners while adding new and innovative functions for more experienced users.

Usability doesn't extend to software brokers, though. Unless you are technically savvy, stay away from these platforms. They assume, and rightly so, that the investor who uses software to trade stocks has had a great deal more experience than the average trader. Ask the broker you are considering the following question: Would you recommend this trading platform to a novice investor? If the answer is yes, this might be a good broker to remember for both the short term and the long term.

While the next thing to look for is important to both long- and short-term traders, if the site isn't easy to use, the offerings of an online broker mean little to the investor.

Online brokers now offer a wide range of functions for traders. While short-term traders might want the ability to sell short and to play with options, futures, commodities, international equities, and often currencies, long-term traders might find the mutual fund offerings, which vary widely from broker to broker, an important consideration.

Ask the broker you are considering the following question: What sort of fees, if any, do you charge for mutual funds? Many brokers waive the trade costs if you hold the fund for a certain period of time. Mutual funds, especially indexed ones, are often good places for investors to ride out market uncertainty. Even short-term traders should consider this feature.

Short-term traders are referred to in the brokerage world as active, serious, or pro traders. Long-term traders are considered a necessary evil, with some brokers requiring a minimum number of trades per year. But you should not ignore online brokers simply because they court the high rollers, the ones who are likely to make trade after trade. These traders are, after all, the brokers' bread and butter. Without them, the brokers would have to charge higher commission rates to pay for all the services they usually offer accountholders at no extra charge.

Research and analysis can be had from numerous online sources, but when your broker makes it easy to access, seamless to use, and available for reference when needed, it becomes a valuable perk that is much needed and much used by both short- and long-term traders.

Perhaps we should take a moment to discuss the necessity of charts, the usefulness of analysts' opinions, and the numerous rating systems available. I mentioned earlier how Caterpillar missed the analysts' estimate and the stock fell significantly because of that news. Analysts offer their opinions based on information provided by their own research, materials offered by the company as well as meetings with management, market trends, and a variety of additional nuances specific to the analyst or the firm that employs them. These opinions are for investors to use at their own risk, and if the analyst is correct, a good decision can help investors profit or save them from losses. Repeatedly correct calls can help the analyst attain rock-star status and huge financial rewards.

Charts are often used by short-term investors as a form of technical analysis. By using information about past events such as price movements and volume of shares traded, *chartists* make trading decisions that they hope will lead to profits and avoid losses.

Among the most popular charts is the one that utilizes the Bollinger Band. Developed by John Bollinger (CFA, CMT), the chart wraps a moving average of stock prices with several bands. The band on the top signifies an overbought market, while the band on the bottom signifies an oversold market. A good chart would have the bands moving in a tight range. Such a chart would show low volatility. If the bands are wide, the stock would show the investor just the opposite. As Bollinger explains on his Web site (http://www.bollingerbands.com), his charts "can aid in rigorous pattern recognition and are useful in comparing price action to the action of indicators to arrive at systematic trading decisions."

Another favorite charting technique involves identifying Heads and Shoulders (HS), a pattern within a stock trading pattern that shows what traders like to call a "trend reversal." The chart of an HS pattern would show a stock that has fallen from a high point to a low. The stock then makes an upward move but fails to get back to its previous high. The stock price then begins to fall. This creates the shoulders, a low on each side with the high separating the two, called the "head." Investors who use this chart and identify this pattern are confident that the stock will then "break out" and head much higher once the head and shoulder pattern occurs. In other words, this chart suggests that you buy at the second low stock price, not the first.

Chart lovers also use an Inverse Head and Shoulders pattern to predict a breakout for a stock. Simply, this involves identifying a stock that has fallen in price. As the stock attempts to go higher, it is met with resistance. The stock falls again, rises, and then falls further than the previous low. It tries to rise again but fails, falling again, but not as low as previously. Chart watchers see this as an inverse head and shoulder and that resistance, drawn from each attempt to go higher, is referred to as the "neckline." At this point, all the investor needs is a signal, usually higher than normal trading volume, and the stock should go higher.

While there are numerous additional types of charts (3D Candlesticks, Renko, Kagi, Three Line Break, Point and Figure, Candlevolume, Equivolume, Shaded Equivolume, Darvas Boxes, as well as charts that graph open and closing prices, high-low patterns, and any combination of technical analysis imaginable), and just as many advocates, we will explain just one more commonly used type of chart, the *cup and handle*.

Investors look for certain specific actions to create a cup and handle chart. The pattern on the chart reveals a stock with a new high, often done in a relatively short time. The stock price begins to do down, and if a good cup is formed, the downward trend is U-shaped. That shape is important once the stock begins to reverse and head higher. V-shaped formations are not considered a good sign for investors. As the stock price increases, it meets its old high and then begins to fall back. This second retreat from the high should not fall as far as the bottom of the bowl before it begins to head up again. This short fall creates the handle and signifies that the stock is about to head higher than the previous two highs (or the rim of the cup) on heavier volume.

There are numerous ratings systems available to investors, and their success rate is subject to method used by the investor. Seemingly everyone has some sort of system for judging the worth of a particular company. Every major brokerage has some sort of system to rate stocks for their clients. In the aftermath of the stock market collapse in 2000, many companies simplified their ratings systems.

SmithBarney/CitiGroup uses the simplified buy, sell, or hold. Charles Schwab uses a letter grade, A designating the highest recommendation, while E would be considered the worst. Goldman Sachs uses an Outperform (an expectation that the stock will outperform the median total return for, as the Web site suggests, the analyst's coverage universe), In-line (an expectation that the stock will perform in the same way that other stocks in the same sector will perform), and Under-perform (a call by the analyst suggesting that the stock will not do as well as similar stocks in the same category). Goldman Sachs also gives stocks additional grades of Attractive, Neutral, and Cautious. Morgan Stanley also uses attractive, in-line, and cautious ratings for its stock picks but uses terminology such as Overweight, Equal weight, Underweight, and Volatile, each essentially meaning the same thing as the Goldman Sachs system. Your broker probably has a system. If not, the Internet offers numerous systems to judge a stock.

Easy Is the Key

You can also appreciate an online broker who makes your portfolio easy to use. The broker should offer intelligent platforms that require little in the way of experience. Ease is key. The research should be plain and clear for everyone and scalable for those who want more detail.

There should be someone there. A live broker can explain how things work, walk you through the correct way to execute a trade, or simply answer a question. Ask the broker you are considering the following question: Can I place a trade with a live broker at no extra cost? If the answer is no, that's not a reason to run for the hills, but it is certainly a consideration. Knowing that there is someone there will make the experience less impersonal. Don't get me wrong; all of the online brokers offer customer service and live brokers, but whether the one you are looking into offers the service for free is something that is worth considering.

Costs were briefly discussed earlier, but they deserve a little more attention. Short-term traders will find this particular subject the only one worth looking at. How much it costs to get in the game depends on how much you commit to the account. If you are able to put down a sizable amount of cash ($50,000 or more), you will find that a good deal of attention is devoted to your effort. You will get cheaper trades, with the costs going down based on the account's activity. This, however, might seem more like a goal for many of us: to have enough money to really play the game, to reap the big rewards, and to take risks like the pros do.

In fact, smaller accounts get the unadvertised price. A lot of advertising dollars are devoted to attracting a very small number of investors to the online brokerages. At the end of this chapter, I will discuss the real world of real wages and the kind of customers that online brokers want.

This is not the first and certainly will not be the last time that I mention prudent and conservative investing as the surest way to real wealth. For many people, the idea of investing is to grow your money, not to create obscene amounts of wealth through spur-of-the-moment decisions. While many will claim that there is a bull market somewhere, and that there are always values to be had, those values are much harder to find than is advertised. Remember the herd? Once news of something meaningful about a stock is widely known, traders will have pushed the stock higher through their sheer number of trades.

To short-term traders, the stock was not priced correctly prior to the news. If they are able to find such gems before the crowd piles in, they will receive the benefit of the herd. Otherwise, the company must have enough real value to justify doing research beyond 50- or 200-day moving averages, beyond charting the peaks and valleys and teacup formations, beyond speculation. Research of that nature makes a long-term trade almost inevitable. Why, then, does the short-term trader turn down the tax benefit of holding the equity for 12 months? Probably for the same reason that folks don't always pick the index fund with the lowest fees.

One last thing to consider: the addictive nature of online trading is hard to shake. It is largely unsupervised, with no buffer between you and your speculative nature but a broadband Internet connection. Add a margin account and the chances of disaster are just one mouse click away.

While many strategies come into play, the loneliness of trading without distraction leads us to believe that we can win using some sort of game theory. In fact, short-term trading is a zero-sum game with yourself. A zero-sum game basically means that both sides are equal when it comes to what they take away from the experience. For instance, the winner takes away exactly the amount that the loser loses. If you trade online, you will get the rush of being solely responsible for the outcome of your decisions, win or lose.

In the Real World...

A zero-sum game works something like this: restaurants need sharp knives for their chefs. Two competing services put in a bid. Each knows what its cost of sharpening is per knife, a figure that includes labor, the to-the-door service, and equipment. It just so happens that the costs are exactly the same for both companies. At a dollar a knife, sharpening 500 knives a week, each business breaks even, sharing the total in equal amounts. But if one company were to charge two dollars instead of one, the game would change. The company charging one dollar would take all of the business, while the higher-priced company would get nothing.

Before I give you the list of brokers, it is important that you understand who is using them. The statistical information given in popular online brokers' surveys conducted by respected news journals such as *Kiplinger's* or *Barron's* is usually based on accounts of $100,000 or more. That's not chump change. These brokers are catering to the high rollers—not the top 20 percent of wage earners, or even the top 10 percent. The top 1 percent.

According to the Tax Policy Center (http://www.taxpolicycenter.org/home/), a nonpartisan joint venture between the Urban Institute and the Brookings Institute, the top 1 percent of the wage earners in this country are the ones with incomes large enough to be included in these surveys. The people in that top 1 percent earn an average of $402,306. Those in the top 0.1 percent earn more than $1.6 million a year, and the truly elite wage earners, the ones in the top 0.01 percent, take home an average of more than $6 million.

This is important for two reasons. The first is to illustrate how few people control the flow of money in this country. You should keep that in mind at all times. The goal is not to become one of them. Even a college degree is no guarantee that you will rise to that kind of income level. (To read more about this, check out *Where Did the Productivity Growth Go?* by Robert Gordon and Ian Dew-Becker of Northwestern University.) The goal is to survive on their table scraps. Sorry if that sounds as bad as it actually is. Money moves markets. Large amounts of money move markets faster. You just want to be there when it happens.

This kind of income does not necessarily suggest that wealth creates short-term volatility. In fact, wealth in many cases is more concerned with preservation of capital rather than risky ventures to increase it. This allows fewer opportunities for the short-term investor.

If you have fully financed your retirement account, built a solid portfolio of taxable mutual funds, constructed a basket of good long-term dividend-paying stocks, and set up your "mad money" portfolio, the account that makes up 10 percent of your total holdings and that you should never replenish, you probably won't be seen as a market mover. Brokers will not, I'm afraid, court you.

The behemoth that this high-income group has become will have an effect on all investors who are not their equals. Lesser investors have to be aware of how commissions and fees work, pay special attention to each detail, and come to grips with the idea that this is a real game with real money. Whatever philosophy short-term traders pursue, they should pursue it with money that they do not need. Truly, how many of us can say that while mustering a good balance of common sense and intuition? Not many, I suspect.

You, as well as they, have the luxury of hiring someone with better tools and more time to research, evaluate, and move on a stock in a structured, less emotional (at least, we hope so) manner to do the job. We know that these money managers will not be relying on a flurry of financial news and prevailing sentiment; instead, they will be scouring prospectuses and financial statements for the right mix of management, products, and markets. Ours are called mutual fund managers. Theirs are called expensive.

While there does seem to be a computer—full of information, technology, trading platforms, charts, and analysis, all displayed in vivid color—between you and a human, don't let that stop you from calling your broker. In many instances, a technical question will be kicked up to a broker who is capable of completing any transaction that might result from the customer's query. If you are unsure of how to place a trade, the fees involved, or whether you will get the right price for your trade, call your broker.

Online brokers can serve a purpose in the investor's life. They are the pit crew for your racing experience. As Dale Earnhardt once said: "Finishing races is important, but racing is more important."

These brokers provide access to mutual funds held outside of 401(k) plans, and many of them offer these funds in individual retirement accounts, both Roth and traditional. They allow access to the stock market, the bond market, and, in some instances, options and futures trading. (The later two are best avoided, although we will discuss what they are in Chapter 20.)

Online brokers are not, however, very good places to leave uninvested cash. Many of them pay only a pittance in interest. Some don't even have a money market fund. Many of those who have one don't automatically direct your money to a money market fund. And the interest paid, even on large accounts, is not very good.

In no special order other than alphabetically, the following list includes many of the most highly publicized brokers. You know the names, and because of the success of their ad campaigns, you are likely to patronize one of these brokers.

Ameritrade (www.tdameritrade.com)

Ameritrade recently merged with TDWaterhouse to form a new company. It continues to have the same platforms for experienced traders, going under the name Apex or Izone, which are browser-based brokers. These platforms do a good job with transactions because of their routing technology, but short-term traders might find their margin rates a bit high (9.5 percent on a $25,000 account balance). The Apex account holders will face a maintenance fee if their balance falls below $2,000 or if they make four or fewer trades in a six-month period. Internet trades cost $9.99, broker-assisted trades are $44.99, and no-load mutual fund transactions are $49.99.

Bank of America (www.bankofamerica.com)

This company bases its fees on account balances, usually combined across all accounts with the bank. To get the firm's best pricing of $5 per trade, premier account holders must have $100,000 in total accounts, and private clients must hold $3 million. Regular fees for regular traders are $14.

E*Trade (www.etrade.com)

This firm offers a wide range of banking opportunities as well as brokerage services. Account balances need to be kept above $2,000. If you make 1,500 or more trades in a quarter, commissions can be as low as $6.99, or $12.99 on accounts of less than $50,000. Margin rates are 9.49 percent. The site has a nice suite of features, a no-fee IRA, and over 6,000 mutual funds to choose from as well.

Charles Schwab (www.schwab.com)

This firm charges traders with account balances of less than $50,000 a fee of $19.95 per trade. Mutual fund offerings are extensive, but the cost might make buying them independently worthwhile (purchases of $0 to $14,999 are charged 0.7 percent of the principal). Schwab also has more than 250 offices nationwide (which matters little to the online trader).

Fidelity (www.fidelity.com)

This firm offers several account balance options as well, ranging from $8 for active traders to $12.95 for inactive accounts of less than $25,000. There are no maintenance fees, and the firm provides access to its family of mutual funds as well as an additional 4,500 funds, 1,100 of which have no transaction fees.

Firstrade Securities (www.firstrade.com)

This firm charges a single flat rate of $6.95 and is used as a gateway broker for direct purchase plans (DPP) and dividend reinvestment plans (DRIPS).

Muriel Siebert (www.siebertnet.com)

The grande dame of the brokerage world focuses on education and customer service while remaining competitive in terms of rates. Rates for larger accounts are open to negotiation; otherwise a straight $14.95 commission is charged. Siebert's Women's Financial Network (http://www.wfn.com/index.asp) offers additional access to her services; it may make you feel warm and fuzzy, but the rates are the same.

optionsXpress (www.optionsexpress.com)

At this firm, the best pricing comes with more frequent trading. If you trade at least nine times per quarter, you pay $9.95 per trade; customers trading less pay $14.95.

Scottrade (www.scottrade.com)

This company offers a bare-bones flat fee of $7 for all customers. Broker-assisted trades cost $27.

Sharebuilder (www.sharebuilder.com)

This broker gives the best rates to traders who sign up for automatic investments via account deductions. Fees can range from $1 to $4, depending on which type of account you sign up for, with fees for real-time trades being as high as $15.95.

This is only a selection of the offerings available in the online brokerage world, and inclusion in it is by no means a recommendation. Online brokers have their place, and you should not decide to trade more simply to get lower commissions. These firms do provide easy access to research and, in many cases, inexpensive mutual fund offerings, but you should use these firms wisely; read about all the fees involved, and remember that online trading is not online investing.

 In the next chapter, we will offer some final thoughts on short-term trading, along with some additional tools and terms that speculative traders often use to reap the rewards they seek.

CHAPTER 20
Some Final Thoughts

S hort-term traders are not necessarily in the market to obtain skills. They understand that risk assessment is incredibly difficult. The problem is not our failure to see the risk or even understand the risk, but that we often choose to ignore what we know. There are several additional investment techniques that I'd like to cover before I turn you loose. They involve a riskier side of the marketplace, a financial underbelly that, once exposed, can offer some reward to those who can stomach the risk.

Information is not knowledge.

Albert Einstein

Among these techniques are *short selling* (which we discussed earlier in Part IV) and *option contracts*. On the surface, options seem to be complicated, but once you understand the terminology, the concept becomes easier to grasp.

Suppose you rented an apartment that you were given the opportunity to own one day. The landlord includes a provision so that you could buy the property for a specific price in the next three months. In this case, you have the *option* to buy and the landlord becomes the *option writer* or *issuer*. The apartment becomes an *underlier*. And the price at which the apartment is sold to you is called the *strike price*. Your agreement with the issuer might include an additional amount of time to buy the apartment beyond the three months.

The landlord, or in this example, the issuer, has offered you a *call option*. A call option allows you to purchase the apartment (the underlier) for a specific price. A *put option* would give you the right to sell the apartment at a specific price.

The option contract you entered into with your landlord for the specific apartment lookes like this:

The underlier: the apartment

The expiration date: three months

The strike price: the agreed upon cost of the apartment.

Had there been some other item involved that specified an amount, there would have been a fourth item in that list: the *notional amount*. If it had been stock, the notional amount would have listed the amount of shares. Had the contract been for oil, the notional amount would have listed how many barrels were being bought or sold.

The expiration date is usually referred to as American, European, or Bermudian. These terms have nothing to do with geography. An *American exercise* simply means that the option can be exercised at any time leading up to the actual expiration of the contract. The *European exercise* restricts the option from being exercised on any date other than the actual expiration date. The *Bermudian exercise* allows for some additional dates when the option contract can be exercised.

A put option is basically a bet that the price of a certain stock will decline. The person who buys a put option does not need to actually sell the stock short. Instead, the person buys a contract giving him or her the right to sell the stock at an agreed-upon price, the strike price, for a specified period of time. The buyer of the put option is hoping that the price of the stock will fall below the strike price. If it does, the buyer will either sell the contract to someone else and take the difference as profit or buy the stock at the lower price and sell it to the seller of the put option at the strike price. This is called a married put.

Married puts are generally used when the investment is considered to be very bullish. If the married put involves stock, the investor buys shares along with the specified number of shares in the contract. No matter what happens to the shares in the put contract, the strike price will remain the same. If the market goes up, then the investor will reap huge rewards. If the market goes down, the investor has time to make his or her decision knowing that the strike price is fixed.

In a married put, the upside is unlimited. The downside is calculated like this: the purchase price of the stock less the strike price and the premium paid.

Another of these techniques is buying *call options*. A call option allows the investor to buy a stock at a certain price for a specified period of time. The difference between a call and a put is that the buyer of a call option hopes that the stock will appreciate in price so that he or she can buy it at the lower strike price.

In our landlord/renter example above, the contract you enter into is considered naked. There is nothing underlying your contract in the form of protection. You could have covered your option by owning another apartment. This would have protected you from being forced to buy the option at the strike price because you owned a similar security.

Investors who purchase call options can cover those purchases by buying the same stock and holding it separately. Investors might opt for such a move if they believe the markets may turn bullish or, at worst, remain neutral. When investors cover their call or create a *covered call*, they retain all the rights of the stock they own including dividends and voting privileges. The upside of such a move allows the investor to profit from the premium on the written call. If the expiration has been assigned, the investor not only gets the premium but the difference between the strike price and the acual stock purchase price. In a situation where the expiration has not been assigned, the investor still gets the premium and receives the gains that may have occurred in the stock's value.

A related technique is the use of *derivatives*. Both put options and call options are a form of derivative. So are futures contracts, swaps, and forward contracts, all of which are speculative investments based on some form of underlying asset that are used to bet on changes in the price of that underlying asset. The assets involved can be anything from stocks and bonds to interest rates, commodities, indexes, and currencies.

Derivatives have been around since records of financial transactions were kept on clay tablets, some dating back to 1750 B.C. There is a reference to derivatives in the Bible as Jacob negotiated with his father-in-law, exchanging seven years of labor for the right to marry Rachel, daughter of Laban. Even Aristotle made mention of derivatives when he spoke of options on olive oil presses. That deal allowed Thales the Milesan access to the presses and the subsequent fortune made with a bumper crop of olives.

But derivatives also come with numerous and well-documented losses of fortune. Consider the worth of the following items:

4 tons of wheat

8 tons of rye

1 bed

4 oxen

8 pigs

12 sheep

1 suit of clothes

2 casks of wine

4 tons of beer

2 tons of butter

1,000 pounds of cheese

1 silver drinking cup

Even in this day and age, these items have great value. But in seventeenth-century Amsterdam, they were worth one tulip bulb. Brought from Turkey, tulip bulbs were considered of great value because of their rarity. To allow more people to purchase bulbs, options contracts were created. Investors believed that a single investment of $1,000 could net them a return of $100,000. At the height of the tulip bulb craze, a single bulb was worth $76,000. Six weeks later, the value of that contract was worth a single dollar.

The most famous example of derivatives can be found in the collapse of Long Term Capital Management, a hedge fund created by John Merriwether, formerly of Salomon Brothers, two Nobel laureates, and a former regulator. An excellent recap of those events, written by David Shireff, can be found at the following link: http://riskinstitute.ch/146480.htm.

Yet another of these techniques is *futures*. The difference between a futures contract and an option contract is the obligation. The option contract offers the investor an opportunity to buy the underlying asset; a futures contract obligates the investor to do so at some designated point in the future. When you see oil futures pricing a barrel of light sweet crude at $70, that is an obligation to purchase that commodity at that price when the contract expires. Those who do not want to purchase the physical commodity can sell the contract before its expiration. Futures trade in an auction market, with volume increasing during periods of market uncertainty.

The final technique we will discuss is *hedging*. This is used by investors to reduce their risk. An example of a hedge is a situation in which an investor who owns the underlying security but is unsure of where the price will go purchases a put option. If the price of the underlying security goes down, the investor will lose money on the stock but make a profit on the put option. With any luck, the investor will break even—less the cost of the hedge.

Economists generally agree that the existence of derivatives is a good thing for the overall economy. While derivatives are essentially a financial contract between two parties, the basis of the agreement is the assumption of risk. Derivatives can be bought and sold on the performance of assets, on the fluctuation of interest rates or currency exchange rates, or simply on the changes in certain indexes. Always speculative, derivatives act as an insurance policy for increased risk, especially when those transactions structured debt obligations and deposits, swaps, futures, and options. Derivatives are traded over the counter (OTC).

Online trading provides all investors with some access to these types of trades as well as access to a wide variety of trading platforms, research and information, and, often, a live person to talk to (however, a trade with a live broker often costs quite a bit more).

Short-term investors are speculative, driven by data, and able to assess their risk tolerance. They will often concern themselves with the costs of margin accounts, are often fixated on the ticker crawler, and are apt to follow the market up (and, in many cases, down).

It is extremely important for short-term investors to take numerous factors into consideration. They need to calculate not only the selling price of the stock, but the tax consequences, broker charges, the effects of inflation, and margin costs when determining the right price at which to sell their holdings.

The main problem with ending a book like this is that, while this seems like a good place for a finish line, it is, in fact, only the beginning. We have methodically "driven" through all of the steps that investors need to take. We began with the easiest tool available, the one that the largest amount of us have access to, our retirement accounts, and from there, we built a working knowledge of what belongs in those accounts and what does not.

We have looked beneath the hood at mutual funds. They have their faults (who or what doesn't?), but they remain, with the right approach, a key ingredient in a well-structured portfolio. If that is as far as you ever get, don't worry.

But if your goals include holding individual stocks, we looked at the fundamentals of why the stock market is no longer the gambler's market of your grandfather's day, but instead a real way to grow wealth. Long-term, you have found, is the best way to do that.

And because all due diligence and no fun makes investing seem dull, we offered a look at how the short-term trader lives. We do offer one caveat, however: discipline is the key to success. Keeping the money in your trading account separate from all other accounts and never adding to it will make the experience much more satisfying—if your speculation does not prove profitable, then your other accounts are not harmed. If you profit in that short-term account, congratulate yourself, but do not add additional money. Reinvest your profits and keep the accounts separate.

For this book, it is an end. For you, it is a beginning.

Glossary of Investment Terms

◆◆◆◆◆◆◆◆◆◆◆◆◆◆◆◆◆◆◆◆◆◆◆◆◆◆◆◆◆◆◆◆◆◆◆

Accumulation plan: This often referred to as a nest egg. It is considered a financial strategy commonly used as part of a retirement plan where the investor accumulates an ever-increasing amount with a specific goal in mind.

Aggressive growth: An investment category that involves seeking maximum capital appreciation by purchasing stocks believed to offer rapid growth potential or by employing risky trading strategies. These funds generally are high risk and volatile.

Alpha: This is used when calculating the risk of a mutual fund and its risk as it relates to the market. When a mutual fund investor is taking on more risk, the reward is rated as an *alpha*. A positive alpha rating is expressed as a percentage, so that a fund that receives an alpha of 2.5 percent, the fund will reward the risk by doing 2.5 percent than the average market return.

Ask price: This is the lowest price a seller will offer a stock to a potential buyer. It is almost always higher than the bid price. The difference between an ask price and a bid price is the spread. Market makers make money of that difference.

Asset: Anything of value owned by a business or an individual.

Asset allocation: An investment strategy that involves seeking both income and capital appreciation by shifting assets between stocks, bonds, and cash to achieve the optimal return. While a balanced fund maintains fixed percentages of stocks and bonds, asset allocation funds are not tied to a specific asset ratio. Also called *flexible allocation*.

Assumed investment rate: A rate that is needed for the purpose of setting premiums and statutory reserves for a guaranteed minimum death benefit. The premiums are those that flow into a separate account.

Average maturity: The average time to maturity for all the securities held by a fund.

Balanced fund: A mutual fund that strives for stability by maintaining a constant ratio of equity to debt securities, usually 60:40. Also called *fixed allocation*.

Beta: This is used as a measure of both risk and volatility. A beta of one could be considered as an even point in both the risk of the investment and the chance that the investment or stock will react to outside stimulus. If a stock were to receive a beta value less than 1, the investment would be considered safer than an investment with a higher beta rating. If a stock receives a beta rating of 1.5, there is a 50 percent chance that the stock will be riskier and more volatile.

Bid price: This refers to the highest price an investor will pay to purchase a stock.

Blue chip: The common stock of a large company with a record of stable growth and earnings over an extended period.

Breakpoint: In a schedule of load fees, the dollar value at which the sales charge percentage changes. Typically, a sales charge schedule contains five or six breakpoints, with the commission declining as the amount invested rises.

Broker: A person who buys and sells securities on behalf of others, receiving a commission for each exchange. See also *dealer*.

Call option: A type of security used to speculate on a stock's price movement. A call is an option to buy a stock at a specified price (the *strike price*) during a specified time period. A call is created by a specialist on an options exchange; once created, it can be traded, and its value will fluctuate as the price of the underlying stock changes. The opposite of a call option is a put option. Option contracts and other derivatives may be used for either speculative or hedging purposes.

Capital: The material assets of a business, including plant and equipment, inventories, cash, receivables, and so on.

Capital gains: Profits realized from the sale of securities that have appreciated while being held. As currently defined, long-term capital gains are gains on securities held for more than one year; short-term capital gains are those on securities held for one year or less.

Capital gains distribution: A payment to investment company shareholders from capital gains that the fund has realized.

Capital gains tax rates: Under present law, all short-term capital gains are taxed as ordinary income. Although the maximum tax rate for individuals, estates, and trusts can be as high as 39.6 percent, the tax on long-term capital gains is guaranteed by law not to exceed 15 percent through 2010. See *capital gains*.

Capital growth: An increase in the market value of securities.

Cash position: A measure of a company's fiscal situation that compares cash to total net assets.

Certificate of deposit: A note issued by a bank or thrift institution guaranteeing that the bank will hold a specified sum of money for a fixed period of time and will pay a specified interest rate. Euro CDs are CDs issued by foreign branches of U.S. banks or U.S. branches of foreign banks.

Check-writing privilege: The ability to withdraw money from an investment account, such as a money market account, by writing checks. The holdings will continue to earn dividends until checks are cleared.

Closed-end investment company: An investment company with a fixed number of shares outstanding that trade on the open market; it holds the type of investments stated in its objective. The market value of a closed-end fund will usually differ from the value of its holdings.

Closed-up fund: An open-end fund that trades actively but does not accept deposits from new investors.

Common stock: A security that represents partial ownership of a corporation and therefore normally carries voting rights. Should a company liquidate, the claims of a holder of common stock rank below those of holders of bonds, other debt, and preferred stock because the company's creditors receive compensation before the owners.

Common stock fund: An investment company whose portfolio consists primarily of common stocks.

Contingent deferred sales charge (CDSC): A fee that is payable when shares are redeemed. See *load fee, back-end load.* Also called a *trailer* or a *redemption fee.*

Contractual plan: A type of accumulation plan under which the total intended investment amount and periodic payments to reach that amount are specified at the time of purchase. The sales charge is based on the total amount to be invested and usually is deducted from the initial payments..

Contrarian: An investor who attempts to move against major market trends at any given time, searching for undiscovered opportunities.

Controlled affiliate: A company in which 25 percent or more of the outstanding voting securities are controlled by one source, as stipulated in the Investment Company Act of 1940.

Conversion privilege: See *exchange privilege.*

Convertible securities: Preferred stocks or bonds that can be exchanged for a given amount of common stock before a specified date.

Conversion ratio: The specified rate at which preferred stocks or bonds can be exchanged for common stocks; it is determined when the convertible security is issued.

Corporate (master or prototype) retirement plan: A corporate or trust agreement that qualifies for special tax treatment because the company is investing for the benefit of its employees. Prototype plans typically take the form of pension or profit-sharing plans; 401(k) plans are also offered.

Current assets: This is a balance sheet reference to all assets, cash and cash equivalents, that can be converted to cash within a year.

Current liabilities: Obligations due within one year.

Custodian: A bank or trust company that holds all the securities and cash owned by an investment company. In some cases, the custodian acts as transfer agent and dividend disbursing agent, although it has no supervisory function with in regard to portfolio policies.

Cyclical stock: A stock whose performance is closely tied to the strength of the economy. Examples are firms in the heating oil, air travel, and housing industries.

Dealer: See *broker*.

Death benefit: The amount guaranteed to the survivors or beneficiaries of an annuity contract if the annuitant dies before the annuitization date; it is contingent upon several factors.

Depreciation: The loss of value of a security or a fixed asset since its purchase.

Discount rate: The rate at which the Federal Reserve loans money to banks, which in turn guides commercial banks in establishing their loan rates for customers.

Distributor: A reseller of open-end investment company shares to interested buyers.

Diversification: Investment in a number of different securities to protect a portfolio from a painful drop in one market area. This risk-reducing strategy is akin to not "keeping all your eggs in one basket."

Diversified investment company: A fund that has not invested more than 5 percent of its total assets in any single company and does not hold more than 10 percent of the outstanding voting securities of any company, as stipulated in the Investment Company Act of 1940.

Dividend: A payment of income on a share of common or preferred stock.

Dollar cost averaging: A method of accumulating capital by investing equal amounts of money at regular intervals. This allows the purchase of more shares when the security's price is low and fewer shares when the price rises. The collective shares are bought at an average price rather than at a particular moment when the market could be skewed, thus reducing the need to time the market correctly.

Dual-purpose fund: A type of closed-end investment company, originally developed in England and introduced in the United States in 1967, designed to serve the needs of two distinct types of investors: (1) those who are interested only in income, and (2) those who are interested solely in capital growth. Two separate classes of shares are issued.

Duration: A gauge of price sensitivity to interest rates. Expressed in years, duration shows the weighted average time required for an investor to realize the currently stated yield.

Earnings: A company's profit.

Earnings per share (EPS): Profit divided by the number of outstanding shares of stock.

Emerging markets: Developing nations, as defined by gross domestic product and various economic measures. Usually these new markets are in Latin America, Eastern Europe, and Asia (excluding Japan). Funds that invest in emerging markets can be high risk.

Equity: Money represented by stock holdings.

Equity income: A category of investment funds seeking income through investments in dividend-producing stock.

Equity securities: Technically, all securities other than debt, although the term may be used to denote common stocks alone or common stocks plus preferred stocks that behave like common stocks.

Exchange privilege: The right to exchange shares of one open-end fund for shares of another within the same family of funds without incurring new sales charges.

Expense ratio: The proportion of net assets represented by total annual operating expenses.

Face-amount certificate: A promise by the issuer of a security to pay the certificate holder a stated amount at a future date. The security may be purchased through periodic payments (installment type) or with a single payment (fully paid)

Fair value: The value determined by the board of directors for those securities and assets that do not have a market quotation readily available, as stipulated in the Investment Company Act of 1940.

Federal funds rate: The rate that Federal Reserve member banks charge each other for overnight loans needed to meet reserve requirements. The rate is set daily by the market, although it can be affected by actions of the Federal Reserve.

Fiduciary: A person or entity that has custody of the assets of another.

Fixed-income security: A preferred stock or debt security that has a stated percentage or dollar income return.

Forward pricing: Pricing mutual fund shares for sale, repurchase, or redemption at a figure computed after the receipt of an order. Pricing is usually done once or twice a day.

Free partial withdrawal: The amount, expressed as a percentage of the investors' account values, earnings, premiums, or the greatest of some or all of these three, that investors are allowed to withdraw free of surrender charges during a specific period of time.

Fully managed fund: A fund without restrictions on the securities that may be held, giving the portfolio manager maximum discretion in all investments.

Fund of funds: An investment company that invests in other investment companies.

Government agency: A unit of government. Debt securities can be issued by government-sponsored enterprises, federal agencies, and international institutions. These securities, such as GNMAs or FNMAs, are not direct obligations of the Treasury, but have government sponsorship or government guarantees.

Growth stock: A stock that has shown better-than-average growth in earnings and is expected to continue to do so through discoveries of additional resources, development of new products, or expanding markets.

Hedge: To offset, or a security that has offsetting qualities. For example, an "inflation hedge" would rise in value as inflation rises, counterbalancing the erosion of value normally expected to result from inflation.

Hedge fund: A mutual fund or investment company that, as a regular policy, "hedge" its market commitments. It does this by holding securities that it believes are likely to increase in value and at the same time shorting securities that it believes are likely to decrease in value. This is an aggressive approach to capital appreciation.

Incentive compensation: A fee paid to an investment company advisor based on the fund's performance relative to specified market indexes. Also called *fulcrum fee.*

Income: Money earned through dividends or interest (but not capital gains). Gross income is the total amount of money earned, while net income is the gross income minus expenses, fixed charges, and taxes. Also referred to as *net investment income*.

Income fund: An investment company whose primary objective is generating income.

Incubator fund: An investment company that operates as a private, closed fund before offering shares to the public.

Individual retirement account: A tax-saving retirement program for individuals, established under the Employee Retirement Income Security Act of 1974.

Inflation: Upward movement in the price level of goods and services, resulting in a decline in the purchasing power of money.

Insured redemption value plan: An insurance program designed to protect investors against loss in long-term mutual fund investments.

Investment advisor: See *investment management company*.

Investment category: The stated purpose or goal of an investment company.

Investment company: A corporation or trust through which investors pool their money to obtain supervision and diversification of their investments.

Investment Company Act of 1940: A federal statute enacted by Congress in 1940 that provides for the registration and regulation of investment companies.

Investment management company: An organization employed by an investment company to advise and supervise the assets of the investment company. Also called *investment advisor*.

Investment trust: See *investment company*.

Issuer: With reference to investment company securities, the company itself.

Junior security: This describes the status of the common shareholder during bankruptcy proceedings. After bond and preferred stock holders (see *senior security*) are satisfied, common stock owners are next in line when the remaining assets are liquidated.

Keogh plan: A tax-saving retirement program for self-employed persons and their employees. Also known as *H.R. 10 plan* or *self-employed retirement plan*.

Large cap: Stocks with an average market capitalization greater than $5 billion. Many of these stocks are considered blue chips.

Leverage: Borrowing money to invest in hopes of achieving greater returns on the new securities. This simultaneously adds debt and builds assets.

Leverage stock: A junior security of a company with a complex capital structure; generally a common stock, but the term may also apply to a warrant or to a preferred stock established with loans.

Liquid: Easily convertible into cash or exchangeable for other values.

Living trust: A trust instrument that becomes effective during the lifetime of the creator, in contrast to a testamentary trust, which is created under a will.

Load fee: A sales charge. *Front-end load:* A sales charge imposed at the time of purchase. *Back-end load:* A sales charge imposed at the time of redemption. *Level load:* A single front- or back-end sales charges without breakpoints, or a 12b–1 fee greater than 1.25 percent imposed annually. *No-load:* The absence of any front, back, or level sales charges.

Management company: See *investment management company*.

Management fee: A fee paid by an investment company to a management company for portfolio supervision and advisory services. See also *incentive compensation*.

Management record: A statistical measure of the performance of an investment company.

Market capitalization: The market value of a fund or stock, calculated by multiplying the market value of each share by the number of shares.

Market maker: This refers to an investment company that buys and sells stock on a continuous basis. Primarily, market makers are used on over-the-counter or Nasdaq trades and they must have a least 100 shares available. Large trades may involve several market makers, and as a result, the trade may come with several different prices.

Market price: The price at which investors are willing to buy or sell a security on the open market. This is the offer (bid/ask) price for closed-end funds.

Maturity: The date when a debt obligation will pay its face value.

Micro cap: Stocks with an average market capitalization of less than $500 million. These are considered high-risk investments.

Mid cap: Stocks with an average market capitalization of between $1 and $5 billion.

Modern Portfolio Theory (MPT): A statistical method of analyzing investments by comparing their return and risk characteristics to each other and to established benchmarks. Elements of MPT include alpha, beta, R^2, and standard deviation.

Money market fund: A mutual fund that invests exclusively in short-term debt securities with the intent of maximizing liquidity, preserving capital, and providing current income. These funds typically maintain a stable net asset value of $1.

Mortality and expense fee (M&E): A fee, expressed as an annual percentage of assets, that pays the insurance company for the risk it incurs in guaranteeing to pay either a specified death benefit or a specified lifetime income to annuitants.

Multisector bond fund: A fund that invests in a vast array of bonds, foreign or domestic, government or corporate, investment grade or high yield.

Municipal bond: These types of bonds can be issued by all 50 states, counties, cities, towns, villages, or school districts for civil projects. The bonds are free from federal income taxes and often free from income taxes in the municipality or state where they were issued.

Mutual fund: See *open-end investment company*.

National Association of Securities Dealers (NASD): The organization of brokers and dealers that regulates the over-the-counter securities markets to prevent fraud and protect investors.

Net assets: The dollar amount of all resources at market value less all liabilities.

Net asset value (NAV): The market price of an open-end mutual fund; the value of all the assets held by the fund divided by the number of outstanding shares. For open-end funds, this is the daily price at which an investor can buy or sell shares.

Net cash inflow/outflow: The amount of money entering or leaving a fund during a specific time period. If a fund has new investments totaling $1 million (inflow) in March, and investors withdraw $300,000 (outflow) during the same period, the net cash inflow would be $700,000.

No-load fund: A fund that does not have sales charges. See *load fee*.

Nondiversified investment company: See *diversified investment company*.

Nonqualified plans: Retirement plans that do not meet the requirements of the Self-Employed Individuals Tax Retirement Act or Internal Revenue Code Sections 401(a), 403(a), or 403(b).

Nontaxable dividend: A dividend paid by a tax-exempt bond, such as a municipal bond.

Objective: The goal of an investor or investment company, such as growth of capital, current income, stability of capital, or any combination of these.

Odd lot: A number of shares that is not a round lot (normally 100 shares) and therefore may incur higher exchange costs than round lots. Not applicable to open-end investment companies.

Open account: An account where a shareholder has reinvestment privileges and the right to make additional purchases without a formal accumulation plan.

Open-end investment company: An investment company whose shares are redeemable at any time at their approximate asset value. In most cases, new shares are offered for sale continuously.

Option: See *warrant*, *put option*, and *call option*.

Optional distribution: A shareholder's decision to receive distributions (capital gains or dividends) in cash or to have them reinvested to purchase more shares.

Par value: The amount that an issuer promises to pay upon the maturity of a bond issue. Also known as the *face value* or *maturity value*.

Payroll deduction plan: An arrangement between a fund, employer, and employee whereby the employer deducts a specified amount of money from the employee's salary to purchase shares in a fund.

Pension plan: A program established by an employer, union, or other member-based organization to pay benefits to employees/members upon their retirement.

Pension portability: The ability of an employee to move accumulated assets from a pension plan to an individual retirement account or another qualified retirement plan.

Pension rollover: The opportunity to take distributions from a qualified pension or profit-sharing plan and, within 60 days of the distribution, reinvest them in an individual retirement account. Under current law, investors who do not transfer the distributed funds to a qualified account within 60 days will be assessed a 20 percent withholding tax plus a 10 percent penalty for early withdrawal.

Performance fund: Generally, an open-end investment company that emphasizes short-term results and has rapid turnover of portfolio holdings. The term may also refer to funds with outstanding records of capital growth, regardless of the policies that achieved those results.

Preferred stock: An equity security that generally carries a fixed dividend, and whose claim to earnings and assets ranks ahead of common stock but behind bonds. Unlike common stock, preferred securities do not allow the investor to vote.

Premium: The percentage above asset value at which shares of a stock or closed-end fund sells, or the percentage by which the conversion value exceeds the price at which a convertible bond or convertible preferred stock sells. Regarding closed-end funds, it is the amount by which the market price exceeds the portfolio value.

Price-to-book ratio: The market price of a stock divided by stockholders' equity. The ratio shows how much investors are willing to pay for each dollar that the company is worth.

Price-to-earnings ratio: Market price divided by profit. The ratio shows how much investors are willing to pay for each dollar of the company's earnings.

Profit-sharing retirement plan: A retirement program in which a company contributes a percentage of its annual gross profit to participating employees. In a Keogh plan, the earnings of the self-employed individual are substituted for gross profit.

Prospectus: The official document that describes an issuer's investment policy, fees, risks, management, and other pertinent information as directed by the Securities and Exchange Commission. A prospectus must accompany any new offer to sell securities.

Proxy: An agreement allowing a stockholder to transfer voting rights to another person if the stockholder will not attend the stockholders' meeting.

Prudent man rule: A law limiting the investments in a fiduciary account to those that a "prudent" investor would make when managing his or her own affairs, thus checking the power of the trustee.

Put option: A type of options contract that gives the investor the right to buy a certain stock at an agreed-upon price. The investor does so in the hope the stock will decline in price.

Qualified plans: Retirement plans that meet the requirements of Section 401(a), 403(a), or 403(b) of the Internal Revenue Code or the Self-Employed Individuals Tax Retirement Act.

R^2: A measure of diversification that determines how closely a particular fund's performance parallels the performance of an appropriate market benchmark over a period. The market is understood to have an R^2 of 100 percent. Therefore, a fund with an R^2 of 85 percent contains 85 percent of the market's diversification and risk. The remaining 15 percent is derived from the fund manager's actions.

Realized: The appreciation or depreciation of a security when it is redeemed. If a stock price increases by $50 to $100 and the shares are sold, the appreciation is realized and the investor receives his or her money. If the shares are not sold, the appreciation is unrealized because it exists only on paper. A security that loses value is said to have depreciated, and the loss may also be realized or unrealized.

Record date: The date by which a shareholder must be registered on an investment company's books in order to receive a dividend.

Redemption in kind: Redemption of investment company shares in a form other than cash, such as other securities. This is permissible for many mutual funds and tax-free exchange funds.

Redemption price: The price at which an investor sells securities, i.e., redeems securities for cash. See *bid price* as applicable to open-end investment companies.

Registered investment company: An investment company that has filed a registration statement with the Securities and Exchange Commission in accordance with the requirements of the Investment Company Act of 1940.

Registrar: A banking institution that maintains the list of a company's shareholders and the number of shares that each of them holds.

Registration statement: A document detailing a security's vital information that must be filed with and approved by the Securities and Exchange Commission before the security can be sold to the public.

Regulated investment company: An investment company that has elected to qualify for the special tax treatment provided by Subchapter M of the Internal Revenue Code; not to be confused with registration under the Investment Company Act of 1940.

Reinvestment privilege: A service offered by most mutual funds and some closed-end investment companies in which distributions may be automatically reinvested in additional full and fractional shares.

Repurchase agreement: The temporary transfer of a security to another person, with the understanding that ownership will revert at a future time and price. This "renting" of a debt security fixes the yield while the security is held by the purchaser and insulates the return from market fluctuations during the period of temporary ownership.

Repurchases: In closed-end companies, the companies' voluntary open-market purchases of their own securities. For open-end companies, the stock taken back at approximate asset value.

Restricted security: A security that has not been registered with the Securities and Exchange Commission and therefore is not available to the public at large, since a security must be registered before it may be sold publicly; frequently referred to as a *private placement* or *letter stock*.

Rollover: Movement of funds from one qualified retirement investment to another without incurring tax liabilities. The investor receives the money and must move it to another qualified account within 60 days or be assessed a 20 percent withholding tax plus a 10 percent penalty for early withdrawal. If the investor does not touch the money but has it moved from custodian to custodian, it is called a *direct transfer*. See also *pension rollover* and *qualified plan*.

Round lot: A fixed unit of trading (usually 100 shares) that forms the basis for the prevailing commission rates on a securities exchange.

Securities and Exchange Commission (SEC): An independent agency of the U.S. government that administers securities transaction laws.

Selling charge or sales commission: A fee paid at the time of purchase to a broker or financial advisor for the service of selling the fund; generally stated as a percentage of the offering price. See *load fee*.

Senior capital: See *senior securities*.

Senior securities: Notes, bonds, debentures, or preferred stocks, whose claim on a company's earnings and assets ranks ahead of that of common stock. Should a company liquidate, the claims of senior security holders rank above those of junior security holders because the company's creditors receive compensation before the owners.

Separate account: An account that is completely separated from the general account of an insurance company, since its assets are generally invested in common stocks.

Shareholder experience: A measure of investment returns, usually expressed in terms of a hypothetical $10,000 investment and including sales charges.

Sharpe ratio: A measure of the portfolio returns compared to total risk. A higher value indicates a greater return per unit of risk. Risk in this calculation is provided by the portfolio's standard deviation. Sharpe ratios cannot stand alone and are effective only when used in comparison to other portfolios or securities.

Short sale: The sale of a security that is not owned in the hope that the price will go down so that the security can be repurchased at a profit. The person making a short sale borrows stock in order to make delivery to the buyer, and must eventually repurchase the stock in order to return it to the lender.

Small cap: Stocks with an average market capitalization of between $500 million and $1 billion. These are considered high-risk investments.

Special situations: Investments in distressed or undervalued securities, including firms that are restructuring, venture capital, mergers, reorganizations, and other such situations.

Specialty or specialized fund: An investment company that concentrates its holdings in a specific industry group, such as technology, natural resources, or gold.

Split funding: An arrangement that combines investment in mutual fund shares and the purchase of life insurance contracts, such as under an individual Keogh plan.

Spread: The difference between the bid price and the ask price of a stock.

Standard deviation: A statistical measure of the month-to-month volatility of a fund's returns. Higher numbers indicate greater variation from a benchmark. If the standard deviations for Fund A and Fund B were 8.0 and 4.0, respectively, then Fund A has experienced twice as much variability as Fund B. Money market funds, which have stable asset values and low risk, have standard deviations that are near zero.

Standardized return: The return net of all fees, calculated according to form N-4 as required by SEC Rule 482.

Subchapter M: A section of the International Revenue Code that provides special tax treatment for regulated investment companies.

Surrender charge: The charge, expressed as a percentage of assets, that an insurance company assesses clients when they surrender all or part of their contract; similar to a contingent deferred sales charge.

Swap fund: See *tax-free exchange fund*.

Tax-free exchange fund: An investment company that permits investors with appreciated securities to exchange them for shares of the fund while avoiding capital gains taxes.

Total return: An investment strategy that strives for both capital appreciation and current income. Also, performance calculated assuming the reinvestment of all income and capital gains distributions.

Trustee: A party with the responsibility for administering assets for the benefit of others.

Turnover ratio: A measure of the change in portfolio holdings; the extent to which an investment company's portfolio changes during a year. A rough calculation can be made by dividing the lesser of portfolio purchases or sales (to eliminate the effects of net sales or redemptions of fund shares) by average assets.

12b-1 fee: A fee covering marketing and distribution costs, named after the 1980 Securities and Exchange Commission rule that permits it.

Uncertified shares: Ownership of fund shares credited to a shareholder's account without the issuance of actual stock certificates.

Underwriter: Principal. See *distributor*.

Unit trust: An investment company or contractual plan that has a fixed portfolio, as opposed to the changeable portfolio available in open-end or closed-end funds.

Valuation date: The day on which the value of a separate account is determined.

Value investing: The policy of buying securities with a market price that an investor believes is below their actual or potential worth

Volatility: Price fluctuation of a security. This can be measured in various ways, most commonly by standard deviation and beta.

Voluntary plan: An accumulation plan without any stated duration or specific requirements as to the total amount to be invested, although the minimum amount that can be invested in each instance may be specified. Sales charges are applicable to each purchase made.

Warrant: An option to buy a specified number of shares of the issuing company's stock at a specified price, often in the form of put or call options. Warrants are tradable securities, with values determined by the performance of the underlying security.

Withdrawal: The option of an open-end shareholder to receive periodic payment from his or her account. The payments may be more or less than investment income during that time period and therefore may imply the selling of shares.

Yield: For stocks, the percentage income return, derived by comparing dividends to market price. For bonds, the interest rate.

Yield to maturity: The rate of return on a debt security that is held to maturity, including appreciation and interest.

Companies that Participate in Direct Stock Purchase Programs

◆◆◆◆◆◆◆◆◆◆◆◆◆◆◆◆◆◆◆◆◆◆◆◆◆◆◆◆◆◆◆◆◆◆◆◆◆◆◆

The following is a list of companies that participate in direct stock purchase programs. Often a third party is involved in the transaction, and that transaction is very often free of fees or commissions. It is strongly suggested that all dividends be reinvested in the purchase of additional shares. This list is not a recommendation to purchase these stocks, however.

- 3M Company (MMM)
- 7-Eleven, Inc. (SE)
- A.M. Castle & Co. (CAS)
- AAR Corp. (AIR)
- Abbott Laboratories (ABT)
- Acadia Realty Trust (AKR)
- ACE Limited (ACE)
- Adams Express Company (ADX)
- ADC Telecommunications (ADCT)
- Advanta Corp. (ADVNB)
- Aetna Inc. (AET)
- AFLAC Incorporated (AFL)
- Agilysys, Inc. (AGYS)
- AGL Resources Inc. (ATG)

- Agree Realty Corporation (ADC)
- Air Products & Chemicals, Inc. (APD)
- AK Steel Holding Corp. (AKS)
- Albany International Corp. (AIN)
- Albemarle Corporation (ALB)
- Albertson's, Inc. (ABS)
- Alcoa Inc. (AA)
- Alexander & Baldwin (ALEX)
- Alfa Corporation (ALFA)
- Allegheny Energy, Inc. (AYE)
- Allegheny Technologies Inc. (ATI)
- Allergan, Inc. (AGN)
- ALLETE, Inc. (ALE)
- Alliant Energy Corporation (LNT)

- Allied Capital Corp. (ALD)
- Allied Healthcare Products (AHPI)
- Allstate Corporation, The (ALL)
- Alltel Corporation (AT)
- Altria Group, Inc. (MO)
- AMB Property Corporation (AMB)
- AMCOL International Corp. (ACO)
- AMCORE Financial, Inc. (AMFI)
- Amerada Hess Corporation (AHC)
- Ameren Corporation (AEE)
- American Capital Strategies (ACAS)
- American Electric Power (AEP)
- American Express Company (AXP)
- American Greetings Corp. (AM)
- American Real Estate Partners, LP (ACP)
- American States Water Co. (AWR)
- AmeriServ Financial, Inc. (ASRV)
- AmeriVest Properties Inc. (AMV)
- AmerUs Group Co. (AMH)
- AMLI Residential Properties (AML)
- AmSouth Bancorporation (ASO)
- Anadarko Petroleum Corp. (APC)
- Angelica Corporation (AGL)

- Anheuser-Busch Companies (BUD)
- Annaly Mortgage Mgmt. (NLY)
- Anthem, Inc. (ATH)
- Aon Corporation (AOC)
- Apache Corporation (APA)
- Apartment Investment & Management Co. (AIV)
- Applied Biosystems Group (ABI)
- Applied Industrial Technologies (AIT)
- Aqua America, Inc. (WTR)
- Arch Chemicals, Inc. (ARJ)
- Arch Coal, Inc. (ACI)
- Archer Daniels Midland Co. (ADM)
- Archstone-Smith Trust (ASN)
- Arrow Financial Corp. (AROW)
- Artesian Resources Corp. (ARTNA)
- ArvinMeritor, Inc. (ARM)
- ASA Limited (ASA)
- Associated Banc-Corp (ASBC)
- Associated Estates Realty (AEC)
- Astoria Financial Corporation (AF)
- AT&T Corp. (T)
- Atmos Energy Corporation (ATO)
- Avery Dennison Corporation (AVY)
- Aviall, Incorporated (AVL)

- Avista Corporation (AVA)
- Avnet, Inc. (AVT)
- Avon Products, Inc. (AVP)
- AVX Corporation (AVX)
- AXA (ADR) (AXA)
- Baker Hughes Incorporated (BHI)
- Baldwin Technology Co. (BLD)
- Ball Corporation (BLL)
- BancorpSouth, Inc. (BXS)
- Bandag, Incorporated (BDG)
- Bank of America Corp. (BAC)
- Bank of Granite Corp. (GRAN)
- Bank of Hawaii Corp. (BOH)
- Bank of New York Co., The (BK)
- Banknorth Group, Inc. (BNK)
- Banta Corporation (BN)
- Barnes Group Inc. (B)
- Bausch & Lomb Inc. (BOL)
- Baxter International Inc. (BAX)
- BB&T Corporation (BBT)
- Beckman Coulter, Inc. (BEC)
- Becton, Dickinson and Co. (BDX)
- Bedford Property Investors, Inc. (BED)
- BellSouth Corporation (BLS)
- Bemis Company, Inc. (BMS)
- Black & Decker Corporation (BDK)
- Black Hills Corporation (BKH)
- Blyth, Inc. (BTH)
- BNP Residential Properties, Inc. (BNP)
- Bob Evans Farms, Inc. (BOBE)
- Boeing Company, The (BA)
- BorgWarner Inc. (BWA)
- Boston Beer Company, Inc. (SAM)
- Boston Private Financial (BPFH)
- Boston Properties, Inc. (BXP)
- BostonFed Bancorp, Inc. (BFD)
- Bowater Incorporated (BOW)
- Bowne & Co., Inc. (BNE)
- Brady Corporation (BRC)
- Brandywine Realty Trust (BDN)
- Brantley Capital Corp. (BBDC)
- BRE Properties, Inc. (BRE)
- Briggs & Stratton Corp. (BGG)
- Bristol West Holdings, Inc. (BRW)
- Bristol-Myers Squibb Co. (BMY)
- Brown Shoe Company, Inc. (BWS)
- Brunswick Corporation (BC)
- Brush Engineered Materials, Inc. (BW)
- BSB Bancorp, Inc. (BSBN)
- Burlington Northern Santa Fe (BNI)
- C.R. Bard, Inc. (BCR)
- Cabot Corporation (CBT)
- Cadmus Communications (CDMS)
- Calgon Carbon Corporation (CCC)

- California Water Service Group (CWT)
- Callaway Golf Company (ELY)
- Campbell Soup Company (CPB)
- Capital One Financial Corp. (COF)
- Capitol Bancorp Ltd. (CBC)
- Caraustar Industries, Inc. (CSAR)
- Carlisle Companies, Inc. (CSL)
- Carnival Corporation (CCL)
- CarrAmerica Realty Corp. (CRE)
- Cascade Financial Corp. (CASB)
- Cascade Natural Gas Corp. (CGC)
- Casey's General Stores, Inc. (CASY)
- Caterpillar Inc. (CAT)
- Cathay General Bancorp (CATY)
- Cavalier Homes, Inc. (CAV)
- CBL & Associates Properties (CBL)
- CBRL Group, Inc. (CBRL)
- Cedar Fair, L.P. (FUN)
- Cendant Corporation (CD)
- CenterPoint Energy, Inc. (CNP)
- CenterPoint Properties (CNT)
- Central Vermont Public Service (CV)
- CenturyTel, Inc. (CTL)
- CH Energy Group, Inc. (CHG)
- Charles Schwab Corp., The (SCH)
- Chart Industries, Inc. (CIDI)
- CharterMac (CHC)
- Chesapeake Corporation (CSK)
- Chesapeake Utilities (CPK)
- ChevronTexaco Corporation (CVX)
- Chiquita Brands International (CQB)
- Chittenden Corporation (CHZ)
- Chubb Corporation (CB)
- Church & Dwight Co., Inc. (CHD)
- CIGNA Corporation (CI)
- Cincinnati Financial Corp. (CINF)
- Cinergy Corp. (CIN)
- Citizens Banking Corp./MI (CBCF)
- Citizens Communications (CZN)
- Citizens, Inc. (CIA)
- City Holding Company (CHCO)
- CLARCOR Inc. (CLC)
- Cleco Corporation (CNL)
- Cleveland-Cliffs Inc. (CLF)
- Clorox Company, The (CLX)
- CMS Energy Corporation (CMS)
- CNF, Inc. (CNF)
- Coca-Cola Bottling Co. (COKE)
- Coca-Cola Company, The (KO)
- Coca-Cola Enterprises (CCE)
- Colgate-Palmolive Company (CL)
- Colonial BancGroup, Inc. (CNB)
- Colonial Properties Trust (CLP)

- Columbus McKinnon Corp. (CMCO)
- Comerica Incorporated (CMA)
- Commerce Bancorp, Inc. (CBH)
- Commercial Net Lease Realty (NNN)
- Community Bank System (CBU)
- Compass Bancshares, Inc. (CBSS)
- Computer Associates (CA)
- ConAgra Foods, Inc. (CAG)
- Connecticut Water Service (CTWS)
- ConocoPhillips (COP)
- Consolidated Freightways (CFWEQ)
- Cooper Industries, Ltd. (CBE)
- Corn Products International, Inc. (CPO)
- Countrywide Financial Corp. (CFC)
- CPI Corp. (CPY)
- Crane Co. (CR)
- Crompton Corporation (CK)
- Crown Holdings Inc. (CCK)
- CRT Properties, Inc. (CRO)
- CSX Corporation (CSX)
- CVS Corporation (CVS)
- DaimlerChrysler AG (ADR) (DCX)
- Dana Corporation (DCN)
- Dean Foods Company (DF)

- Deere & Company (DE)
- Delphi Corporation (DPH)
- Delta Air Lines, Inc. (DAL)
- Delta Natural Gas Co. (DGAS)
- Diebold Incorporated (DBD)
- Dollar General Corp. (DG)
- Dominion Resources, Inc. (D)
- Donaldson Company, Inc. (DCI)
- Dover Corporation (DOV)
- Dover Motorsports, Inc. (DVD)
- Dow Chemical Company (DOW)
- Dow Jones & Co. (DJ)
- DPL Inc. (DPL)
- DTE Energy Company (DTE)
- Duke Energy Corporation (DUK)
- Duke Realty Corp. (DRE)
- Duquesne Light Holdings (DQE)
- Dynegy Inc. (DYN)
- E-Z-EM, Inc. (EZM)
- E.I. du Pont de Nemours (DD)
- Eastern Company, The (EML)
- EastGroup Properties Inc. (EGP)
- Eastman Chemical Co. (EMN)
- Eastman Kodak Company (EK)
- Eaton Corporation (ETN)
- Ecolab Inc. (ECL)
- El Paso Corporation (EP)
- EMC Insurance Group (EMCI)

- EMCEE Broadcast Products (ECIN)
- Emerson Electric Co. (EMR)
- Empire District Electric Co. (EDE)
- Energen Corporation (EGN)
- Energy East Corporation (EAS)
- Energy West, Incorporated (EWST)
- EnergySouth, Inc. (ENSI)
- Enesco Group, Inc. (ENC)
- Engelhard Corporation (EC)
- Entergy Corporation (ETR)
- Entertainment Properties Trust (EPR)
- Equifax Inc. (EFX)
- Equitable Resources, Inc. (EQT)
- Equity Office Properties Trust (EOP)
- Equity Residential (EQR)
- Essex Property Trust, Inc. (ESS)
- Estee Lauder Co., The (EL)
- Exelon Corporation (EXC)
- Exxon Mobil Corporation (XOM)
- F.N.B. Corporation (FNB)
- Fannie Mae (FNM)
- FBL Financial Group (FFG)
- Federal Signal Corp. (FSS)
- FedEx Corporation (FDX)
- Ferro Corporation (FOE)
- FFLC Bancorp, Inc. (FFLC)
- Fifth Third Bancorp (FITB)
- FINOVA Group Inc., The (FNVG)
- First Commonwealth Financial (FCF)
- First Federal Capital (FTFC)
- First Financial Holdings (FFCH)
- First Horizon National Corp. (FHN)
- First Midwest Bancorp Inc. (FMBI)
- First Niagara Financial (FNFG)
- First United Corporation (FUNC)
- FirstEnergy Corp. (FE)
- FirstMerit Corporation (FMER)
- Fleming Companies, Inc. (FLMIQ)
- Florida Public Utilities Co. (FPU)
- Foothill Independent Bancorp (FOOT)
- Ford Motor Company (F)
- Fortune Brands, Inc. (FO)
- FPL Group, Inc. (FPL)
- Franklin Resources (BEN)
- Freddie Mac (FRE)
- Fulton Financial Corp. (FULT)
- Gannett Co., Inc. (GCI)
- GATX Corporation (GMT)
- GenCorp Inc. (GY)
- General Electric Company (GE)
- General Growth Properties (GGP)
- General Mills, Inc. (GIS)
- General Motors Corporation (GM)

- Genuine Parts Company (GPC)
- Georgia-Pacific Corporation (GP)
- Gillette Company, The (G)
- Glacier Bancorp, Inc. (GBCI)
- Glenborough Realty Trust (GLB)
- Glimcher Realty Trust (GRT)
- Goodrich Corporation (GR)
- Goodyear Tire & Rubber (GT)
- Gorman-Rupp Company (GRC)
- Graco Incorporated (GGG)
- Great Plains Energy Inc. (GXP)
- Great Southern Bancorp (GSBC)
- Green Mountain Power Corp. (GMP)
- Greenbrier Companies, The (GBX)
- GreenPoint Financial Corp. (GPT)
- Guidant Corporation (GDT)
- H&R Block, Inc. (HRB)
- H.J. Heinz Company (HNZ)
- Hancock Holding Co. (HBHC)
- Harley-Davidson, Inc. (HDI)
- Harleysville Group Inc. (HGIC)
- Harris Corporation (HRS)
- Harsco Corporation (HSC)
- Hartford Financial Services (HIG)
- Hartmarx Corporation (HMX)
- Hasbro, Inc. (HAS)
- Hawaiian Electric Industries (HE)
- Health Care Property Investors (HCP)
- Health Care REIT, Inc. (HCN)
- Healthcare Realty Trust (HR)
- Hercules Incorporated (HPC)
- Herman Miller, Inc. (MLHR)
- Hershey Foods Corporation (HSY)
- Hewlett-Packard Company (HPQ)
- Hibernia Corporation (HIB)
- Hillenbrand Industries (HB)
- Hingham Institution for Savings (HIFS)
- Home Depot, Inc., The (HD)
- Home Properties, Inc. (HME)
- Honeywell International (HON)
- Hormel Foods Corporation (HRL)
- IDACORP, Inc. (IDA)
- IKON Office Solutions, Inc. (IKN)
- Illinois Tool Works Inc. (ITW)
- Independent Bank Corp. (INDB)
- Independent Bank Corp. (IBCP)
- IndyMac Bancorp, Inc. (NDE)
- Ingersoll-Rand Company Ltd. (IR)
- Insteel Industries, Inc. (IIIN)
- Integra Bank Corporation (IBNK)
- Intel Corporation (INTC)
- Interchange Financial (IFCJ)
- International Business Machines (IBM)
- International Flavors & Fragrances (IFF)
- International Paper Company (IP)

- Interpublic Group of Companies, Inc. (IPG)
- Invacare Corporation (IVC)
- Investors Financial Services (IFIN)
- iStar Financial Inc. (SFI)
- ITT Industries, Inc. (ITT)
- J.C. Penney Company, Inc. (JCP)
- Jefferson-Pilot Corporation (JP)
- John H. Harland Company (JH)
- Johnson & Johnson (JNJ)
- Johnson Controls, Inc. (JCI)
- JPMorgan Chase & Co. (JPM)
- Kaman Corporation (KAMNA)
- Keithley Instruments (KEI)
- Kellogg Company (K)
- Kellwood Company (KWD)
- Kelly Services, Inc. (KELYA)
- Kennametal Inc. (KMT)
- Kerr-McGee Corporation (KMG)
- KeyCorp (KEY)
- KeySpan Corporation (KSE)
- Kilroy Realty Corporation (KRC)
- Kimberly-Clark Corp. (KMB)
- Kimco Realty Corp. (KIM)
- Knight-Ridder, Inc. (KRI)
- Kramont Realty Trust (KRT)
- La-Z-Boy Incorporated (LZB)
- Laclede Group, Inc., The (LG)
- Lafarge North America Inc. (LAF)
- Lancaster Colony Corp. (LANC)
- LaSalle Hotel Properties (LHO)
- Lear Corporation (LEA)
- Lehman Brothers Holdings (LEH)
- Lexington Corporate Properties Trust (LXP)
- Libbey Inc. (LBY)
- Liberty Media Corp. (L)
- Liberty Property Trust (LRY)
- Limited Brands, Inc. (LTD)
- Lincoln National Corp. (LNC)
- LION Inc. (LINN)
- Liz Claiborne, Inc. (LIZ)
- Lockheed Martin Corp. (LMT)
- Long Island Financial (LICB)
- Longs Drug Stores Corp. (LDG)
- Louisiana-Pacific Corp. (LPX)
- Lowe's Companies, Inc. (LOW)
- LSB Bancshares, Inc. (LXBK)
- LTC Properties, Inc. (LTC)
- Lubrizol Corporation (LZ)
- Luby's, Inc. (LUB)
- Lucent Technologies Inc. (LU)
- Lyondell Chemical Co. (LYO)
- M&T Bank Corporation (MTB)
- Macerich Company, The (MAC)
- Mack-Cali Realty Corp. (CLI)
- Manitowoc Company, Inc. (MTW)
- Manpower Inc. (MAN)
- Manufactured Home Communities, Inc. (MHC)

- Marcus Corporation, The (MCS)
- Marriott International Inc. (MAR)
- Marsh & McLennan Companies, Inc. (MMC)
- Marshall & Ilsley Corporation (MI)
- Masco Corporation (MAS)
- MASSBANK Corp. (MASB)
- Massey Energy Company (MEE)
- Mattel, Inc. (MAT)
- May Department Stores Co. (MAY)
- Maytag Corporation (MYG)
- McCormick & Company (MKC)
- McDermott International (MDR)
- McDonald's Corporation (MCD)
- McGraw-Hill Companies (MHP)
- McKesson Corporation (MCK)
- MDU Resources Group (MDU)
- Meadowbrook Insurance Group (MIG)
- MeadWestvaco Corp. (MWV)
- Media General, Inc. (MEG)
- Medtronic, Inc. (MDT)
- Mellon Financial Corp. (MEL)
- Memry Corporation (MRY)
- Mercantile Bankshares (MRBK)
- Merchants Bancshares, Inc. (MBVT)
- Merck & Co., Inc. (MRK)
- Meridian Bioscience, Inc. (VIVO)
- Merrill Lynch & Co., Inc. (MER)
- Met-Pro Corporation (MPR)
- MGE Energy, Inc. (MGEE)
- Michaels Stores, Inc. (MIK)
- Microsoft Corporation (MSFT)
- Mid-State Bancshares (MDST)
- Middlesex Water Company (MSEX)
- Middleton Doll Co. (DOLL)
- Milacron Inc. (MZ)
- Millipore Corporation (MIL)
- Mills Corporation, The (MLS)
- Modine Manufacturing Co. (MODI)
- Monmouth Capital Corp. (MONM)
- Monmouth Real Estate Investment Corp. (MNRTA)
- Morgan Stanley (MWD)
- Motorola, Inc. (MOT)
- MTS Systems Corporation (MTSC)
- Myers Industries, Inc. (MYE)
- Mylan Laboratories Inc. (MYL)
- Nashua Corporation (NSH)
- National City Corporation (NCC)
- National Commerce Financial (NCF)
- National Fuel Gas Co. (NFG)
- National Health Investors (NHI)
- National Penn Bancshares (NPBC)

- Nationwide Financial Services (NFS)
- Nationwide Health Properties (NHP)
- NCR Corporation (NCR)
- New Jersey Resources Corp. (NJR)
- New York Times Co., The (NYT)
- Newell Rubbermaid Inc. (NWL)
- Newport Corporation (NEWP)
- Nicor Inc. (GAS)
- NIKE, Inc. (NKE)
- NiSource Inc. (NI)
- Nordson Corporation (NDSN)
- Norfolk Southern Corp. (NSC)
- North Fork Bancorp (NFB)
- Northrop Grumman Corp. (NOC)
- Northwest Natural Gas (NWN)
- NorthWestern Corp. (NTHWQ)
- NSTAR (NST)
- Nucor Corporation (NUE)
- Occidental Petroleum Corp. (OXY)
- Office Depot, Inc. (ODP)
- OGE Energy Corp. (OGE)
- Ohio Casualty Corp. (OCAS)
- Old National Bancorp (ONB)
- Old Republic Intl. Corp. (ORI)
- Olin Corporation (OLN)
- OM Group, Inc. (OMG)
- Omega Healthcare Investors (OHI)

- Omnicare, Incorporated (OCR)
- Omnicom Group Inc. (OMC)
- ONEOK, Inc. (OKE)
- Otter Tail Corporation (OTTR)
- Owens & Minor, Inc. (OMI)
- Owens Corning (OWENQ)
- Pall Corporation (PLL)
- Pan Pacific Retail Properties (PNP)
- Parkway Properties, Inc. (PKY)
- Paychex, Inc. (PAYX)
- Pennichuck Corporation (PNNW)
- Pentair, Inc. (PNR)
- People's Bank (PBCT)
- Peoples Bancorp of NC (PEBK)
- Peoples Bancorp/IN (PFDC)
- Peoples BancTrust Co., The (PBTC)
- Peoples Energy Corp. (PGL)
- Pep Boys (PBY)
- Pepco Holdings, Inc. (POM)
- PepsiAmericas, Inc. (PAS)
- PepsiCo, Inc. (PEP)
- PerkinElmer, Inc. (PKI)
- Petroleum & Resource Corp. (PEO)
- PFF Bancorp, Inc. (PFB)
- Pfizer Inc. (PFE)
- PG&E Corporation (PCG)
- Phelps Dodge Corp. (PD)

- Piedmont Natural Gas Co. (PNY)
- Pier 1 Imports, Inc. (PIR)
- Pinnacle West Capital (PNW)
- Pitney Bowes Inc. (PBI)
- Pizza Inn, Inc. (PZZI)
- PMC Commercial Trust (PCC)
- PNC Financial Services (PNC)
- PNM Resources, Inc. (PNM)
- PolyOne Corporation (POL)
- Post Properties, Inc. (PPS)
- Potlatch Corporation (PCH)
- PPG Industries, Inc. (PPG)
- PPL Corporation (PPL)
- Praxair, Inc. (PX)
- Prentiss Properties Trust (PP)
- Procter & Gamble Co., The (PG)
- Progress Energy, Inc. (PGN)
- ProLogis (PLD)
- Protective Life Corp. (PL)
- Provident Bankshares Corp. (PBKS)
- Providian Financial Corp. (PVN)
- Public Service Enterprise Group (PEG)
- Puget Energy, Inc. (PSD)
- Quanex Corporation (NX)
- Questar Corporation (STR)
- R.R. Donnelley & Sons Co. (RRD)
- RadioShack Corporation (RSH)
- Rayonier Inc. (RYN)
- Raytheon Company (RTN)
- Reader's Digest Association (RDA)
- Redwood Trust, Inc. (RWT)
- Regions Financial Corp. (RF)
- Reliv' International, Inc. (RELV)
- Republic Bancorp, Inc. (RBNC)
- Reynolds & Reynolds (REY)
- RGC Resources Inc. (RGCO)
- RLI Corp. (RLI)
- Robbins & Myers, Inc. (RBN)
- Rockwell Automation (ROK)
- Rockwell Collins, Inc. (COL)
- Rohm and Haas Company (ROH)
- Rollins, Inc. (ROL)
- Rouse Company, The (RSE)
- Rowe Companies, The (ROW)
- RPM International Inc. (RPM)
- Russell Corporation (RML)
- Ryder System, Inc. (R)
- S&T Bancorp, Inc. (STBA)
- Sanderson Farms, Inc. (SAFM)
- Sara Lee Corp. (SLE)
- Saul Centers, Inc. (BFS)
- SBC Communications Inc. (SBC)
- SCANA Corporation (SCG)
- Schawk, Inc. (SGK)
- Schering-Plough Corp. (SGP)

- Schnitzer Steel Industries (SCHN)
- Scientific-Atlanta, Inc. (SFA)
- Sears, Roebuck & Co. (S)
- Selective Insurance Group (SIGI)
- SEMCO Energy, Inc. (SEN)
- Sempra Energy (SRE)
- Senesco Technologies, Inc. (SNT)
- Sensient Technologies (SXT)
- ServiceMaster Company (SVM)
- Sherwin-Williams Company (SHW)
- Sierra Pacific Resources (SRP)
- SIFCO Industries, Inc. (SIF)
- Sizeler Property Investors (SIZ)
- Sky Financial Group, Inc. (SKYF)
- Snap-on Incorporated (SNA)
- Solutia Inc. (SOLUQ)
- Sonoco Products Company (SON)
- Sotheby's Holdings, Inc. (BID)
- Source Capital, Inc. (SOR)
- South Jersey Industries (SJI)
- Southern Company, The (SO)
- Southern Union Company (SUG)
- SouthTrust Corporation (SOTR)
- Southwest Gas Corporation (SWX)
- Southwest Water Co. (SWWC)
- Southwestern Energy Co. (SWN)
- Sovereign Bancorp, Inc. (SOV)
- Spartech Corporation (SEH)
- Sprint Corp. (FON)
- Standard Register Company (SR)
- Stanley Works, The (SWK)
- State Bancorp, Inc./NY (STB)
- State Street Corporation (STT)
- Sterling Bancorp (STL)
- Stride Rite Corp., The (SRR)
- Suffolk Bancorp (SUBK)
- Summit Properties Inc. (SMT)
- Sun Bancorp, Inc. (SUBI)
- Sunoco, Inc. (SUN)
- SunTrust Banks, Inc. (STI)
- Superior Industries International (SUP)
- SUPERVALU Inc. (SVU)
- Susquehanna Bancshares (SUSQ)
- Synovus Financial Corp. (SNV)
- Sysco Corporation (SYY)
- Tanger Factory Outlet Centers (SKT)
- Target Corporation (TGT)
- Taubman Centers, Inc. (TCO)
- TCF Financial Corporation (TCB)
- TECO Energy, Inc. (TE)
- Tektronix, Inc. (TEK)
- Telephone & Data Systems (TDS)
- Temple-Inland, Inc. (TIN)
- Tennant Company (TNC)
- Tenneco Automotive Inc. (TEN)
- Texas Instruments Inc. (TXN)

- Textron Inc. (TXT)
- Thomas & Betts Corporation (TNB)
- Thomas Industries Inc. (TII)
- Thornburg Mortgage, Inc. (TMA)
- Tidewater Inc. (TDW)
- Tiffany & Co. (TIF)
- Timken Company, The (TKR)
- Tompkins Trustco, Inc. (TMP)
- Torchmark Corporation (TMK)
- Toro Company, The (TTC)
- Total System Services (TSS)
- Transocean Inc. (RIG)
- Tribune Company (TRB)
- TriCo Bancshares (TCBK)
- Tuesday Morning Corp. (TUES)
- Twin Disc, Incorporated (TDI)
- TXU Corporation (TXU)
- Tyco International Ltd. (TYC)
- Tyson Foods, Inc. (TSN)
- U.S. Bancorp (USB)
- UAL Corporation (UALAQ)
- UGI Corporation (UGI)
- UIL Holdings Corporation (UIL)
- Union Pacific Corp. (UNP)
- UniSource Energy Corp. (UNS)
- United Bancorp, Inc. (UBCP)
- United Bankshares, Inc. (UBSI)
- United Mobile Homes, Inc. (UMH)
- United Parcel Service (UPS)
- United Technologies Corp. (UTX)
- Unitil Corporation (UTL)
- Unitrin, Inc. (UTR)
- Universal Health Realty (UHT)
- Unocal Corporation (UCL)
- UnumProvident Corp. (UNM)
- USEC Inc. (USU)
- USG Corporation (USG)
- UST Inc. (UST)
- V.F. Corporation (VFC)
- Valley National Bancorp (VLY)
- Valspar Corporation, The (VAL)
- Vectren Corporation (VVC)
- Verizon Communications (VZ)
- Visteon Corporation (VC)
- Vulcan Materials Company (VMC)
- W.R. Grace & Co. (GRA)
- Wachovia Corporation (WB)
- Waddell & Reed Financial (WDR)
- Wal-Mart Stores, Inc. (WMT)
- Walgreen Company (WAG)
- Walt Disney Company, The (DIS)
- Washington Mutual Inc. (WM)
- Washington Real Estate Investment Trust (WRE)
- Washington Trust Bancorp (WASH)
- Waste Management, Inc. (WMI)
- Wayne Savings Banc (WAYN)
- Waypoint Financial Corp. (WYPT)

- Webster Financial Corp. (WBS)
- Weingarten Realty Investors (WRI)
- Weis Markets, Inc. (WMK)
- Wells Fargo & Company (WFC)
- Wendy's International (WEN)
- WesBanco, Inc. (WSBC)
- West Pharmaceutical Services (WST)
- WestAmerica Bancorp. (WABC)
- Westar Energy, Inc. (WR)
- Western Digital Corp. (WDC)
- Weyerhaeuser Company (WY)
- WGL Holdings, Inc. (WGL)
- Whirlpool Corporation (WHR)
- Whitney Holding Corp. (WTNY)
- William Wrigley Jr. Co. (WWY)
- Wilmington Trust Corp. (WL)
- Winn-Dixie Stores, Inc. (WIN)
- Wisconsin Energy Corp. (WEC)
- Worthington Industries (WOR)
- WPS Resources Corp. (WPS)
- Wyeth (WYE)
- Xcel Energy Inc. (XEL)
- Xerox Corporation (XRX)
- XL Capital Ltd. (XL)
- XTO Energy Inc. (XTO)
- Yahoo! Inc. (YHOO)
- York International Corp. (YRK)
- Yum! Brands, Inc. (YUM)
- Zions Bancorporation (ZION)

Index

About the Author

◆◆◆

Paul Petillo is the founder and managing editor of BlueCollarDollar.com and also the author of *Building Wealth in a Paycheck-to-Paycheck World*.